REVISE
SECOND E

MW00668115

Special
Programs
& Services
in Schools

Creating Options, Meeting Needs

Bonnie M. Beyer
Eileen S. Johnson

PRO>ACTIVE PUBLICATIONS

*We dedicate this book to all students who have been
the recipients of special programs and services in schools and
to the parents, teachers, support personnel, school administrators,
and community members who strive daily to ensure that
all children are provided with the opportunity to learn.*

*A special dedication is extended to our children
Beth, Jim, Len, Alex, and Brian, and grandson, Stephen,
who have benefited from the educational programs
and special services available in schools.*

Special Programs & Services in Schools, Revised Second Edition

DEStech Publications, Inc.
439 North Duke Street
Lancaster, Pennsylvania 17602 U.S.A.

Proactive Publications is an Imprint of DEStech Publications, Inc.

Printed in the United States of America
10   9   8   7   6   5   4   3   2   1

Entry under main title:
Special Programs & Services in Schools: Creating Options, Meeting Needs—Revised, Second Edition

A Proactive Publications book
Includes index p. 219

ISBN: 978-1-60595-175-1

THROUGHOUT the history of American education, schools have attempted to nurture and support the growth of children and youth through the development of curricular programs and support services that address the needs of all students and help them achieve their highest academic potential. This is a daunting task that has increased the activities of professional educators and service providers in their roles of working with parents, guardians, families, communities, and legislative bodies to serve the best interest of all students in our schools.

Chapter 1 explores the history of the *Elementary and Secondary Education Act* from its roots in 1965 to its present reauthorization as *No Child Left Behind* and the 2010 Department of Education proposal *Blueprint for Reform: Reauthorization of the Elementary and Secondary Education Act*. It provides an introduction to subsequent chapters by outlining NCLB funding programs and options available to schools for the development and implementation of educational programs, health and safety initiatives, support programs and services, and educational options available to parents and students. Chapter 2 discusses curriculum, assessment of student learning, and accountability measures for educational service providers along with College- and Career-Ready initiatives ensuring a highly qualified workforce to teach students and lead our nation's schools. Supplemental services for students at-risk of academic failure or dropping out of school and additional funded educational and support programs are also presented. Included is a discussion of the Common Core Standards, Race to the Top, NCLB waivers, and STEM initiatives.

Specialized education services in the schools are presented and discussed in Chapters 3, 4, and 5. Chapter 3 presents the current status, controversies, and future trends in special education programs serving students with disabilities, including an update of IDEA initiatives. Also addressed are the changing roles and responsibilities of both special and general education teachers and the increased incorporation of parental involvement in the education of their children. Legal processes and procedures are presented along with suggestions for application and administration of special education programs and services. Chapter 4 presents and discusses programs serving students with gifts and talents. The impact of gifted and talented education programs is discussed along with definitions and means of identifying students with gifts and talents. Program development, implementation, and delivery models are presented within the parameters of legal and funding issues. Chapter 5 addresses the needs of English language learners in the schools. Bilingual and English as a second language (ESL) instructional options are discussed and evaluated along with instructional leadership considerations. The roles of the teacher, parent, community, and school administrator are analyzed along with considerations related to assessment of learning and the Common Core State Standards. Proposed reauthorization initiatives and funding opportunities under the *Blueprint for Reform* are discussed.

Parents and students are increasingly faced with options to traditional public school education formats. Chapter 6, Alternative Educational Opportunities, goes beyond the alternative school option for students at risk of academic failure and dropping out of school. This chapter explores a variety of options available to parents and students starting with options within public school systems such as magnet, schools-within-schools, charter schools, and public school choice. Other alternatives such as private and contract schools, home schooling, online schools and distance education are presented along with the impact of vouchers, tax credits, school choice, competition, and alternative funding sources on financing public education. NCLB waivers and college- and career-ready initiatives are addressed. Chapter 7 continues the discussion of educational options for students with the presentation of applied education programs from their earliest beginnings as vocational education to their current status of technical education and school-to-work programs serving industrial and corporate needs. The future trends in applied educational programs along with models of reform and innovative programs including college- and career-ready initiatives are also presented.

Service to students, parents, and the community goes beyond academic programs in elementary and secondary schools. Chapters 8, 9, and 10 address the special needs of students beyond the classroom that can impact a student's ability to learn. Chapter 8 discusses health and human services options in the schools, presenting the roles of the school nurse, social worker, and school counselor in addressing the health and general well-being of students. Health and social issues such as communicable disease, substance abuse, sexually transmitted disease, teen-age pregnancy, and child abuse and neglect are some of the topics presented. Food services in schools, childhood obesity, and physical education programs are also discussed. Finally, the chapter looks at the concept of full-service schools in the form of school-linked or school-based health clinics. Chapter 9 builds upon topics from the previous chapter and presents prevention programs in schools. The variety of programs discussed includes substance abuse, violence, health-related issues, suicide, and drop-out prevention. Student intervention and crisis management programs are assessed along with current controversies and future trends in prevention program development and management. In summary, Chapter 10 addresses student support services in the schools. Guidance and counseling services along with mentoring programs for children and youth are presented and discussed. School-community partnerships such as service learning, internships, and field-based activities are explored along with school-based programs such as before- and after-school programs and activities, tutorial programs, and childcare services. Case studies are included in the chapters, allowing the educator an opportunity to assess their understanding of special programs in schools through the application of knowledge to practice.

The role of educator has expanded beyond the original concept of student and teacher working together toward academic achievement. All the programs addressed in this book are essential to ensure that students are ready to learn and that teachers, support staff, and school administrators are providing the services and support systems to ensure that all students have the best opportunity possible to achieve academically and become well-prepared, active, contributing members of society in the world beyond school

New in this Edition

The following is a brief list of laws which have appeared since the first edition of this book was published. The consequences of each of these new initiatives—for students and school administrators—represent an important addendum to this revised, second edition. Concomitant changes and updates have been made to the text, case studies and references.

- Common Core State Standards
- Blueprint for Reform: Reauthorization of the Elementary and Secondary Education Act
- Science, Technology, Engineering, and Mathematics (STEM)
- Race to the Top
- NCLB Waivers
- IDEIA Updates
- Completely revised chapter on English Language Learners
- College- and Career-Ready Initiatives
- Blueprint for Reform Proposals and Diverse Learners
- Case Studies Incorporated in Chapters
- Updated Data and Research Base

CHAPTER 1

Title Programs of the Elementary and Secondary Education Act

Introduction

THE *Elementary and Secondary Education Act* (ESEA or the Act) was established in 1965 during the administration of President Lyndon B. Johnson. The Act was part of President Johnson's War on Poverty and a response by the federal government to unequal educational opportunities for disadvantaged children and youth particularly within lower socio-economic groups. Since the Constitution of the United States does not provide for a free public education for its citizens but rather defers that choice to the individual states as part of the 10th Amendment to the Constitution, the federal government can influence public primarily education through legal action, such as the 1964 Supreme Court decision in *Brown v. The Board of Education of Topeka*, or through programs that offer funds or funding grants for educational purposes. The U.S. government greatly expanded its influence in the educational arena with the implementation of ESEA and the funds that are made available for the education of disadvantaged children and youth throughout the United States.

The *Elementary and Secondary Education Act* is divided into sections, referred to as Titles, addressing specific elementary and secondary educational topics. These sections of ESEA have maintained certain basic components over time, such as the emphasis on mathematics and reading and the emphasis and aid to educationally disadvantaged children, yet changes and additions have been made with each reauthorization in an attempt to address specific educational and financial concerns, as well as public and political demands of a particular era. Sections of the original *Elementary and Secondary Education Act of 1965* are entitled:

Title I: Educationally Deprived Children
Title II: Libraries and Textbooks
Title III: Supplementary Education
Title IV: Cooperative Research
Title V: State Education Departments
Title VI: Handicapped Children
Title VI: Bilingual Education
Title VIII: Dropout Prevention and Education
(U.S. Government, 1965)

1

A quick comparison of these Title headings with the Title headings of the most recent reauthorization in 2001 demonstrates some of the immediate differences and expansion of the Act:

Title I: Improving the Academic Achievement of the Disadvantaged
Title II: Preparing, Training, and Recruiting High Quality Teachers and Principals
Title III: Language Instruction For Limited English Proficient and Immigrant Students
Title IV: 21st Century Schools
Title V: Promoting Informed Parental Choice and Innovative Programs
Title VI: Flexibility and Accountability
Title VII: Indian, Native Hawaiian, and Alaska Native Education
Title VIII: Impact Aid Program
Title IX: General Provisions
Title X: Repeals, Redesignations, and Amendments to Other Statutes
          (U.S. Government, 2001)

Major funding for the education of disadvantaged children was and still is provided to the States and subsequently from the State Education Agency (SEA) to the Local Education Agency (LEA) through direct funding, funding grants, or contracts. A comparison of the original contents and intent of ESEA through subsequent reauthorizations to the most current, demonstrates the expansion of services and opportunities and the attempts by the federal government to provide equal educational opportunities for all children. A full outline of the *No Child Left Behind Act of 2001: Reauthorization of the Elementary and Secondary Education Act of 1965* is available in the Appendix.

Historical Background

Following its original implementation in 1965, Congress has reauthorized the *Elementary and Secondary Education Act* in 1978, 1981, 1988, 1994, and most recently in 2001 (Table 1.1). Contents of the Act have come to reflect the political climate, Congressional composition, and expressed educational goals of the elected administration at that particular time in history. Title I of the Act is the basic federal funding vehicle. The original Act directed funding toward a targeted group of students identified as disadvantaged and falling within lower socioeconomic categories. Schools were quick to access the funds. However, in 1978 the Act was reauthorized as *Revisions to the Elementary and Secondary Education Act* (P.L. 95-561) to address the improper distribution of federal funds by the States and schools. Financing was restructured allowing use of federal monies to serve both a targeted population of individually identified students or the application of funds on a school wide or district wide basis based on 75% percent or more of students in a school or district meeting federal guidelines for identifying socio-economically disadvantaged students. In 1981, Congress passed the *Education Consolidation and Improvement Act* (P.L. 97-35), which addressed restrictions on State monitoring requirements and selection of schools. The

Table 1.1. Reauthorizations of the Elementary and Secondary Education Act.

1965 *Elementary and Secondary Education Act* (P.L. 89-10)
1978 *Revisions to the Elementary and Secondary Education Act* (P.L. 95-561)
1981 *Education Consolidation and Improvement Act* (P.L. 97-35)
1988 *Hawkins-Stafford Elementary and Secondary Education Improvements Act of 1988* (P.L.100-297)
1994 *Improving America's Schools Act of 1994: Reauthorizing the Elementary and Secondary Education Act of 1965* (P.L.103-382)
2002 *No Child Left Behind Act of 2001: Reauthorization of the Elementary and Secondary Education Act of 1965* (P.L. 107-110)

Act also eliminated requirements for parental involvement and loosened fiscal regulations. During this time, program sections were changed from Title to Chapter (i.e., Title I to Chapter 1, Title II to Chapter 2), but the basic components remained the same. The *Hawkins-Stafford Elementary and Secondary Education Improvements Act* provided guidance to the education of economically disadvantaged children from 1988 to 1993. At that time, the Act once again addressed funding issues, mathematics, and literacy, but also reemphasized the importance of parental involvement and encouraged the increase of pre-school and secondary school programs.

In 1994, the ESEA was reauthorized as *Improving America's Schools Act of 1994: Reauthorizing the Elementary and Secondary Education Act of 1965*. Section designations were changed from "Chapter" back to" Title," and the application of funds on a school wide or district wide basis was lowered from 75% to 50% of the student population falling into an identifiable lower social-economic category, thus allowing more students the opportunity to benefit from federal funding. School districts were encouraged to apply Title I ideas and newly defined requirements of parental involvement, professional development, curriculum planning, regular assessment of student learning, and the use of highly trained and qualified teachers and teacher aids to all students and programs in a school district rather than only to those students identified as falling within a low socio-economic category. The intent was to encourage states and local school districts to improve education overall while providing equal opportunities for disadvantaged children.

Improving America's Schools Act of 1994 was signed into law by Congress on October 20, 1994 and was designed to work in conjunction with *Goals 2000: Educate America Act (Goals 2000)*, which was approved by Congress in March 1994 and signed into law by President Clinton on March 31, 1994. *Goals 2000* was the most aggressive educational plan to that point and mandated setting high expectations for student achievement. Title I of *Goals 2000* formalized into law eight National Education Goals, and stated the expectation that all the goals would be met by the year 2000 (Table 1.2).

In order to receive funds under this plan, the States were responsible for developing comprehensive improvement plans geared to high standards of achievement for all students. States had the option of using a plan currently in place or developing a new State plan to meet federal requirements. Reform plans were to be sent by each State to the U. S. Secretary of Education for approval. One of the components of the *Improving America's Schools Act of 1994* dealt with high standards and regular assessment of student learning in grades 3, 6, and 8. Though past reauthorizations were directed toward increased student competency in mathematics and reading, none prior to 1994 required testing at specified intervals to assess student learning. Under the Act, schools and LEAs were held accountable for student achievement results based upon an approved state assessment plan. Additionally, an intensive professional development program was required to support the development of highly qualified teachers, para-professionals, and school principals.

The ESEA's most recent update and revision occurred in 2001 and is entitled *No Child Left Behind Act of 2001: Reauthorization of the Elementary and Secondary Education Act of 1965*. The Act is more commonly referred to and known as *No Child Left Behind* (NCLB). This most recent reauthorization received strong bipartisan support in Congress, yet has become the most politically contentious to date due to the strong emphasis and requirements in Title I on accountability measures directed toward improving student achievement, the emphasis in Title II on the requirement for highly qualified teachers and principals, and some sections in Title V related to parental choice, innovative programs, and charter schools. Chapter 2 of this text will provide a more in-depth review of Titles I and II of the *No Child Left Behind* reauthorized ESEA of 2001. In a continued effort to improve educational opportunities for all children, the school- wide or district-wide basic funding formula was once again lowered, this time from 50% to 40%, encour-

Table 1.2. Goals 2000: Educate America Act.

Title I - National Education Goals
1. **School Readiness**   All children in America will start school ready.
2. **School Completion**   All students in America will be competent in the core academic subjects.
3. **Student Achievement and Citizenship**   The high school graduation rate will increase to at least 90 percent.
4. **Teacher Education and Professional Development**   All teachers will have the opportunity to acquire the knowledge and skills needed to prepare U.S. students for the next century.
5. **Mathematics and Science**   U. S. students will be first in the world in math and science.
6. **Adult Literacy and Lifelong Learning**   Every adult American will be literate and possess the skills necessary to compete in the economy of the 21st century.
7. **Safe, Disciplined, and Alcohol and Drug-free Schools**   Every school in America will be safe, disciplined, and alcohol and drug-free.
8. **Parental Participation**   Every school will promote parental involvement in their children's education.

U. S. Government (1994) Goals 2000: Educate America Act. 20 USC 5801. Washington, DC: U.S. Government Printing Office.

aging districts to adopt proven research-based educational improvement programs throughout a district and at the same time enabling a higher number of students to benefit from federal funding, resources, and the application of research-based instruction.

There have been no revisions to the *Elementary and Secondary Education Act* since the *No Child Left Behind Act of 2001*, although the Department of Education issued a *Blueprint for Reform of the Elementary and Secondary Education Act* in 2010 (U.S. Department of Education, 2010c). "The Obama administration's blueprint to overhaul the No Child Left Behind Act (NCLB) will support state and local efforts to help ensure that all students graduate prepared for college and a career" (U.S. Department of Education, 2010e). Priorities in this blueprint are:

- College- and Career-Ready Students
- Great Teachers and Leaders in Every School
- Equity and Opportunity for all Students
- Raise the Bar and Reward Excellence
- Promote Innovation and Continuous Improvement
  (U.S. Department of Education, 2010a).

While this blueprint has been in development, implementation of the blueprint has already begun, such as specialized incentive programs and waivers developed and granted by the government such as: "Race to the Top" incentives, individual state applications for accountability waivers of NCLB requirements related to student academic achievement goals, teacher evaluations, and school principal evaluations. Along with the accountability measures have been efforts to standardize curriculum and assessment across the nation, such as moves towards a common core curriculum and standardized testing. Appendix B of this book outlines the ESEA Reauthorization: A Blueprint for Reform proposal (U.S. Department of Education, 2010b). Appendix C offers a comparison of NCLB and the Blueprint for Reform developed by the Department of Education (U.S. Department of Education, 2010d).

Over the years, the Act has consistently strived to address educational needs in such areas as low academic achievement in reading and mathematics, bilingual/ESL education, education of migrant children, educational opportunities for indigenous American populations, and gifted and talented programs among others. The original emphasis was on mathematics and reading programs at the elementary level, offering States Title I monies, which were then distributed to local school districts in an effort to increase student achievement in these basic skills. School districts developed specialized programs primarily in the elementary grades, but also on the secondary level particularly in mathematics and reading—in the 9th and 10th grades. These specialized programs have offered educational support to low-achieving students in the form of summer enhancement classes, pull-out programs, private tutorials, class instructional aides, Title I instructors, professional development, computer assisted instruction, before- and after-school programs, math and reading camps, early education opportunities, parent education programs, and services extended to homeless, delinquent, and migrant children.

Originally the program was directed at a targeted student population of economically disadvantaged children, making it necessary to address the needs only of individuals or small groups of students in one-on-one sessions, often referred to as pull-out programs. These programs are so named because students were taken out, or "pulled-out," of the classroom during the regular school day to receive specialized instruction. Provision of these programs to students often required separate classrooms or smaller breakout rooms for small student groups or individualized instruction. It was not unknown for Title I instruction to take place in school hallways, behind partitions, or even in converted closets of schools, particularly within low socio-economic districts and over-crowded schools where additional classroom space was not available. Over the years, it became apparent that pull-out programs were not as effective as desired, there was minimal or no increase in student academic achievement, and learning in other academic subjects was affected due to the fact that students were being taken out of the regular classroom during instructional time and missing instruction in subjects such as history, science, geography, music, or physical education (Anderson and Pellicer, 1999).

Generally, with each reauthorization, Title sections have been retained, expanded, or incorporated into other Titles, and new Title sections have been added based on current and projected future student populations and their educational needs. Mathematics and literacy have remained as integral parts of the funded programs, yet over the years additional attention has been paid to at-risk students, safe and drug free schools, parental involvement, early childhood education, education of migrant children, rural schools, programs for the gifted and talented, and increased educational opportunities for indigenous peoples. As the nation has grown and changed since 1965, so has the *Elementary and Secondary Education Act* been revised to address the changing educational requirements of students and schools.

A review of the contents of the most recent reauthorization of ESEA, including subsections, provides the reader with a more comprehensive view of the educational programs funded and supported under *No Child Left Behind*. A more detailed view of NCLB contents can be found in Appendix A. An ambitious scholar may want to compare and contrast the development of ESEA programs over the years, particularly changes due to political influences or a comparison of the 1994 and 2001 reauthorizations and their emphasis on assessment of learning, accountability, and highly qualified teachers, staff, and school principals.

States or local school districts have the option to refuse funding under Title I and would thus not be required to meet the federal guidelines and requirements such as assessment of student learning and highly qualified teachers and principals. Rejection of federal funds does not, however, exempt schools and school districts from meeting state standards. It is important to keep in mind that the provision of free public education is a role designated to the States and that the federal government's involvement in education is only a result of the acceptance of federal funds to supplement state and local educational programs.

General Overview of NCLB Title Programs

For the purposes of this book, discussion of Title programs will be based on the most current reauthorization of the ESEA more commonly referred to as *No Child Left Behind*. Title I: Improving The Academic Achievement of the Disadvantaged and Title II: Preparing, Training, And Recruiting High Quality Teachers and Principals have been the most highly questioned and discussed sections of the Act in its most recent reauthorization and will therefore be addressed in Chapter 2 in an effort to provide for a more detailed exploration of these sections. The following review of Titles III through X will hopefully assist the reader in developing a more comprehensive understanding of the extent of the Act and its impact on educational opportunities for all children. Title descriptions will attempt to show what's new in NCLB and provide information as applicable in such areas as accountability, flexibility, programs and instruction, expectations for student performance, parental involvement, or appropriate use of funds. Throughout NCLB, a strong emphasis has been placed on the application of curriculum and instruction that is tied to scientifically based research and demonstrated effectiveness (U.S. Government, 2002).

Language Instruction for Limited English Proficient and Immigrant Students (Title III)

The goal of Title III, Language Instruction for Limited English Proficient and Immigrant Students, is to assist Limited English Proficient (LEP) students gain both oral and written proficiency in the English language and to help these students "meet the same challenging state standards required of all students" (U.S. Department of Education, 2002; p. 62). English proficiency is the goal of this program. Flexibility is afforded to school districts to choose the method of instruction used to meet this goal; however, instructional programs must be based on scientific research. As stated by the U.S. Department of Elementary and Secondary Education:

> State education agencies and districts have the flexibility to implement language instruction programs based on scientifically based research on teaching limited English proficient children. In addition, professional development is to be informed by scientifically based research that demonstrates its effectiveness in increasing children's English proficiency or teachers' knowledge and skills, and is of sufficient intensity and duration to have a positive and lasting impact on the teachers' performance in the classroom (U.S. Department of Education, 2002; p. 64).

States are required to establish standards and benchmarks. Annual achievement objectives for LEP students must relate to gains in English proficiency. Ninety-five percent of funds received by the states under this Title must be directed to the local level in the form of sub grants. In return, LEAs are responsible for meeting annual achievement goals and for making adequate yearly progress. Failure to meet annual yearly progress as established by the State will require the LEA to develop an improvement plan. Sanctions are required if the LEA fails to make annual yearly progress for four consecutive years. More detailed information regarding LEP, bilingual, and English as a second language programs can be found in Chapter 6.

21st Century Schools (Title IV)

Safe and Drug-Free Schools and Communities

The purpose and rationale of the Safe and Drug-Free Schools and Communities program is to:

> . . . prevent violence in and around schools; prevent the illegal use of alcohol, drugs, and tobacco by

young people; and foster a safe and drug-free learning environment that supports academic achievement. Without safe and orderly learning environments, teachers cannot teach and students cannot learn. Students and school personnel need a secure environment, free from the dangers and distractions of violence, drug use, and lack of discipline, in order to ensure that all children achieve to their full potential (U.S. Department of Education, 2002; p. 66).

There are two main components to the Safe and Drug-Free Schools (SDFS) program. There is a state formula grant program, and there are national programs. Under the state program, 80 percent of funding is provided to the SEA and 20 percent to the office of the governor. Five percent of the state funding may be used for state-level activities related to SDFS. This money may be used for program evaluation, training, and for providing services to LEAs and community groups. The remaining 75 percent is available for distribution to LEAs for prevention programs and program compliance. Governors' funding grants may be allocated to schools and communities for services to children and youth who may be dropouts, pregnant or parenting, suspended, or expelled. School districts and communities can access these funds from the office of the governor through grants and contracts. States are required to conduct a needs assessment and develop a plan that includes performance measures for prevention activities. Plans are to be developed in consultation with parents, students, and community-based organizations and made available for public review. Additionally, the office of the governor may not duplicate prevention efforts formulated by SEAs and LEAs; program funds are to supplement, not supplant, other funding; and, the state and local agencies must cooperate with national evaluation and data collection activities.

Each state is required to establish a uniform management and reporting system to collect information on school safety and drug use among young people. This information will be publicly reported so that citizens have the information they need to ensure that their local schools are free from violence and drug use, and, in cases where schools fall short, to encourage improvement and track progress over time (U.S. Department of Education, 2002; p. 67).

The national programs initiative provides discretionary funding for efforts by state and local educational agencies to improve drug and violence prevention. This program comprises a variety of new or revised initiatives, each with specific provisions as to who may apply for federal monies and what funds may be used. The approved discretionary funding initiatives are categorized and entitled as: Hate Crime Prevention; National Coordinator Program; Community Service Grant Program; School Security Technology and Resource Center; National Center for School and Youth Safety; Grants to Reduce Alcohol Abuse; and Mentoring Programs (U.S. Department of Education, 2002; p. 70).

Gun-Free Requirements

This section of Title IV requires states to have in effect a law prohibiting guns and other explosive devices such as bombs, rockets, and grenades in schools. Under this law, a student in possession of a gun or other dangerous weapons in school must be expelled from school for one year. The law clarifies that a student must be expelled not just for possessing a gun in school, but also for bringing a gun to school (U.S. Department of Education, 2002, p. 71). Schools have the option of modifying an expulsion on a case-by-case basis. The modification must be in writing and submitted to the state. The only exceptions to this law are

. . . firearms that are inside a locked vehicle on school property, and firearms that are brought to school or possessed in school for activities approved and authorized by the district, if the district adopts appropriate safeguards to ensure student safety (U.S. Department of Education, 2002; p. 71).

Schools may provide educational services to expelled students in an alternative setting and as circumstances require; the expulsion must be administered consistent with the *Individual with Disabilities Act* for students with identified disabilities. Additionally, districts are required to refer offending students to the juvenile delinquency or criminal justice system. In order to receive ESEA funds, States must show that they are in compliance with the *Gun-Free Schools Act,* collect expulsion data from school districts, and annually report to the U.S. Department of Education the names of schools that have expelled students, the number of students expelled, and the type(s) of firearms involved.

21st Century Community Learning Centers

21st Century Community Learning Centers focuses funding efforts on providing services to students, parents, and the community outside of regular school hours, particularly for those students attending low- performing schools, in an effort to help students meet academic achievement standards. These services may focus on improving student academic achievement, recreation programs, the arts, drug prevention, youth development programs, and literacy services for parents. Such programs can be before or after school, in the evenings, on weekends, or during the summer. Funding is no longer restricted to school districts under NCLB, but is now also available to governmental agencies, faith-based and community organizations, as well as public or private entities to develop and provide these services. A good example of how this type of collaboration can serve children and communities is a $12 million initiative between the City of Detroit, the Detroit Public Schools, and seven nonprofit groups for after-school programs "to create after-school activities that will help kids stay out of trouble" (Feighan, 2004). The grant was secured from the state education department through an initiative called Michigan State 21st Century Community Learning Centers, and the programs provided by over 50 community-based organizations and directed toward boosting academic achievement and creating safe environments for children and youth.

The responsibility of the state is to ensure that funding grants go to serve children who attend schools with a high percentage of low-income students or attend those schools eligible for school-wide programs. Transportation needs must also be addressed to ensure that children and their families can participate in the programs. States must create program planning and monitoring guidelines, establish performance indicators, evaluate the effectiveness of programs, and ensure that funded community learning centers will be sustained after the grant period.

Environmental Tobacco Smoke

Smoking is prohibited in buildings used to provide children under 18 with health care, day care, education, or library services as part of the *Pro-Children Act* of 2001. This section of NCLB covers children's services that are funded through the U.S. Department of Education, the Department of Health and Human Services, and the Department of Agriculture Special Supplemental Nutrition Program for Women, Infants, and Children. States and state agencies, which include schools and school districts, must prohibit smoking in any building that provides services to children (U.S. Department of Education, 2002; p. 76).

Promoting Informed Parental Choice and Innovative Programs (Title V)

Title V, Promoting Informed Parental Choice and Innovative Programs, is the repository for a wide variety of programs, topics, and interests ranging from schools of choice, charter schools, physical education, gifted education, apprenticeship and exchange programs, to women's educational equity and community technology centers. The stated purpose of Title V is to:

. . . assist local education reform efforts that are consistent with and support statewide reform efforts. They also support state and local efforts to implement promising education reform programs, provide a continuing source of innovation and educational improvement, help meet the special education needs of at-risk and high-need students, and support programs to improve school, student, and teacher performance (U.S. Department of Education, 2002; p. 77).

The funding received by states and districts under Title V can be utilized in a broad range of programs designed to improve teacher quality and the academic achievement and quality of education for students. To ensure that federal funding reaches schools and teachers closest to students, "States must distribute 100 percent of the funds that they receive *beyond what they received in FY 2002* to districts" (U.S. Department of Education, 2002; p.77). In addition, States are required to use their share of federal funds to support efforts directed toward school renovations, technology, school choice programs, and the implementation of other associated reform efforts.

The following sections provide a broad overview of the contents of Title V and will provide the reader with a more detailed view of some of the most often discussed topics that are part of this section of NCLB. It is suggested that the reader refer to Appendix A to review all the topics and programs contained in Title V. Specific topics such as special education (Chapter 3), gifted and talented programs (Chapter 4), foreign language assistance and ESL programs (Chapter 5), vocational education (Chapter 7), programs serving high-need and at-risk students (Chapters 3, 9, and 10), health issues (Chapter 8), elementary and secondary school counseling (Chapter 10), character education, parental involvement, community education, and educational equity (Chapter 6) are presented and discussed in depth in other chapters of this book. The reader should refer to the Table of Contents or Index to locate a particular program or topic that may be of specific interest.

Voluntary Public School Choice

The Voluntary Public School Choice program provides funding to establish or expand programs that allow a greater choice in where parents may send their children to school. NCLB requires that options be made available to parents and students that would allow them to move from a low-performing school to a school that can provide a higher-quality education. School choice provides parents and students with the option to choose high-quality educational programs rather than remain in a school that does not meet state educational standards. It promotes competition among schools, which is intended to multiply high-quality educational programs for students in all schools. This, hopefully, will eventually eliminate the need for any parent or student to have to choose to go to another school because of low-quality academic programs. The program helps SEAs and LEAs implement public school choice policies

> . . . by providing funds for transportation, tuition transfer payments to the schools that students choose to attend, increasing the capacity of high-demand schools to serve greater numbers of students, and disseminating information about open-enrollment options (U.S. Department of Education, 2002; p. 83).

Grants are available to states, school districts, or partnerships developed between one of these agencies and another organization. Per-pupil funding is provided to a local school district to support the education of an individual child. Therefore, the funding follows the child to the new school. This cuts down on the tendency to misuse funds for purposes other than instruction of students meeting eligibility criteria or whole-school programs specified under ESEA. School choice programs are evaluated under this Title on the basis of:

1. the extent to which programs promote educational equity and excellence;
2. the characteristics of participating students; and

3. the programs' effects on the academic achievement of participating students, particularly those who move from low- to higher-performing schools, and on the overall quality of participating schools and districts (U.S. Department of Education, 2002; p. 84).

Increased accountability for student performance and empowerment of parents are key factors in this program.

Voluntary Pubic School Choice offers options to parents of children in low-performing schools and increases accountability for student performance. The program requires evaluation of the effects of the program on academic achievement of student participants, the characteristics of students participating in the program, and the extent to which the program promotes educational equity and excellence. The federal government evaluates SEAs to determine whether these goals are being achieved. The program thus

> . . . authorizes competitive awards to state education agencies (SEAs) school districts or partnerships that include an SEA or a district and another organization. Funding is available to establish or expand programs that provide students and parents with greater public school choice. Grants are for up to five years, and grantees may use up to one year for planning or program design (U.S. Department of Education, 2002; p. 83).

Magnet Schools

Magnet schools were initially developed during the 1960s under Title IV of the *Civil Rights Act of 1964* and were developed as an option to eliminate, reduce, or prevent the isolation of minority groups in elementary and secondary schools. Magnet schools are designed to offer innovative educational programs not available in regular schools and to provide opportunities for students to learn and interact in racially diverse environments. Discretionary grants are provided through the Magnet School Assistance Program (MSAP) to school districts that are under a court-ordered or federally approved voluntary desegregation plan:

> Districts (or a consortium of local school districts) that receive an award must use it to reduce, eliminate, or prevent minority group isolation, increase student academic achievement, continue the magnet school program after assistance is no longer available, and implement services to improve the academic achievement of all students attending the magnet school program (U.S. Department of Education, 2002; p. 86).

Magnet School Assistance grants provide school districts with the capacity to offer programs not generally found in local public schools and provide opportunities for students to learn in a racially diverse environment. Funds may be utilized on programs to improve academic achievement based on state designed content standards in reading, mathematics, science, English, history, geography, foreign languages, music, or art. Funding may also be directed toward programs that support the improvement of vocational, technological, and professional skills (Table 1.3).

Charter Schools

Charter schools provide a form of flexibility and innovation available to states and local school districts to provide educational options not available within a traditional public school system.

> The Charter School Program (CSP) was authorized in October 1994, under Title X, Part C of the Elementary and Secondary Education Act of 1965 (ESEA), as amended, 20 U.S.C. 8061-8067. The program was amended in October 1998 by the Charter School Expansion Act of 1998 and in January 2001 by the No Child Left Behind Act of 2001 (U.S. Department of Education, 2003b; p. 2).

Table 1.3. Magnet School Funding Objectives.

Support federal technical assistance and dissemination of successful programs.
Expand national activities to include technical assistance and dissemination activities. Requires the U.S. Department of education to collect and disseminate information on successful magnet school programs.
Build a grantee's capacity to operate magnet school programs.
Expands the uses of funds to include professional development in order to operate magnet school programs after the grant period has ended.
Provides more flexibility in administering magnet school programs.
A district may use their grant to serve students who are not enrolled in the magnet program.
Increases flexibility in designing magnet schools.
Enables grantees to have flexibility in designing magnet schools for students in all grades.
Allows more funds to be used for planning.
Increases the cap on the amount of funds that may be used for planning, form 10 to 15 percent in a project's third year.

U. S. Department of Education, Office of Elementary and Secondary Education (2002). *No child left behind: A desktop reference.* Author: Washington, D. C., p. 85.

Title V provides competitive grants to both individual charter schools and States for the planning, design, or initial implementation of charter schools and to evaluate the effectiveness of those schools. Monies may also be utilized for dissemination of information about successful charter schools to assist other schools in the development of a public CSP. Charter schools are held under the same standards as other schools in hiring and maintaining a highly qualified teaching and administrative staff and in the development and maintenance of superior programs. Funding for this section of NCLB is unique in that it lifts restrictions on awards:

> Eligibility has been extended beyond state education agencies (SEAs), in partnership with districts or non-profit groups or colleges, to also include districts, which may partner with other districts or non-profit groups or colleges. Private school children and teachers are authorized to participate. Restrictions on the number of grants that can be made and the total amount of funding each grantee may receive have been lifted (U.S. Department of Education, 2002; p.89).

Collaboration among school personnel, parents, and community members is encouraged in the development of school curricula and special programs that emphasize citizenship, respect, responsibility, trustworthiness, justice, and giving as aspects of character.

Part B, Subpart 2 of Title V awards grants to offset the cost of acquiring, constructing, or renovating a charter school. This section of NCLB is aimed at increasing the number of charter schools as well as expanding the number of students an existing charter school may serve. Grant money must be placed in a reserve account and used to guarantee or insure debt to finance charter school facilities, insure leases of personal and real property, assist in identifying potential lending sources, encouraging private lending, and facilitating bond issues by charter schools or other public entities for the benefit of charter schools (U.S. Department of Education, 2002; p. 81).

Elementary and Secondary School Counseling

Counseling services in schools provide essential support to the educational, social, and emotional development of children and youth. School counselors help students understand peer and family relationships, develop and understand socially acceptable behaviors, develop decision-making skills, and assist students in career and academic planning. School counselors work closely with teachers, families, the community, and other specialists such as school psychologists, social workers, and child and adolescent psychiatrists in addressing the special needs of students. This section of NCLB provides support for the development, evaluation and dissemination of research-based programs that identify effective strategies for serving children and youth at both the elementary and secondary school levels:

> Programs may also include in-service training for teachers, instructional staff, and appropriate school personnel, including training in appropriate identification and early intervention techniques. Programs must involve parents of participating students in the design, implementation, and evaluation of counseling programs and also involve community groups, social service agencies, or other public or private entities in collaboration efforts to enhance the program and promote school-linked integration of services (U.S. Department of Education, 2002; p.88).

Previous support for school counseling services provided by ESEA was directed toward elementary schools only. There is now a provision under which secondary schools may also benefit from funding support under NCLB. Additionally, the new law expands the list of professionals who may provide counseling services in schools. NCLB supports not only the work of school counselors, social workers, and school psychologists, as has been the case in the past, but now also allows child psychiatrists and other qualified psychologists to receive payment from program funds. Expanding existing programs, developing new preventative initiatives, and increasing the capacity of counseling programs in schools are emphasized in this part of the Act.

School counselors play an important role in the education of children and youth, and school counseling programs are intertwined throughout many aspects of educational programs. More detailed information and an investigation of the role of the school counselor and school counseling programs can be found throughout this book.

Access to Technology

A variety of additional programs and services are available under Title V of NCLB to support the educational needs of students, families, and the community as a whole. Access to technology is an important factor in a number of these programs. For instance, funding is available for utilizing technology to develop and disseminate challenging course work for gifted and talented students who would not ordinarily have the chance to take such courses. Students in rural schools or in schools without a highly qualified instructor to teach a specific course now have the opportunity to take advanced courses via the Internet with funding opportunities available to districts. Distance learning can be utilized as part of the *Star Schools Program*, which provides opportunities for districts to "enrich regular classroom instruction and provide high quality instruction in remote or high poverty locations where students otherwise do not have access to specialized courses . . ." (U.S. Department of Education, 2002; p.95). The Internet and other telecommunications vehicles can be utilized to provide professional development opportunities for teachers in the core curriculum areas, and in the use of technology and student assessment tools. Community Technology Centers promote the development of model programs that will increase community access to technology, particularly in urban, rural, and economically distressed communities. Grants are available to expand access to computers and related services to enhance technology proficiency and learning inside and outside the classroom, as well as in the broader community.

Specialized Support Programs

Educational support is offered through Foreign Language Assistance, Arts in Education, Smaller Learning Communities, Reading Is Fundamental, Women's Educational Equity and the Carol M. White Physical Education programs also available as part of Title V. Each program addresses increased academic achievement and/or student development. Smaller Learning Communities is unique in its attempt to address the problems of secondary schools with high student enrollment. The program supports LEA efforts to create multiple learning communities within large high schools, specifically, "(It) supports strategies to (1) restructure the high school by creating academies, houses, schools-within-a-school, and (2) engage students through teacher advisors, mentoring, alternative scheduling, and other innovations designed to personalize high school and thereby, improve student achievement" (U.S. Department of Education, 2002; p.91). This concept has a research-based foundation in studies conducted during the last century across the nation on school restructuring, empowerment, shared leadership, and community involvement and their effects on student achievement (Short & Greer, 1997). The historical perspective, educational initiatives, and current status of these restructuring efforts, as presented by the authors, is an example of the type of research-based initiatives consistently referred to in NCLB.

Parental Involvement

Research has shown that parental involvement in a child's education can have a positive impact on student achievement. Title V addresses the need for programs that not only link the student, school, and parent, but also offers the opportunity to establish Parental Assistance Information Centers that give information, training, and support to parents and to organizations that work with parents. Competitive grants are awarded to nonprofit organizations or consortia of nonprofit organizations and school districts

> . . . to establish, expand, or operate Parents as Teachers, Home Instruction Programs for Preschool Youngsters, or other early childhood parent education programs. Because parents are their children's first and most influential teachers, these programs help train parents in positive parenting skills, and provide the information and support that parents need to give their child a solid foundation for school success (U.S. Department of Education, 2002; p.103).

To further support the need for early education and parental involvement, Reading is Fundamental-Inexpensive Book Distribution provides for the distribution of books and other reading materials in an effort to increase disadvantaged children's motivation to read and help them keep up academically with their peers. Priority funding and distribution of books to children from birth to high school age is given to

> . . . programs that serve a significant number or percentage of children with special needs, including low-income children, children at risk of school failure, children with disabilities, foster children, homeless children, migrant children, children without access to libraries, institutionalized or incarcerated children, and children whose parents are institutionalized or incarcerated (U.S. Department of Education, 2002; p.92).

Character Education

Funding for this section of the Act is unique in that it lifts restrictions on awards.

Eligibility has been extended beyond state education agencies (SEAs), in partnership with districts or non-profit groups or colleges, to also include districts, which may partner with other districts or non-profit groups or colleges. Private school children and teachers are authorized to participate. Restrictions on the number of grants that can be made and the total amount of funding each grantee may receive have been lifted (U.S. Department of Education, 2002; p.89).

Collaboration among school personnel, parents, and community members is encouraged in the development of school curricula and special programs that emphasize citizenship, respect, responsibility, trustworthiness, justice, and giving as aspects of character.

Cultural Apprenticeship and Exchange Program

The Educational, Cultural, Apprenticeship, and Exchange Programs for Alaska Natives, Native Hawaiians, and Their Historical Whaling and Trading Partners in Massachusetts promotes the development of programs to learn about these groups' links in history and their shared cultures and traditions. It aims to increase the understanding of cultural diversity and use technology to "teach about the cultural and trading relationships among Alaska Natives, Native Hawaiians, and the people of Massachusetts" (U.S. Department of Education, 2002; p.101). Grants and contracts are available to Alaskan, Hawaiian, and Massachusetts' museums, heritage/cultural centers, and educational organizations that will encourage intergenerational internships, apprenticeship programs, and cultural exchanges among the target populations.

NCLB Flexibility and Accountability (Title VI)

Title VI, Flexibility and Accountability, defines and outlines the relationship among student academic achievement, SEA and LEA accountability, and assessment. It also explains the flexibility and opportunities available to state and local agencies through transferability of funds. The Title VI section of NCLB defines how states may pay for the development and administration of additional state assessments and standards. If a state has already developed educational standards, then the money may be utilized to administer assessments or carry out other activities designed to demonstrate student academic achievement results. Additionally, states may utilize the Grants for Enhanced Assessment Instruments funding vehicle to improve state assessment instruments or to offer competitive grants.

Flexibility is a key component of NCLB. Funding transferability allows state and local educational agencies the opportunity to consolidate a variety of ESEA funds for the purpose of assisting the SEA and LEA in making adequate yearly progress (AYP) in school improvement programs and narrowing the academic achievement gaps of students as required under NCLB. It gives them more control over resource allocation decisions.

State Flexibility or "State-Flex" Authority allows states to collaborate with local education agencies in the implementation of innovative programs to improve student achievement. It requires that achievement data be used to gauge success of the program(s) and that parents are informed of outcomes associated with the flexible use of funds. If the state fails to make adequate yearly progress and academic achievement objectives are not met within two years of the implementation of the program(s), federal flexibility authority is withdrawn. Funds may be consolidated under any of the following ESEA authorities in order to assist SEA and LEA collaboratives in making adequate yearly progress in narrowing achievement gaps:

1. Improving the Academic Achievement of Disadvantaged Children: State Administration
2. Reading First: Formula Grants to State Education Agencies, State Uses of Funds
3. State Grants for Improving Teacher Quality
4. Enhancing Education Through Technology
5. Safe and Drug-Free Schools and Communities Governor's Funds
6. 21st Century Community Learning Centers
7. Innovative Programs (U.S. Department of Education, 2002, p. 115).

Local Flexibility or "Local-Flex" Demonstration allows LEAs to consolidate certain federal funds available under ESEA to meet district learning achievement objectives. It requires school districts to set achievement objectives, to use disaggregated achievement data to gauge student success, to ensure that parents are informed of the achievement outcomes as a result of the flexible use of funds, and withdraws flexibility authority if objectives are not met. Under Local-Flex, local school districts may consolidate and use ESEA funds for educational purposes under the following NCLB categories:

- Title II: Teacher and Principal Training and Recruiting
- Title II: Enhancing Education Through Technology
- Title IV: Safe and Drug-Free Schools and Communities
- Title V: Innovative Programs (U.S. Department of Education, 2002, p. 118).

Rural Education Initiatives

The Rural Education Initiative is composed of two separate programs: Small, Rural School Achievement and the Rural and Low-Income School initiative. Consolidation of federal funds is once again the key to the Small, Rural School Achievement program along with accountability for student performance.

> Districts are authorized to combine their allocations under the Improving Teacher Quality, State Grants for Innovative Programs (formerly Title IV), Safe and Drug-Free Schools and Communities, 21st Century Community Learning Centers, and Educational Technology State Grants programs. Districts are authorized to use their consolidated funds to carry out activities authorized under Title I, Teacher Quality, Educational Technology, Bilingual Education, Innovative Programs, and Safe and Drug-Free Schools programs (U.S. Department of Education, 2002; p. 118).

The Rural And Low-Income School initiative is a new program under NCLB and provides additional funds for rural schools that serve high concentrations of low-income students. A school district may not participate in the Rural and Low-Income School initiative if it is eligible to receive funds under the Small, Rural School Achievement program.

Funding Sources and Information

It is imperative that states and local school districts be aware of funding opportunities for supplemental educational programs and services. These opportunities are clearly defined within the contents of the Act. Additionally, the federal government regularly posts funding opportunities on the Internet and through mailings to educational agencies. Larger school districts may have a grant coordinator and writer as part of the central office staff who will seek out funding opportunities and work with content area specialists in the district to secure funds. In mid-size to smaller districts, that task may fall on school administrators and teachers. The state education agency (SEA) or intermediate school district (ISD) may serve as resources to the local school district (LEA) by providing grant writing workshops or information on funding opportunities. State departments of education can also provide information and resource links to assist in financing special and supplementary programs addressing student needs.

American Indian, Native Hawaiian, and Alaska Native Education (Title VII)

Title VII, Indian, Native Hawaiian, and Alaska Native Education, is divided into three sections: Indian Education, Native Hawaiian Education, and Alaska Native Education. Although the funding requirements of the Act are the same for each group, the needs and educational challenges of each are unique. Hence, the following sections touch upon specific issues and educational concerns related to each group.

American Indian

Meeting the educational and culturally related needs of American Indian children and youth is of the essence in program development and dissemination. As pointed out in NCLB, fourth-grade American Indian students fall below basic levels in reading, math, and history; high school graduation rates are low; and students are less likely to attend college. In an ongoing attempt to solve the problem of educational underachievement among American Indian students,

> . . . the federal government continues to work with school districts, Indian tribes and organizations, postsecondary institutions, and other entities toward the goal of ensuring that programs that serve Indian children are of the highest quality and provide for not only the basic elementary and secondary educational needs but also the unique educational and culturally related academic needs of these children (U.S. Government, 2003; p. 124).

Funding is available to public school districts and Bureau of Indian Affairs (BIA) operated or supported schools. Acceptable funded activities under this program include:

- Culturally related activities that support the application;
- Early childhood and family programs;
- Enrichment programs that directly support the attainment of challenging state academic content and student academic achievement standards;
- Integrated educational activities;
- Career preparation activities;
- Activities concerning substance abuse and to prevent substance abuse;
- Activities that incorporate American Indian and Alaska Native specific curriculum content, consistent with state standards, into the curriculum; and
- Family literacy services (U. S. Government, 2003; p. 125).

Additional acceptable special services address the needs of bilingual and bicultural programs, health and nutrition services, school retention, school-business partnerships, and incentive programs directed toward higher education.

Native Hawaiian

Native Hawaiian students, as noted in NCLB, continue to begin school lagging behind other students in terms of readiness factors such as vocabulary test scores, scoring below the national norms of standardized education achievement tests at all grade levels They are often overrepresented among students qualifying for special education programs and underrepresented in gifted and talented programs, are more likely to be retained in grade level, and are excessively absent in secondary school. NCLB combines six prior programs into one comprehensive grant program. These include: Native Hawaiian Family-Based Education Centers; Native Hawaiian Curriculum Development, Teacher Training and Recruitment Program; Native Hawaiian Gifted and Talented Program; Native Hawaiian Higher Education Program; Native Hawaiian Special Education Program; and Native Hawaiian Community-Based Education Learning Centers. Funding opportunities set priorities on reading and literacy among K-3 students, addressing the needs of at-risk children, fields in which Native Hawaiians are underemployed, and the use of the Hawaiian language in instruction (U. S. Government, 2003; pp. 127–129).

Alaskan Native

No Child Left Behind points out that the educational achievement of many Alaskan Native children is below national norms, with Native performance low on standardized tests, high drop-out rates, and under-representation in higher education. A large majority of Alaskan Native children attend small and isolated rural schools due to the vast size of the state and distribution of its population, thus making it necessary to develop and implement innovative programs to serve this unique demographic. New NCLB requirements include cultural exchange programs, parenting education, dropout prevention, and community engagement programs. To provide more flexibility in the use of available funds, the following three programs have been combined into one: the Alaska Native Educational Planning, Curriculum Development, Teacher Training and Recruitment program; the Alaska Native Home-Based Education for Preschool Children program; and the Alaska Native Student Enrichment program.

Emphasis in funding is placed on the educational and cultural needs of Alaska Native students. Priority is given to Alaska Native regional nonprofit organizations or consortia that include at least one Alaska Native regional nonprofit organization.

> Competitive grants and contracts are awarded to eligible applicants, which include Alaska Native organizations, educational entities with experience in developing or operating Alaska Native programs or programs of instruction conducted in Alaska Native languages, cultural, and community-based organizations, and state education agencies (SEAs) or school districts, if they apply as part of a consortium involving an Alaska Native organization (U. S. Government, 2003; p. 130).

Acceptable funded activities under this program are:

- developing and implementing plans, methods, and strategies to improve the education of Alaska Natives;
- developing curricula and educational programs that address the educational needs of Alaska Native students;
- professional development activities;
- family literacy services;
- student enrichment programs in science and mathematics;
- research and data-collection activities to determine the educational status and needs of Alaska Native children and adults;
- remedial and enrichment programs to assist Alaska Native students in performing at a high level on standardized tests;
- education and training of Alaska Native students enrolled in a degree program that will lead to certification or licensing as teachers;
- parenting education;
- activities carried out through Even Start and Head Start programs and other early learning and preschool programs;
- career preparation activities to enable Alaska Native children and adults to prepare for meaningful employment;
- providing operational support and purchasing equipment to develop regional vocational schools in rural areas of Alaska, including boarding schools, for Alaska Native students in grades 9 through 12 or above, to provide students with the necessary resources to prepare for skilled employment opportunities (U.S. Government, 2003; p. 131).

Impact Aid Program (Title VIII)

Title VIII, Impact Aid, furnishes financial assistance to school districts that educate children living on federal property, whose parents are employed on federal property, who have a parent on active military duty, or a parent who is a foreign military officer. These formula and competitive grants can be utilized for facilities maintenance, construction or renovation of school facilities, or to serve children with disabilities. Federal property may include Indian lands, military bases, low-rent housing assisted under the US Housing Act of 1937, and school facilities owned by the US Department of Education.

General Provisions of NCLB (Title IX)

Title IX provides an overview of what is new in NCLB and the general requirements and provisions that affect all programs under the *No Child Left Behind Act*. Table 1.4 provides a complete summary of the general provisions.

NCLB Repeals, Redesignations, and Amendments to Other Statutes (Title X)

The McKinney-Vento Homeless Education Assistance Improvements provides formula grants to states to be distributed to districts to address the many challenges presented by homeless children and youth. Grant monies are to be utilized to facilitate the enrollment, attendance, and academic success of homeless children and youth. Issues such as transportation, residency requirements, immunizations, guardianship, and missing birth certificates and school records present a challenge to schools. Each state is required to establish or designate an Office or Coordinator for Education of Homeless Children and Youth. School districts may use funds for tutoring and

Table 1.4. NCLB Title IX—General Provisions.

Increases Accountability for Student Performance
• Allows development of content standards. State education agencies (SEAs) may use Title I administrative funds to develop challenging academic content standards and academic assessments. This may include, for example, developing additional academic content standards for science or for grades not yet included in state standards for math and reading.
• Prohibits federally sponsored national testing except international comparisons and other assessments explicitly provided by law, such as the National Assessment of Educational Progress (NAEP).
Reduces Bureaucracy and Increases Flexibility
• Provides authority to consolidate administrative funds. SEAs and school districts may consolidate administrative funds to eliminate duplication in conducting administrative functions to enhance the effectiveness and coordination of programs.
• Provides authority to submit a consolidated application. SEAs may apply for programmatic funds through a consolidated application process, rather than applying for funds on a program-by-program basis.
• Streamlines reporting for participation in U.S. Department of Education programs into a single annual consolidated report to reduce costly duplication and burden, and encourage effective program implementation.
• Continues the U.S. Department of Education's authority to grant waivers from many statutory or regulatory requirement of the No Child Left Behind Act. However, there are certain limitations and exceptions to this waiver authority set forth in the statute.
Empowers Parents
• Requires options to attend safe public schools. SEAs must establish and implement a policy to allow students attending persistently dangerous public schools or who become victims of violent crimes while at school to attend safe public schools within the district.
Other Major New Requirements
• Prohibits teacher testing. Program funds cannot be used for mandatory teacher or para-professional national testing

U. S. Department of Education, Office of Elementary and Secondary Education (2002). *No child left behind: A desktop reference.* Author: Washington, D. C., p. 134.

supplemental instruction, providing health services, professional development for staff, transportation costs, preschool programs, and coordination and collaboration with local agencies in an effort to provided more comprehensive services to homeless children, youth, and their families both in and out of school.

Unsafe School Choice Option

The safety of children and youth is a concern both in and out of school. If students do not feel safe, they cannot concentrate on learning and improve their academic achievement. Students as victims of crime in schools have been a topic of discussion in newspapers, magazines, on radio and television, the Internet, and social media networks. The *Unsafe School Choice Option* allows parents, regardless of income, to remove their children from a dangerous school setting. Any state receiving funds under any portion of ESEA is required to:

- Establish an *Unsafe School Choice Option* policy.
- Identify "persistently dangerous" schools.
- Identify types of offenses that are considered to be violent criminal offenses.
- Provide a safe public school choice option.
- Include a certification of compliance in application to ESEA funds (U.S. Department of Education, 2002; p. 137).

Whether a student is a victim of a violent crime on school property or attends a school that is considered "persistently dangerous," both elementary and secondary students are given the option of transferring to a safe public school, including charter schools, in the district.

Summary

The *Elementary and Secondary Education Act* has grown over the years from a program originally developed to close the achievement gap in mathematics and reading of children from lower socio-economic families to what we see today as a program that can serve all students through the implementation of research-based instruction and assessment of learning programs. *No Child Left Behind* provides states and school districts with a comprehensive guide to improving academic achievement for all students. It is also a program to close the academic achievement gap that exists among students from various social, cultural, and economic backgrounds across the United States and its territories. Closing this gap is not an easy task, and the effort has been ongoing since ESEA was first implemented in 1965.

Questions for Consideration

1. What are the similarities and differences between *Improving America's Schools Act of 1994* and the *No Child Left Behind Act of 2001*?

2. How have national and international politics influenced changes that have been made to ESEA programs over the years?

3. What are the similarities and differences between the 1994 and 2001 reauthorizations of ESEA and the emphasis on assessment of learning, accountability, and highly qualified teachers, staff, and school principals?

4. What do you consider to be the reasons for resistance to implementation of *No Child Left Behind Act of 2001* by some states and local school districts?

5. What efforts are required to ensure that all students achieve academically to set standards? Is it reasonable to require a set standard of academic achievement of all students? What should be the level of academic achievement for all students?

6. Is it reasonable to say some students should achieve to a set standard of academic achievement and others do not? Who or what group of students, if any, would be exempt from the requirement? Explain your answers demonstrating both sides of the argument.

7. Develop a plan showing how states and local schools can help all students meet the same high standards of academic achievement.

References

Anderson, L. W. & Pellicer, L. O. (1999). Synthesis of research on compensatory and remedial education. In Allan C. Ornstein and Linda S. Behar-Horenstein, *Contemporary Issues in Curriculum.* (2nd Ed.). pp. 244–251. Boston: Allyn and Bacon.

Brown v. Board of Education of Topeka, 347 U.S. 483, 74 S.Ct. 686 (1954).

Feighan, M. (2004). $12M in grants to Detroit aid after-school activities. *The Detroit News.* Section B. Metro. September 17, 2004, p. 1B.

Short, P. M. & Greer, J.T., (1997). *Leadership in empowered schools: Themes from innovative efforts.* Upper Saddle River, NJ: Merrill, an imprint of Prentice Hall.

U. S. Department of Education, Office of Elementary and Secondary Education (2002). *No child left behind: A desktop reference.* Author: Washington, D. C.

U.S. Department of Education (2003a). *Local educational agency identification and selection of school attendance areas and schools and allocation of Title I funds to those areas and schools; Non-regulatory guidance.* Washington, DC: U. S. Government. Retrieved on April 19, 2004, from http://www.ed.gov/progrmas/titleiparta/wdag.doc

U.S. Department of Education (2003b). *No child left behind: Charter school program, Title V, Part B: Non-regulatory guidance.* Washington, DC: U.S. Government Printing Office.

U.S. Department of Education (2010a). *ESEA blueprint for reform.* Office of Planning, Education, and Policy Development. Washington, DC. Retrieved from http://www2.ed.gov/policy/elsec/leg/blueprint/blueprint.pdf

U.S. Department of Education (2010b). *ESEA reauthorization: A blueprint for reform.* Retrieved from http://www2.ed.gov/policy/elsec/leg/blueprint/index.html

U.S. Department of Education (2010c). *ESEA reauthorization: A blueprint for reform.* NCLB and the Blueprint Powerpoint nclb_and_blueprint. ppt Retrieved from http://www2.ed.gov/policy/elsec/leg/blueprint/index.html

U.S. Department of Education (2010d). *Elementary and secondary education: A blueprint for reform. The reauthorization of the elementary and secondary education act.* Retrieved from http://www2.ed.gov/policy/elsec/leg/blueprint/publicationtoc.html

U.S. Department of Education (2010e). *Obama's administration educational reform plan emphasizes flexibility, resources and accountability.* Retrieved from http://www.ed.gov/news/press-releases/obama-administrations-education-reform-plan-emphasizes-flexibility-resources-and

U.S. Government (1965). *Elementary and secondary education act.* (P.L. 89-10). Washington, DC: U.S. Government Printing Office.

U.S. Government (1978). *Revisions to the elementary and secondary education act.* (P.L. 95-561). Washington, DC: U.S. Government Printing Office.

U.S. Government (1981). *Education consolidation and improvement act.* (P.L. 97-35). Washington, DC: U. S. Government Printing Office.

U.S. Government (1988). *Hawkins-Stafford elementary and secondary education improvements act of 1988.* (P.L. 100-297). Washington, DC: U.S. Government Printing Office.

U.S. Government (1994a). *Goals 2000: Educate America act.* 20 USC 5801. Washington, DC: U.S. Government Printing Office.

U. S. Government (1994b). *Improving America's schools act of 1994: Reauthorizing the elementary and secondary education act of 1965.* (P.L. 103-382). Washington, DC: U.S. Government Printing Office.

U. S. Government (2002). *No child left behind act of 2001: Reauthorization of the elementary and secondary education act of 1965* (P.L 107-110). Washington, DC: U.S. Government Printing Office.

CHAPTER 2

Curriculum, Assessment, Accountability, and Quality

Introduction

AS we have seen in Chapter 1, the *Elementary and Secondary Education Act* (ESEA or the Act) has an extensive history dating to 1965 and demonstrating the federal government's role in the education of economically disadvantaged and handicapped children. The key principles of the most recent reauthorization of the Act, *No Child Left Behind* (NCLB), are assessment, accountability, flexibility, choice, and quality. These principles laid the foundation of, and act as a guide to, the implementation of every program authorized under *No Child Left Behind*. NCLB places a strong emphasis on assessment of learning with increased accountability for student performance; flexibility in the use of federal funds for states, school districts, and schools; more rights and choices for parents of disadvantaged children; and an emphasis on the implementation of educational programs and practices that have been demonstrated through rigorous scientific research to be effective.

Assessment of Learning

Assessment of learning can be a vital component in improving student academic achievement and should be an integral part of the instructional process. The classroom teacher uses data gained through testing to improve instruction and learning. Testing data can also be utilized to determine professional development needs, individual student needs, effectiveness of the learning environment, curriculum development, and school improvement strategies. Over the years, regular classroom assessment of learning has been shown to be effective in helping educators understand cognitive processes, identify individual student needs, and develop instructional approaches such as collaborative learning, differentiated instruction, and constructivist learning. These and other strategies and the use of regular classroom assessment measures have brought gains in student achievement. Standardized testing, on the other hand, is utilized to determine outcome measures of student achievement over a longer period of time as opposed to shorter term mastery of a text chapter or unit of instruction. It is questionable whether required standardized assessments of learning have any impact on individual student learning, and it is has been claimed that they only provide data related to classroom and school ranking.

> The mistake we have made at all levels is to believe that once-a-year standardized assessments alone can provide sufficient information and motivation to increase student learning. In fact, this belief

in the power of standardized testing has blinded public officials and school leaders to a completely different application of assessment . . . day-to-day classroom assessment . . . that has been shown to trigger remarkable gains in student achievement (Stiggins, 2004, pp. 22–23).

Formative classroom assessment based on what is taught day-to-day provides a direct measure of individual student achievement. Standardized testing provides an indirect measure of general student achievement. Standardized test results appear to reflect directly on the classroom teacher. A public ranking of schools may in itself be enough motivation for educators to improve classroom instruction; however, as educators concentrate on test preparation, content standards, and learning benchmarks, standardized tests may also be counterproductive to improvements in student academic achievement. On the other hand, standardized tests do provide information to state departments of education and federal funding granting authorities related to accountability of the use of federal monies and taxpayer dollars.

No Child Left Behind

States were required under the previous reauthorization of ESEA, *Improving America's Schools Act of 1994,* to develop standards in reading/language arts and mathematics and to assess student knowledge in these areas in grades 3, 6, and 8. NCLB required that states develop and implement annual assessments of learning for all students in reading/language arts and mathematics in grades 3 through 8 by the 2005–2006 school year and annual science assessments in the same grades by 2007–2008. "These assessments must be aligned with state academic content and achievement standards and involve multiple measures, including measures of higher-order thinking and understanding" (U. S Department of Education, 2002; p. 4). Measuring higher-order thinking is essential in determining students' ability to be reflective, to analyze, to question their own thinking and practice, identify logical flaws in arguments, evaluate premises from which arguments are launched, search for evidence to support their claims, and explore likely consequences of decisions and actions (Noddings, 2004). States are required to report assessment results to the Secretary of Education and disseminate them to school districts in a timely manner so that the results can be used as a guide in program development directed toward improve student achievement.

Children With Disabilities

Participation in annual assessments of learning is mandated for all students, including children with disabilities and limited English proficiency. Reasonable accommodations are to be made for these students. In the case of students with significant cognitive disabilities, alternate assessments may be developed. There is currently a one percent cap on the number of student test scores a state has the discretion to consider not utilizing when reporting test results to the Secretary of Education. The Department of Education (DOE) has offered additional flexibility on reporting test scores of students with serious cognitive disabilities.

The policy guidance outlines the means by which states can seek an exemption to the current one percent cap on the number of proficient scores from alternate assessments that may be included in calculations for determining adequate yearly progress (AYP) under the new law. To exceed the cap, states must provide the following information:

- An explanation of circumstances that result in more than one percent of all students statewide having the most significant cognitive disabilities and who are achieving a proficient score on alternate assessments based on alternate achievement standards;
- Data showing the incidence rate of students with the most significant cognitive disabilities; and
- Information showing how the state has implemented alternate achievement standards.

Without this flexibility, (test) scores would have to be measured against grade-level standards and considered "not proficient" when states measure AYP. The number of those scores may not exceed 1 percent of all students in the grades tested. In other words, students will be assessed by the achievement of standards deemed appropriate for their intellectual development, thus allowing states to more accurately gauge their progress (U.S. Department of Education, 2004a; p. 1).

Additional information on students with disabilities and special education services in the schools can be found in Chapter 3.

Limited English Proficient Students

New policies have also been initiated for limited English proficient (LEP) students. NCLB provides more than $13 billion for LEP students for English language acquisition and improved academic achievement. The DOE recognizes that due to language barriers or lack of formal education prior to immigrating to the United States, LEP students often have difficulty participating in state assessments.

The new flexibility will allow LEP students, during their first year of enrollment in U.S. schools, to have the option of taking the reading/language arts content assessment in addition to taking the English language proficiency assessments. They would take the mathematics assessment with accommodations as appropriate. States may, but would not be required to, include results from the mathematics and, if given, the reading/language arts content assessments in AYP calculations, which are part of the accountability requirements under NCLB.

. . . the other new flexibility would, for AYP calculations, allow states for up to two years to include in the LEP subgroup students who have attained English proficiency. This is an option for states and would give states the flexibility to allow schools and local education agencies (LEAs) to get credit for improving English language proficiency from year to year (U.S. Department of Education, 2004e; pp. 1–2).

NCLB also requires the administration of the *National Assessment of Educational Progress* (NAEP) in mathematics and reading to students in fourth and eighth grades. Since the 1960s, the NAEP has become the standard for monitoring the academic progress of students in America's schools. The results of these tests form data for the Department of Education to assist in determining and monitoring the rigor of state-developed academic achievement standards. For further information, see Chapter 5, which explores in depth English as a Second Language (ESL) and bilingual education programs serving limited English proficient students.

Accountability

With clearly defined goals for student learning and assessment, it stands to reason that teachers in the classroom must be well prepared and competent to instruct students. NCLB has implemented accountability factors for teachers, paraprofessionals, and school leaders to ensure they have the qualifications and are prepared to teach children in K–12 classrooms. Because of the accountability factors built into NCLB, many states that did not develop school improvement plans as required under *Improving America's Schools Act of 1994* were left attempting to develop improvement plans to meet requirements of the *No Child Left Behind Act of 2001*.

. . . when this administration took office, only 11 states were in compliance with the 1994 ESEA. One of the first tasks we undertook was to address those states that were not in compliance with that law. In less than a year, we entered into compliance or timeline agreements with states to ensure that they would be in compliance with a law that had been in effect for seven years but really had never been enforced. This was critical, for, as you may know, many of the principles of NCLB (development of standards, assessing students, identifying schools for improvement, to name a few) have their roots in the 1994 ESEA reauthorization (Paige, 2004).

Curriculum standards and assessment instruments provide the foundation for generating information related to student learning and achievement. If a student is not making adequate yearly progress in learning, assessment should indicate there is a problem. If a school has large numbers of students who are not learning, there is a problem. If a district has multiple schools with students who are not learning, there is a problem. Assessment of learning assists in determining where achievement gaps exist so that curriculum can be realigned to address deficiencies. To support student learning and to ensure all students are receiving a quality education, NCLB requires that all teachers are educationally prepared and qualified to teach in each of their subject area(s). Additional support, to ensure student academic progress, is provided to schools and parents through supplemental educational services, technical assistance to schools and teachers, professional development programs, public school choice, flexibility in use of federal funds, and identified funding for transportation and additional supplemental services for students in schools not meeting adequate yearly progress (AYP).

States and schools are required to report adequate yearly progress of student academic achievement, identify schools and school districts in need of improvement, offer students the option to transfer to another public school that has met adequate yearly progress in assessments of learning, provide transportation for students exercising the public school choice option, provide professional development to teachers and school principals, provide supplemental education services from a public or private-sector provider, and ultimately, to take corrective actions if a school or school district fails to make adequate yearly progress for four years consecutively. In the case of an individual school, these corrective actions may include:

- replacing school staff
- implementing a new curriculum
- decreasing management authority at the school level
- appointing an outside expert to advise the school
- extending the school day or school year
- reorganizing the school internally (U.S. Department of Education, 2002; p. 6).

Similarly, sanctions for a school district may include:

- deferring or reducing administrative funds
- implementing a new curriculum (with professional development)
- replacing personnel
- establishing an alternative governance arrangement
- appointing a receiver or trustee to administer the district in place of the superintendent and school board
- abolishing or restructuring the school district (U.S. Department of Education, 2002; pp. 6–7).

Failure to demonstrate adequate yearly progress in student achievement can result in a sequence of events leading from identifying a school for improvement, taking corrective actions such as those shown above, to the complete restructuring of a school or school district.

Reporting progress in meeting annual assessment goals is an essential element of accountability. State report cards, school district report cards, and an annual state report to the Secretary of Education are required as a means to inform the public of the status of their schools. State report cards must show assessment results for all students, graduation rates for secondary schools, school district performance, and professional qualifications of teachers. School district report cards are required to provide information on student achievement and information on schools identified for improvement. State reports to the Secretary of Education must contain information on progress in developing and implementing academic assessments, reports on student achievement, teacher quality, names of schools needing improvement, supplemental service programs, and public school choice options (U.S. Department of Education, 2002). A more complete listing of required state activities is presented in Table 2.1.

Highly Qualified Teachers, Paraprofessionals, and School Leaders

Teachers

No Child Left Behind requires that all teachers and paraprofessionals who provide instruction in Title I schools and programs are highly qualified in the subject area in which they teach.

The requirement that teachers be highly qualified applies to all public elementary or secondary school teachers employed by a local educational agency who teach a core academic subject. "Highly qualified" means that the teacher:

1. Has obtained full State certification as teacher or passed the State teacher licensing examination and holds a license to teach in the State, and does not have certification or licensure requirements waived on an emergency, temporary, or provisional basis;
2. Holds a minimum of a bachelor's degree; and
3. Has demonstrated subject matter competency in each of the academic subjects in which the teacher teaches, in a manner determined by the State and in compliance with Section 9109(23) of ESEA (U.S. Department of Education; 2004b, p. 7).

Table 2.1. Key Activities for State Education Agencies.

State education agencies (SEAs) must:

- Produce an annual report card.
- Develop and implement annual assessments in reading, language arts, and mathematics in grades 3–8 and at least once in grades 10–12, by 2005–2006.
- Develop and implement standards in science by 2005-06 and assessments in science by 2007–08.
- Annually assess the English proficiency of students who are learning the English language.
- Ensure the prompt dissemination of state assessment results (before the beginning of the next school year).
- Participate in biennial state-level NAEP assessments of fourth- and eighth-grade reading and mathematics.
- Define and implement an adequate yearly progress definition for the state, school districts, and schools.
- Annually review the progress of each school district to determine whether schools receiving assistance are making adequate yearly progress and whether each district is carrying out its responsibilities; SEAs also must publicize the results of this review.
- Establish a statewide system of support for districts and schools in need of improvement.
- Establish a statewide system of support for districts and schools in need of improvement.
- Establish a program for making academic achievement awards to schools that significantly close the achievement gap or exceed adequate yearly progress for two or more years.
- Publish and disseminate to parents and the public information on any corrective action taken by the state.
- Develop a list of approved providers of supplemental educational services and support, monitor, and disseminate information about these providers of supplemental educational services on the same basis as other eligible entities.
- Ensure that students in schools previously identified for improvement under the IASAQ provisions are offered school choice and, if the school had been identified for two years or more, supplemental services, at the beginning of the 2002–03 school year.
- Ensure that schools provide instruction by highly qualified instructional staff (U.S. Department of Education; 2002, p. 10).

All teachers must be qualified in the core academic subjects as defined by NCLB; new teachers who teach in Title I programs hired after the beginning of 2002–2003 and all teachers in core academic subjects as of the end of the 2005–2006 school year (U.S. Department of Education, 2003; p. 1). The core academic subjects are: English, Reading, Language Arts, Mathematics, Science, Foreign Languages, Civics and Government, Economics, Arts, History, and Geography. NCLB defines science as including biology, chemistry, physical science, physics, and earth/space science. It is delegated to each state to define how it will determine whether a teacher is highly qualified within the guidelines of NCLB. Each state has the flexibility to set standards and definitions of what is considered highly qualified. Additionally, each state has the opportunity to seek guidance and come to an agreement with the Department of Education related to the definition of highly qualified for their state, particularly within the multi-subject areas such as science and social studies. An Internet search of state departments of education websites will provide detailed information on how each state is responding to and complying with the requirements of NCLB. It will also disclose differences in compliance among states, demonstrating the flexibility built into the Act.

Flexibility

There has been particular anxiousness on the part of state and local agencies related to rural teachers, multi-subject teachers, and science teachers meeting NCLB highly qualified teacher standards. Following a great deal of confusion and questioning on the part of State Education Agencies (SEAs) and Local Education Agencies (LEAs) and subsequent appeals to the Department of Education, the DOE in 2004 issued new guidelines granting greater flexibility for identifying highly qualified teachers in these three areas. The Department of Education offered the following guidance:

I. Rural Teachers

> ... Often, the teachers in (rural) areas are required to teach more than one academic subject. This new flexibility is designed to recognize this challenge and provide additional time for these teachers to prove they are highly qualified.

- Under this new policy, teachers in eligible, rural districts who are highly qualified in at least one subject will have three years to become highly qualified in the additional subjects they teach. They must also be provided professional development, intense supervision or structured mentoring to become highly qualified in those additional subjects.

II. Science Teachers

> Science teachers, like rural teachers, are often needed to teach in more than one field of science. Some states allow such science teachers to be certified under a general science certification, while others require a subject-specific certification (such as physics, biology or chemistry). In science, where demand for teachers is so high, the Department is issuing additional flexibility for teachers to demonstrate that they are highly qualified.

- Now, states may determine—based on their current certification requirements—to allow science teachers to demonstrate that they are highly qualified either in "broad field" science or individual fields of science (such as physics, biology, or chemistry).

III. Multi-subject Teachers

> Current teachers do not have to return to school or take a test in every subject to demonstrate that they meet highly qualified requirements. *No Child Left Behind* allows states to create an alternative method (High, Objective, Uniform State Standard of Evaluation or HOUSSE) for teachers. This alternate process could become unnecessarily protracted and repetitive as instructors go through the HOUSSE process for each subject.

- Under the new guidelines, states may streamline this evaluation process by developing a method for current, multi-subject teachers to demonstrate through one process that they are highly qualified in each of their subjects and maintain the same high standards in subject matter mastery (U.S. Department of Education, 2004d; p. 1).

New definitions and flexibility in determining highly qualified teacher requirements for rural teachers, science teachers, and multi-subject teachers do not change other existing flexibility guidelines related to middle-school teacher requirements, testing flexibility, special education teachers, or HOUSSE for current teachers. Each state has provided its own definition of High, Objective, Uniform State Standard of Evaluation to offer a means for current teachers who do not meet the definition of highly qualified to demonstrate knowledge and competence in the subject they currently teach. Generally, a teacher can meet HOUSSE standards by developing a portfolio of professional material demonstrating competency in a particular subject area.

> High, Objective, Uniform State Standard of Evaluation (HOUSSE): NCLB allows states to develop an additional way for current teachers to demonstrate subject-matter competency and meet highly qualified teacher requirements. Proof may consist of a combination of teaching experience, professional development, and knowledge in the subject garnered over time in the profession (U. S. Government, 2004d; p. 2).

NCLB gives general guidelines for HOUSSE, and each state provides its own definition of what is acceptable compliance under these standards.

Special Education Teachers

Congress updated guidelines for programs supporting education of children with disabilities in 2004. The most recent reauthorization is entitled *Individuals with Disabilities Education Improvement Act of 2004* (U. S. House of Representatives, 2004). The guidelines modified NCLB highly qualified teacher requirements to apply more specifically to special education teachers. Prior to this change, any middle or secondary special education teachers responsible for direct instruction of students were required to be qualified in the subject they teach. The newly developed guidelines for a highly qualified special education teacher are as follows:

1. All special education teachers must be fully certified in special education by completing state-approved preparation program or passing a licensing exam.
2. Temporary or emergency certifications in special education are prohibited.
3. Teachers must have earned a bachelor's degree.
4. Teachers of students with significant cognitive impairments (those who are in the "1% alternate achievement" category) must be fully certified in special education and have content competence in at least elementary education.
5. Both new and veteran secondary teachers of multiple subjects must be fully certified in special education and either meet the current requirements of the *No Child Left Behind Act of 2001* for the core academic subjects they teach or pass a "high, objective, uniform state standard of evaluation" (HOUSSE) as an alternative (AACTE Briefs, 2004).

ESL and Bilingual Education Teachers

English as a second language or bi-lingual education teachers who provide instruction in core academic subjects must also be highly qualified in the subject(s) they teach, and fluent in English and any other language in which they provide instruction (U.S. Department of Education, 2004d; p. 2).

Paraprofessionals

Paraprofessionals are required to have "at least two years postsecondary education, or for an applicant with a high school diploma, demonstrate necessary skills on a formal state or local assessment" (U.S. Government, 2002; p. 8). These requirements do not apply to those paraprofessionals who only assist in parent involvement or are used for translation services. Paraprofessionals are not allowed to provide instructional services unless under the direct supervision of a certified teacher.

School Administrators and Teacher Leaders

No Child Left Behind provides funding for state grants to recruit, train, and provide professional development opportunities for teachers, school principals, and assistant principals. These initiatives must be based on programs and practices that have been demonstrated effective through rigorous scientific research. Funds are available for partnerships between high-need districts and schools/colleges of arts and sciences, as well as schools/colleges of education that prepare teachers. A key activity of a state agency for higher education is to identify and prioritize needs across the state and award partnership grants to school districts and institutions of higher education, enabling them to develop and provide professional development and technical assistance activities for school leaders.

Funding Grant Programs and Partnerships

NCLB offered a number of new discretionary grant programs and partnership opportunities. One such program was the Advanced Certification or Advanced Credentialing funding grant that encourages advanced training of teachers particularly in conjunction with the National Board for Professional Teaching Standards. Math and Science Partnerships is another program directed toward improving student competencies in mathematics and science. This program focuses on recruiting, training, and advising teachers in these fields, providing ongoing professional development, and aligning mathematics and science curriculum with state, local, and post-secondary standards. The Early Childhood Educator Professional Development grant "aims to enhance the school readiness of young children, particularly those who are disadvantaged, and prevent them from encountering difficulties once they enter school" (U. S. Department of Education, 2004; p. 44). This discretionary grant program supports professional development activities based on scientifically based research and the training of early childhood educators to provide developmentally appropriate school-readiness services.

> The program will provide two-year grants to partnerships consisting of: (1) one or more institutions of higher education or another public or private entity that provides professional development for early childhood educators who work with children from low-income families in high-need communities; (2) one or more local or state public agencies, Head Start agencies, or private organizations; and (3) an entity that has demonstrated experience in providing training to educators in early childhood programs in identifying and preventing behavior problems in children or working with children who are victims or suspected to be victims of abuse (U. S. Department of Education, 2004; p. 45)

Troops to Teachers and Transition to Teaching are alternative teacher certification programs encouraging former military and mid-career professionals to enter the teaching profession and help relieve shortages in high-need areas such as mathematics, science, and special education.

Supplemental Programs

Literacy Initiatives

Title I funds of the *Elementary and Secondary Education Act* were historically directed toward improving academic achievement in reading for economically disadvantaged children. *No Child*

Left Behind continued this tradition. Reading First, Early Reading First, the William F. Goodling Even Start Family Literacy Program, Improving Literacy Through School Libraries, and National Writing Project represent funding programs available under NCLB to address serious deficiencies in children's ability to read. These programs are:

> . . . designed to help states, school districts, and schools, address this issue and to ensure that every child can read at grade level or above by the end of third grade through the implementation of instructional programs and materials, assessments, and professional development grounded in scientifically based reading research (U.S. Department of Education, 2002; p 11).

NCLB recognizes the importance of an early introduction to development of the linguistic and cognitive domains of children. "An extensive body of evidence is now available stressing the importance of early reading skills, including phonological awareness and vocabulary development. Early Reading First is designed to improve these skills" (U.S. Department of Education, 2002; p 14). Integrated literacy services are provided for parents and their children through the William F. Goodling Even Start Family Literacy Program.

> The basic premise behind Even Start's family literacy approach is that the four components of adult education, early childhood education, parenting education, and interactive literacy activities for parents and their children build on each other and that families need to receive all four services in order to bring lasting change and improve children's school success (U.S. Department of Education, 2002; p. 17).

These programs are further supported by funds available through Early Childhood Educator Professional Development. Theories of human development and learning have emphasized the need for early stimulation and encouragement of curiosity in infants and young children. Research indicates that much of a child's intellectual development has taken place by the age of six. Early childhood programs such as Head Start, Even Start, Jump Start, Follow Through, and early literacy programs such as those supported by *No Child Left Behind* play an important role in encouraging and supporting school readiness for economically disadvantaged children (Parkay & Hass, 2000). Another funding opportunity offered by NCLB that addresses narrowing the educational gap between advantaged and disadvantaged children when they start elementary school is Ready-to-Learn Television. This program supports the "distribution of programming and printed materials to increase school readiness for young children in limited English proficient households and to increase family literacy (U. S. Government, 2002; p. 61).

Improving Literacy Through School Libraries is "designed to improve literacy skills and academic achievement of students by providing them with access to up-to-date school library materials; technologically advanced school library media centers; and professionally certified school library media specialists" (U. S. Department of Education, 2002; p 21). The National Writing Project is a "nonprofit educational organization that supports programs to train classroom teachers to teach writing effectively to their students" (U.S. Department of Education, 2002; p 54). Funding grants are available for the organization, or to contract with nonprofit educational organizations and institutes of higher education, to develop and provide professional development programs to train teachers to teach writing.

Programs Serving Migratory, Delinquent, and At-Risk Students

Both *Improving America's Schools Act of 1994* and *No Child Left Behind* have demonstrated awareness of the special needs of migratory children, neglected and delinquent youth, and school dropouts. NCLB addresses the needs of these children and youth at-risk of not achieving to their highest potential in a variety of ways. Migratory children are faced with multiple challenges as they move from state to state. Differences in curriculum, poor record keeping and transferring of information between schools, social isolation, absence of health records, cultural or language differences, and general disruption of their education results in poor academic achievement and early dropout rates of these students from schools. To address this set of problems, a national information system has been established to electronically transfer health and educational information for all migrant children served by the Migrant Education Program (MEP). It also requires state and local education agencies to share migrant student records with other states and districts at no cost. Migrant children must be included in annual assessments of learning. To keep parents of migrant children informed, school districts are required to provide parents with report cards in a language and format they can understand. States are required to report disaggregated results of migrant student achievement along with other annual assessment reports. Additionally, MEP encourages family literacy services for parents and other family members of migrant students, and advocacy and outreach to migrant children and their families on such topics as education, health, nutrition, and available social services (U.S. Department of Education, 2002, pp. 23–25).

The Prevention and Intervention Programs for Children and Youth Who Are Neglected, Delinquent, or At-Risk provides financial assistance to educational programs for children and youth in state-operated institutions or community day programs. It also provides assistance to LEA programs involving collaboration with correctional facilities. The focus of these programs is to provide transitional services between the correctional facility or institution and the school district and to "concentrate on providing student participants with the knowledge and skills needed to make a successful transition to secondary school completion, vocational or technical training, further education, or employment" (U.S. Department of Education, 2002, p. 26). Success of these programs is measured by how students maintain and improve academic achievement, accrue school credits, make the transition to a regular school program, complete secondary school or obtain employment, and participate in postsecondary education or job-training programs.

Sagor (1993) defines at-risk students as those who, on the basis of several risk factors, are unlikely to graduate from high school and may be without the skills and self-esteem necessary to be successful in leading a fulfilling life. School Dropout Prevention aims funding at schools with dropout rates higher than their state average. It is a grant program to SEAs and LEAs to implement sustainable, research-based, and coordinated school dropout prevention and reentry programs. Funding can be used for counseling and mentoring programs for at-risk students, reduction in student-teacher ratios, professional development, and implementing comprehensive school reform models.

History and Civic Education

No Child Left Behind offers funding opportunities in Titles I and II for the development of instructional programs, partnerships, professional development, and exchange opportunities. Civic Education is designed to "improve the quality of civics and government education, foster civic competence and responsibility, and improve the quality of civic and economic education through cooperative education exchange programs with emerging democracies" (U. S. Government, 2002; p. 55). Teaching Traditional American History provides funds to districts to design and implement research-based professional development programs for teachers that will support student achievement by improving teachers' knowledge, understanding, and appreciation of American history. Enhancing Education Through Technology stresses the use of technology in curriculum planning and instruction to engage students in learning and improve academic achievement.

NCLB Updated

The *Elementary and Secondary Education Act* has not been rewritten or reauthorized since its reiteration in 2001, which is more commonly known and easily recognized as *No Child Left Behind.* Alternatives, incentives, and changes to the academic curriculum have been authorized by the Department of Education, including initiatives such as Race to the Top, waivers from NCLB requirements available to state departments of education, the Common Core Curriculum, emphasis on STEM (Science, Technology, Engineering, and Mathematics) academic preparation, and greater emphasis on both teacher and school administrator preparation, certification, and evaluation of performance. A blueprint for revising the Elementary and Secondary Education Act was issued in 2010 (U.S. Government, 2010a).

> This blueprint builds on the significant reforms already made in response to the American Recovery and Reinvestment Act of 2009 around four areas: (1) Improving teacher and principal effectiveness; (2) Providing information to families to help them evaluate and improve their children's schools; (3) Implementing college- and career-ready standards; and (4) Improving student learning and achievement in America's lowest-performing schools by providing intensive support and effective interventions (U. S. Government, 2010b).

Expanded ESEA Flexibility Waivers

States have been granted the option to request flexibility in meeting certain requirements of NCLB. These waiver options were first published in 2004, updated in 2011, and updated again in 2012 (U.S. Department of Education, 2013a). The goal of the waivers is to improve the academic achievement of all students. The four basic principles of the waivers are:

- Implementation of college- and career-ready expectations for all students;
- State-developed differentiated recognition, accountability and support;
- Support for effective instruction and leadership; and
- Reduction of duplication and unnecessary burden (U.S. Department of Education, 2013b).

Race to the Top

The American Recovery and Reinvestment Act of 2009 (ARRA) was designed to stimulate the economy, support job creation, and invest in critical sectors, including education (U.S. Government, 2009). The ARRA supports investments in innovative strategies directed toward school reforms aimed toward improved academic performance of students, long-term gains in school and school system capacity, and increased productivity and effectiveness of local and state school systems.

> The ARRA provides $4.35 billion for the Race to the Top Fund, a competitive grant program designed to encourage and reward States that are creating the conditions for education innovation and reform; achieving significant improvement in student outcomes, including making substantial gains in student achievement, closing achievement gaps, improving high school graduation rates, and ensuring student preparation for success in college and careers; and implementing ambitious plans in four core education reform areas:
>
> - adopting standards and assessments that prepare students to succeed in college and the workplace and to compete in the global economy;
> - building data systems that measure student growth and success, and inform teachers and principals about how they can improve instruction;
> - recruiting, developing, rewarding, and retaining effective teachers and principals, especially where they are needed most; and
> - turning around our lowest-achieving schools (U.S. Department of Education, 2009, p. 2).

Race to the Top is designed to reward States that develop educational reforms directed toward raising student achievement and have clearly developed plans to maintain the reform efforts into the future. States are selected to receive a grant on the basis of points. These points are clearly defined and encompass a variety of educational reform topics such as: developing and adopting common core standards; improving principal and teacher effectiveness based on performance; improving the effectiveness of teacher and principal preparation programs; intervening in the lowest-achieving schools and LEAs; ensuring successful conditions for high-performing charters and other innovative schools; emphasis on science, technology, engineering, and mathematics (STEM); and improving early learning outcomes. A full list of the selection criteria, priories, and points can be found in Table 2.2.

Table 2.2. Race to the Top Programs Criteria, Priority, and Points.

Selection Criteria

  A. State Success Factors (125 points)

    (A)(1) Articulating State's education reform agenda and LEAs' participation in it (65 points)

    (A)(2) Building strong statewide capacity to implement, scale up, and sustain proposed plans (30 points)

    (A)(3) Demonstrating significant progress in raising achievement and closing gaps (30 points)

  B. Standards and Assessments (70 points)

    (B)(1) Developing and adopting common standards (40 points)

    (B)(2) Developing and implementing common, high-quality assessments (10 points)

    (B)(3) Supporting the transition to enhanced standards and high-quality assessments (20 points)

  C. Data Systems to Support Instruction (47 points)

    (C)(1) Fully implementing a statewide longitudinal data system (24 points)

    (C)(2) Accessing and using State data (5 points)

    (C)(3) Using data to improve instruction (18 points)

  D. Great Teachers and Leaders (138 points)

    (D)(1) Providing high-quality pathways for aspiring teachers and principals (21 points)

    (D)(2) Improving teacher and principal effectiveness based on performance (58 points)

    (D)(3) Ensuring equitable distribution of effective teachers and principals (25 points)

    (D)(4) Improving the effectiveness of teacher and principal preparation programs (14 points)

    (D)(5) Providing effective support to teachers and principals (20 points)

  E. Turning Schools Around the Lowest-Achieving (50 points)

    (E)(1) Intervening in the lowest-achieving schools and LEAs (10 points)

    (E)(2) Turning around the lowest- achieving schools (40 points)

  F. General Selection Criteria (55 points)

    (F)(1) Making education funding a priority (10 points)

    (F)(2) Ensuring successful conditions for high-performing charters and other innovative schools (40 points)

    (F)(3) Demonstrating other significant reform conditions (5 points)

Priorities

- Priority 1: Absolute Priority—Comprehensive Approach to Education Reform
- Priority 2: Competitive Preference Priority–Emphasis on Science, Technology, Engineering, and Mathematics (STEM) (15 points, all or nothing)
- Priority 3: Invitational Priority—Innovations for Improving Early Learning Outcomes
- Priority 4: Invitational Priority—Expansion and Adaptation of Statewide Longitudinal Data Systems
- Priority 5: Invitational Priority—P-20 Coordination, Vertical and Horizontal Alignment
- Priority 6: Invitational Priority—School-Level Conditions for Reform, Innovation, and Learning (U.S. Department of Education, 2009, p. 2).

In the overview of Race to the Top programs the reader will recognize words and phrases such as common core curriculum, science, technology, engineering, and mathematics (STEM), assessment, evaluation of performance, teacher and administrator preparation and early learning, terms with which the educational community has become familiar.

Common Core State Standards Initiative

The Common Core Standards have been developed and established to provide consistent standards nationwide with the goal of preparing students for success in college and the world of work. The Council of State School Officers (CCSSO) and the National Governors Association (NGA) led the development of the Common Core State Standards which are based on the following mission statement:

> The Common Core State Standards provide a consistent, clear understanding of what students are expected to learn, so teachers and parents know what they need to do to help them. The standards are designed to be robust and relevant to the real world, reflecting the knowledge and skills that our young people need for success in college and careers. With American students fully prepared for the future, our communities will be best positioned to compete successfully in the global economy (CCSSO, 2012)

The Common Core Standards are a single set of high-quality standards for grades K–12 in the areas of mathematics and English language arts. They are the result of the CCSSO and the NGA working together with representatives from participating states, researchers, educators, national organizations, and community groups. They reflect feedback received from the general public, teachers, parents, business leaders, and content area experts and are informed by the standards of other high performing nations (CCSSO, 2010a). As stated by the Council of Chief State School Officers,

> The criteria used to develop the college- and career-readiness standards, as well as these K–12 standards are:
> - Aligned with college and work expectations;
> - Include rigorous content and application of knowledge through high-order skills;
> - Build upon strengths and lessons of current state standards;
> - Informed by top-performing countries, so that all students are prepared to succeed in a global economy and society; and,
> - Evidence and/or research-based (CCSSO, 2010a).

Implementation and instructional resources have been developed by the CCSSO (2010b), the NGA Center for Best Practices (2011), and individual states. Professional organizations and states that have adopted the standards, have developed instructional materials and presented workshops and webinars, to assist school administrators and classroom teachers in the introduction, adaptation, and incorporation of the standards into classroom instruction and assessment. Learning expectations are clearly outlined for grades K through 12 in English language arts and mathematics (CCSSO, 2010b). In addition to the common core elements for mathematics and English language arts, additional resources have been developed to assist in adaptation of the standards for English language learners, special education students, and common core standards for English language arts and literacy in history/social studies, science, and technical subjects.

Science, Technology, Engineering, and Mathematics (STEM)

The Blueprint for Reform of the Elementary and Secondary Education Recovery (U.S. Government, 2010b) was developed in response to the *American Recovery and Reinvestment Act of 2009* (U.S. Government, 2009). Part of this blueprint is an initiative to develop high performance standards and student achievement in Science, Technology, Engineering, and Mathematics (STEM) and is listed as a priority under Race to the Top for inclusion in applications for available federal grant funding.

> President Obama has identified an overarching goal to improve our STEM education compared to other nations, and identified three overarching priorities to ensure more students develop the skills needed to succeed in the STEM fields: improving the quality of math and science teachers so more students have opportunities for high-quality STEM learning and are motivated to pursue STEM degrees and careers; improving undergraduate teaching practices so more well-prepared STEM students persist to a degree in these fields; and expanding STEM education and career opportunities for underrepresented groups, including women and minorities (U.S. Government, 2013).

The U.S. Department of Education released in 2010 a Blueprint for Reform: Reauthorization of the Elementary and Secondary Education Act in which STEM and Race to the Top are addressed along with a full proposal for reauthorization of the Act (U.S, Department of Education, 2010a). Along with this proposal the Department of Education has also developed and published a comparison between the current NCLB legislation and the proposed Blueprint for Reform (U.S. Department of Education, 2010b). More detailed information on both the Blueprint for Reform and the comparison between NCLB and the Blueprint can be found in Appendix B and Appendix C of this text.

Instructional Leadership and Assessment

School Administrators

The challenge for school administrators is to know and understand NCLB, Race to the Top, Common Core Curriculum, STEM and their funding sources; ensure that all teachers are given the support to become and to remain highly qualified in their area of expertise; evaluate test results; and implement programs to ensure that adequate yearly progress (AYP) is attained. Appropriate and targeted allocation of resources is the most obvious method of supporting teachers and instructional activities. Supplies, space, support staff, instructional materials, facility maintenance, scheduled preparation time, maintenance of an environment conducive to learning, funds for professional development, and time to attend conferences or participate in district-developed workshops are all areas to be taken into consideration in budget development. Evaluation of teaching and instructional materials used is another method to ensure higher- quality performance in the classroom.

Teacher Leaders

NCLB stresses accountability and summative assessment of student learning. Teachers are the key to ensure students do learn. Remaining current in content knowledge and applying proven research-based instructional methodologies to classroom teaching are tasks facing the teacher as instructional leader. It is important that instructional skills are addressed and evaluated regularly and opportunities are taken by teachers to update and improve their skills through professional development, shared peer observation and evaluation, updating content area knowledge through additional coursework, and remaining current with research literature and best practices.

As a counterpoint to all the emphasis on assessment *of* learning, it may be time for teachers and administrators to consider assessment *for* learning. NCLB emphasizes summative assessment of student learning as opposed to formative assessment while the student is in the process of learning. Black and Wiliam (1998) have demonstrated through research that formative assessment can raise student achievement.

Assessment for learning is any assessment for which the first priority in its design and practice is to serve the purpose of promoting students' learning. It thus differs from assessment designed primarily to serve the purposes of accountability, or a ranking, or of certifying competence. An assessment activity can help learning if it provides information that teachers and their students can use as feedback in assessing themselves and one another and in modifying the teaching and learning activities in which they are engaged. Such assessment becomes "formative assessment" when the evidence is actually used to adapt the teaching work to meet learning needs (Black, Harrison, Lee, Marshall, and Wiliam 2004, p. 10).

Formative assessment requires an adjustment to classroom teaching, interaction with and among students, and a change in the type of feedback given to students by the teacher. The main research findings by Black, *et al.*, (2004) and subsequent suggestions for improved instruction, categorize classroom work into four major areas: questioning, feedback through grading, peer assessment, self-assessment, and the formative use of summative tests.

Effective questioning is important in determining the level of student understanding and in promoting a critical exploration of topics and ideas. Questioning that stresses the use of increased "wait time," can promote more class discussion and critical thinking on the part of students. Moving beyond memorized fact responses by students, increased "wait time" can promote brainstorming and a broader participation of students in class discussions. Increased "wait time" provides the classroom teacher with the opportunity to assess the students' knowledge base and determine misconceptions or gaps in knowledge. Finally, the use of effective questioning assists the teacher in gaining information that can be directed toward future lesson planning and instruction that will address student needs.

Feedback through grading alters the established tradition of grading an assignment with numerical percentages and letter grades. Instead, narrative feedback is provided to students without the accompanying grade. Research has shown that, "while student learning can be advanced by feedback through comments, the giving of numerical scores or grades has a negative effect, in that students ignore comments when marks are also given" (Black, *et al.*, 2004, p. 13). Narrative feedback does require more work initially; yet, as the teacher becomes more accustomed to the process and students use the feedback to direct their own studying, it becomes evident that targeted and useful feedback increases student learning. As an addition to effective questioning, the teacher can use narrative feedback to encourage students, help students identify weak areas and guide their learning, solicit comments from and promote discussion with students, and encourage critical thinking. Narrative feedback also gives the teacher the opportunity to show that assessment for learning is not competitive and summative, but rather a process directed toward increased personal learning and intellectual development.

Peer assessment and self-assessment can be valuable tools in developing habits and skills in teamwork, collaboration, objectivity, and analysis. If students understand a learning goal, they are more apt to determine what it is they need to do to reach that goal. Students, however, need assistance in learning these skills. When teachers share rubrics by which students will be evaluated and provide concrete examples, the student has a better understanding of the learning goal. It is essential to help students understand that learning is a process and they have the ability to assess their own progress toward the learning goal in an objective and effective manner.

The formative use of summative tests can help students both prepare for, and evaluate performance on, a test. Teachers play an essential role in assisting students in developing study skills and a review plan prior to taking a test. Creating a list of key words or developing possible test questions assist students in directing their study prior to an examination. It is just as important for a teacher to assist students in developing the skills to assess their personal test results. Helping students understand and even develop a rubric for scoring a test will assist the student in understanding what and why certain elements may have been missed or overlooked in response to test questions. Teachers that provide time for individual and group post-test discussion of questions and responses help students understand what learning goals have not been reached and what needs to be reviewed or relearned.

Preparing students for classroom assessments helps students develop test-taking skills, study skills, and the ability to anticipate the content of tests that require not just rote memory, but critical thinking skills directed toward the synthesis and application of knowledge. Black, *et al.*, (2004) have shown through rigorous research studies how formative assessment *for* learning can have a positive impact on summative assessment *of* learning.

Summary

No Child Left Behind very clearly sets out the obligations of state and local educational agencies related to student achievement. NCLB also clearly defines the rights of parents and students when achievement goals are not being met. Since Congress first approved NCLB, efforts have been made by the U. S. Department of Education not only to clarify NCLB and its requirements, but to also meet with educational representatives from around the nation to amend and adjust requirements as needed, which is evidenced by the approval of state requested waivers, Race to the Top, and support for the Common Core and STEM curriculum. These efforts are ongoing and continue to address issues and concerns expressed by educators and the public related to rural schools, teacher certification requirements, combined academic programs, special education services, English language learners, testing, school performance requirements, and funding of services. The Department of Education issued A Blueprint for Reform: Reauthorization of the Elementary and Secondary Act in which outlines a proposal for the next reauthorization of the Act (U.S. Department of Education, 2010a)

State and local educational agencies have an obligation to provide children with the best-qualified teachers in all subjects and to improve instructional pedagogy to assist students in learning and developing higher-order thinking skills. States and schools have been given the flexibility to utilize federal funding and grants from a variety of sources in such a way as to provide the necessary resources to meet the various obligations of the Act and state adopted curricula. This flexibility includes the ability to transfer funds between grants and programs to meet unique needs and circumstances. Accountability requirements have emerged as an issue. Yet, as pointed out by Secretary of Education, Ron Paige, prior to the adoption of the most recent reauthorization of the *Elementary and Secondary Education Act*, only 11 states had met the requirements of *Improving America's Schools Act of 1994* (Paige, 2004). This has prompted the necessity of the federal government to more closely monitor the allocation and use of federal funds, to assess the effectiveness of academic programs on student learning, to ensure teachers and school administrators are academically prepared and qualified in their areas of expertise, to report to the nation the achievement level of students in schools, districts, and states across the nation, and to provide educational alternatives for students in failing schools.

Questions for Consideration

1. What is the role of the state in determining and maintaining accountability for highly qualified teachers and programs under NCLB?

2. What role does the school administrator play in determining and maintaining accountability under NCLB?

3. What new initiatives have been developed since the *No Child Left Behind Act of 2001*?

4. What impact has *Race to the Top, Blueprint for Reform*, and STEM curriculum made related to the original mandates of NCLB?

5. What important issues need to be addressed by the school administrator related to special education teachers and paraprofessionals?

6. What are school and state report cards and what role do they have in supporting high standards and student achievement?

7. How do NCLB and the states address the application of highly qualified teacher requirements for rural teachers, science teachers, and multi-subject teachers?

8. Discuss the differences, advantages, and disadvantages of formative and summative assessments. Describe the appropriate use of each type of assessment.

References

AACTE Briefs (2004). IDEA reauthorized. In *American Association of Colleges for Teacher Education Briefs*, 25(17), p. 1.

Black, P., Harrison, C., Lee, C., Marshall, B., & Wiliam, D. (2004). Working inside the black box: Assessment for learning in the classroom. In *Phi Delta Kappan: The Professional Journal for Education*, 86(1), pp. 9–21.

Black, P., & Wiliam, D. (1998). Inside the black box: Raising standards through classroom assessment. In *Phi Delta Kappan: The Professional Journal for Education*, 80(2), pp. 139–148.

Council of Chief State School Officers (CCSSO) (2010a). *Introduction to the common core standards.* Retrieved from http://www.corestandards.org/assets/ccssi-introduction.pdf.

Council of Chief State School Officers (CCSSO) (2010b). *Read the common core standards.* Retrieved from http://www.corestandards.org/the-standards

Council of Chief State School Officers (CCSSO) (2012). *Common core state standards initiative: Preparing America's students for college and career.* Retrieved from www.corestandards.org.

NGA Center for Best Practices (2011). *Providing governor's ideas that work.* Retrieved from http://www.nga.org/cms/center

National Governors Association Center for Best Practices, Council of Chief State School Officers (2010). *Common core state standards: Preparing America's students for college and career.* Washington, DC: Author.

Noddings, N. (2004). War, critical thinking, and self-understanding. In *Phi Delta Kappan: The Professional Journal for Education*, 85(7), 488–495.

Paige, R. (2004). *Memo to editorial writers. Re: No child left behind implementation.* Issued March 11, 2004. Retrieved from http://www.ed.gov/print/news/opeds/edit/2004/03112004.html

Parkey, F. W., & Hass, G. (2000). *Curriculum planning: A contemporary approach.* (7th Ed.) Boston: Allyn and Bacon.

Sagor, R. (1993). *At-risk students: Reaching and teaching them.* Swampscott, MA: Watersun Publishing Company, Inc.

Stiggins, R. (2004). New assessment beliefs for a new school mission. In *Phi Delta Kappan: The Professional Journal of Education*, 86(1), 22–27.

U.S. Department of Education (2003). *Key policy letters signed by the education secretary or deputy secretary.* Released March 24, 2003. Retrieved from http://www.ed.gov/policy/elsec/guid/secletter/030324.html

U.S. Department of Education (2004a). *Additional guidance offered to states to help students with significant cognitive disabilities.* Released March 2, 2004. Retrieved from http://www.ed.gov/print/news/pressreleases/2004/03/03022004.html

U.S. Department of Education (2004b). *Improving teacher quality state grants: Title II, Part A. Non-regulatory guidance.* Revised January 16, 2004. Author: Washington, D.C.

U.S. Department of Education (2004c). *LEA and school improvement: Non-Regulatory guidance.* Released January 7, 2004. Retrieved from http://www.ed.gov/policy/elsec/guid/schoolimprovementguide.doc

U.S. Department of Education (2004d). *New no child left behind flexibility: Highly qualified teachers.* Released March 15, 2004. Retrieved from http://www.ed.gov/print/nclb/methods/teachers/hqtflexibility.html

U.S. Department of Education (2004e). *Secretary Paige announces new policies to help English language learners.* Released February 19, 2004. Retrieved from http://www.ed.gov.news/pressreleases/2004/02/02192004.html

U.S. Department of Education (2004f). *Secretary Paige issues new policy for calculating participation rates under no child left behind.* Released March 29, 2004. Retrieved from http://ewww.ed.gov/rint/news/pressreleases/2004/03/03292004.html

U.S. Department of Education (2004g). *Title I, Paraprofessionals: Non-regulatory guidance.* Released March 1, 2004. Retrieved from http://www.ed.gov/policy/elsec/guid/paraguidance.doc

U.S. Department of Education (2009). *Race to the top program executive summary.* Issued November 2009. Retrieved from http://www2.ed.gov/programs/racetothetop/executive-summary.pdf

U.S. Department of Education (2010a). *ESEA reauthorization: A blueprint for reform.* Retrieved from http://www2.ed.gov/policy/elsec/leg/blueprint/index.html

U.S. Department of Education (2010b). *ESEA reauthorization: A blueprint for reform.* NCLB and the Blueprint Powerpoint nclb_and_blueprint. ppt Retrieved from http://www2.ed.gov/policy/elsec/leg/blueprint/index.html

U.S. Department of Education (2013a). *ESEA flexibility index page.* Retrieved from http://www2.ed.gov/policy/elsec/guid/esea-flexibility/index.html

U.S. Department of Education (2013b). *ESEA flexibility policy document.* Updated June 7, 2012. Retrieved from http://www2.ed.gov/policy/elsec/gui/esea-flexibility-acc.org

U.S. Department of Education, Office of Elementary and Secondary Education (2002). *No child left behind: A desktop reference.* Author: Washington, D. C.

U.S. Government (2009). *American recovery and reinvestment act of 2009.* Retrieved from http://www2.ed.gov/policy/gen/leg/recovery/factsheet/overview.html

U.S. Government (2010a). *ESEA reauthorization: A blueprint for reform.* Retrieved from http://www2.ed.gov/policy/elsec/leg/blueprint/index.html

U.S. Government (2010b). *A blueprint for reform: The reauthorization of the elementary and secondary education act.* Retrieved from http://www2.ed.gov/policy/elsec/leg/blueprint/publicationtoc.html

U.S. Government (2013). *Improving science, technology, engineering, and mathematics (STEM) education.* Retrieved from http://www2.ed.gov/about/overview/budget/budget13/crosscuttingissues/stemed.pdf

U.S. House of Representatives (2004). *Individuals with disabilities education improvement act of 2004* (H. R. 1350). Issued December 3, 2004. Retrieved from http://www.vesid.nysed.gov/specialed/idea/home.html

CHAPTER 3

Special Education Services in the Schools

Introduction

SERVICES and programs for students with disabilities in American public schools have evolved substantially over time and continue to develop and change with educational reform and shifts in legislation. Such programs have contributed significantly to the education of countless numbers of individual students for whom academic success would otherwise have been out of reach. Even more important, however, is the fact that the inception of such programs in the schools prompted a new wave of investigation into the efficacy of various teaching strategies, instructional models, and individual differences that ultimately transcended special education programs to impact education in general.

More than most programs offered through public schools, special education services have been fraught with controversy. Personnel shortages, quality of teacher preparation programs, staffing requirements, funding issues, student eligibility for services, program implementation and integration, and the rights of students, parents, and schools have all, at one time or another, been the source of contention among professionals and the general public. Indeed, the need for and even the legality of such programs continue to be challenged (Heward, 2006; Rozycki, 2002).

This chapter provides an overview of the history of special education programs in American public schools and will describe the current status of these programs, including categories of recognized disabling conditions, determination of eligibility, the referral process, procedural safeguards and due process, and current controversies. Next, funding issues, personnel considerations, and administrative issue are explored and, finally, current controversies and future trends likely to be seen in the provision of special education will be described.

History of Special Education

It is important to know where we have been in the provision of special services for students with disabilities in order to understand where we are now and where we hope to go in the future. In order to fully understand the evolution of special education programs, the concomitant political climate, social attitudes, and prevailing scientific thought must be considered. History is replete with examples of individuals who have, in one way or another, contributed to the education and development of students with special needs. In the 1700s, several individuals contributed to a general shift in thinking about individuals with disabilities and what they could accomplish. Jacob Rodrigues Pereine was among the first to suggest that persons who were deaf could be taught to communicate and developed a rudimentary form of sign language. Thomas Gallaudet, who developed a formal system of sign language, established the first institution in the United States to serve students with hearing impairments. Phillipe Pinel, a French physician, fostered the idea that individuals with mental illness were human beings with specific disorders and not violent criminals or animals. His contributions to psychology include the recognition that mental illnesses could be differentiated according to symptoms and treated accordingly, and that various disorders could be caused by psychological or social stress, physiological damage, or heredity. He insisted that mental institutions should exist primarily to offer treatment and therapy and not be places where those with mental illnesses were simply hidden from society. Through his humanitarian work with institutionalized patients, Pinel pioneered the field of occupational therapy and developed the use of natural remedies in place of medication where possible (Gargiulo, 2003; Neal, 2001).

Known as the "Father of Special Education," Jean Marc-Gaspard Itard, was another French physician who specialized in diseases of the ear and teaching young children with hearing impairments. He made a significant contribution to the understanding of cognitive development through his work with the "wild boy of Aveyron," an adolescent living in isolation without clothing or language, and presumed to have been reared by wild animals due to his animal-like behaviors. Itard attempted to civilize this child, whom he named Victor, through a program of sensory stimulation and behavior modification. Although Victor failed to fully develop language or more than basic self-help and social skills, he successfully demonstrated that even individuals with severe impairments in language, cognitive abilities and social functioning could benefit from careful and consistent education and training (Itard,1962).

Itard's ideas and practices influenced many subsequent educators, such as Edouard Seguin. A student of Itard's, he is credited with furthering the development of sensory-motor learning techniques for students with mental impairments. Additionally, Seguin was among the first to utilize comprehensive assessment as a basis for planning individual education programs for students, based remediation efforts on specific areas of deficit, and promoted the idea that early intervention was a key element of a successful outcome. Maria Montessori, the first female to earn a medical degree in Italy, was strongly influenced by the work of Itard and Seguin, and became an expert in early childhood education, achieving world recognition for her work with children having cognitive impairments and those from poor, urban backgrounds. These early pioneers in the education of children with cognitive impairments contributed significantly to today's practice of individualized instruction and the use of positive reinforcement techniques, promoting the belief among educators that all children have a capacity to learn (Gargiulo, 2003, Plucker, 2003).

Thus, early efforts to educate and provide services to children with disabilities, especially those with cognitive, visual, and hearing impairments, were most often undertaken by physicians with strong humanitarian views rather than by professional educators. Most education and treatment programs for such individuals continued to take place in specialized residential institutions, sometimes referred to as schools, and were most often funded by private benefactors rather than government agencies. These institutions were originally established in America in the nineteenth century to provide training and education to individuals with disabilities, who were viewed during that era as "blessed innocents" and "wise fools." However, due to a host of factors, residential institutions gradually regressed over the course of the early part of the twentieth century toward mere custodial care. Philosophical shifts from a humanistic perspective to a more psychoanalytic orientation in psychiatry, as well as changes in society's views of individuals with mental impairments and illness—largely a function of popular media- led to a disparaging view of physically or mentally disabled individuals as morally depraved. Practices such as forced sterilization and routine sedation increased, and physicians and other "experts" routinely recommended that children with disabilities be removed from society altogether.

Additional factors such as overcrowding and lack of funding added to the deterioration of custodial institutions (Gargiulo, 2003; Shonkoff & Meisels, 1990; Varin, 1998).

Special classes and programs for students with disabilities did not begin to appear in American public schools until the second half of the nineteenth century, and often represented isolated attempts to meet the needs of a select group of students such as those with visual or physical impairments (Gargiulo, 2003). These early classes and programs for students with disabilities were largely self-contained, often socially and logistically isolated from regular classrooms and schools, and their implementation and development were sporadic at best. Indeed, what has come to be known as special education, an area or sub-discipline within the field of general education, for all practical purposes did not exist until the middle of the twentieth century.

Paul & Morse (1997) described three waves in the evolution of contemporary special education. The first wave occurred during the 1960s against a backdrop of radical social change and political upheaval. Challenges to traditional views of race, class, and social inequities brought about by the civil rights movements also caused professional educators to question the efficacy of the traditional medical model approach to service provision for students with disabilities. An increasing public policy of deinstitutionalization and its concomitant shift toward a continuum of community-based services and opportunities brought about the need for advocacy, rights to treatment, education, and due process. The second wave occurred during the early 1970s and lasted until the mid-1980s. This wave was characterized by increased attention to program development and the specific training and preparation of educators to teach students with a variety of disabling conditions. More importantly, however, were legislative efforts to support the rights of consumers to participate in policy and programming decisions that affected them. Public laws such as The Handicapped Children's Early Education Act (PL 91-230) provided a basis for participation and advocacy through parental involvement. The Developmental Disabilities Assistance and Construction Act established the existence of disability councils to plan and coordinate comprehensive services. Section 504 of the Rehabilitation Act of 1973 guaranteed the civil rights of individuals with disabilities and prohibited discrimination against such individuals in education, employment, and other activities. This was extended even further in 1990 with the Americans with Disabilities Act, which provided legal protection for persons with disabilities in all programs and activities regardless of whether federal funds were used. Finally, in 1975, the passage of PL 94-142, the Education of the Handicapped Act (EHA) ensured the rights of all children to a free, appropriate, public education. This legislation encompassed six major components that have, since its passage, altered the face of public education. These six components include:

- *A Free Appropriate Public Education (FAPE)*   All children, regardless of disability, must receive an education appropriate to their needs and abilities at no cost to the parents, and must be provided with any and all related services necessary to benefit from a program of education.
- *Least Restrictive Environment (LRE)*   Children with disabilities are to be educated, to the maximum extent appropriate, with students without disabilities. However, educational placements for students with disabilities must be consistent with their educational needs.
- *Procedural Safeguards and Due Process*   Safeguards and due process ensure that parents or guardians have the right to confidentiality of records, the right to inspect all records, the right to obtain an independent evaluation, the right to receive written notification in their native language of proposed changes to their child's classification or educational placement, and the right to an impartial hearing in the event of a disagreement regarding educational plans for their child.
- *Nondiscriminatory Assessment*   Prior to placement in any special education program, students must be evaluated by a multidisciplinary team in all areas of suspected disability using tests and instruments that are racially, culturally, and linguistically unbiased.

- *Parental Participation*   Parent participation legislation requires that schools make every effort to ensure that parents partake in a meaningful way in the decision-making processes that affect their child's education.
- *Individualized Education Plan (IEP)*   An educational plan must be personalized for each individual student and developed with input from special education teacher(s), general education teacher(s), and the parent(s) or legal guardian(s). The plan should include:
  —A description of the student's present level of academic functioning.
  —Annual goals and accompanying educational objectives.
  —Related services to be provided.
  —The degree to which the student will participate in general education programs.
  —Plans for initiating services and the anticipated length of service delivery.
  —Methods of annual evaluation to determine if instructional objectives and annual goals are being met.

An amendment to this legislation resulted in an extension of FAPE to all preschool children aged 3-5 with disabilities (PL 99-457) and offered incentives to provide services for infants and toddlers experiencing developmental delays or severe physical or mental conditions expected to result in delays. In addition, PL 101-476, which renamed PL 94-142 as the Individuals with Disabilities Education Act (IDEA), required states to provide all adolescents with disabilities with a transition plan that will coordinate and promote the student's movement to independent living, vocational training, additional educational experiences, and employment.

According to Paul & Morse (1997), the third wave of contemporary special education in America's public schools was characterized by the intellectual and institutional reform spurred by the publication of *A Nation at Risk* (National Commission on Excellence, 1983). This report focused on economic consequences of poor academic preparation among America's youth and on the relatively poor performance of American students in math and science compared to students from other nations. As a result, a shift in educational philosophy, from one of equity to one of excellence, took place and businesses became much more actively involved in the schools in a variety of capacities. Debates as to the efficacy and validity of special education programs and a relative lack of convincing research data on either side of the issue led to the Regular Education Initiative. This policy minimized the role of pull-out programs for students with disabilities and significantly increased the inclusion model of special education programming. Finally, questions about the very nature of knowledge itself, including the validity of empirical research methods and the role of context in understanding human phenomena, have become entrenched in modern educational scholarship (Young, 2001). Not surprisingly, the nature and even existence of disabilities and the best practice for meeting the educational needs of all students were questioned (Kauffman, 2003; Nelson, 2003; Polsgrove, 2003). Paul and Morse (1997) claimed that we are currently still experiencing the third wave, and its outcomes and ultimate effects are yet to be identified.

Current Status of Special Education

The Individuals with Disabilities Act and subsequent amendments continue to be the driving force behind current approaches to special education. In 1997, reauthorization of this legislation emphasized the improvement of educational outcomes for students with disabilities by promoting high expectations, improving access to the general education curriculum and high state standards, increasing participation in state and local assessments, and requiring states and local schools to include students with disabilities in their education reform and accountability systems (Kleinhammer-Tramill & Fiore, 2003). The 2004 reauthorization (NASP, 2004; Wright, 2006) of IDEA, known as the Individuals with Disabilities Education Improvement Act (IDEIA), makes minor changes to provisions regarding professional preparation of special education teachers, student discipline, paperwork, and litigation. The Individuals with Disabilities Education Improvement Act (IDEIA) is the nation's special education law. First enacted in 1990, IDEA earmarked billions of dollars in federal funding to help states and local communities provide special education opportunities for approximately six million students with varying degrees of disability. Part A of IDEA contains the general provisions, including purposes of the Act and definitions. Part B, the most frequently discussed portion of the Act, discusses the education of school-aged and preschool children, the funding formula, evaluations for services, eligibility determinations, Individualized Education Programs (IEPs) and educational placements. It also outlines detailed procedural safeguards, discipline provisions, as well as the withholding of funds, and judicial review. Part B also includes the Section 619 program, which provides services to children ages 3 through 5 years old. Part C of IDEIA outlines early intervention and other services for infants and toddlers with disabilities and their families (from birth through age 3). These services are provided in accordance with an Individualized Family Service Plan (IFSP) developed through collaboration between families of infants and toddlers with disabilities and the appropriate state agency. Part C also gives grants to states to help support these programs for infants and toddlers with disabilities. Part D furnishes support for various national activities designed to improve the education of children with disabilities, including personnel preparation activities, technical assistance, and special education research (U.S. Department of Education). In the paragraphs that follow, key aspects of special education programming, including information on student eligibility for services, decision-making processes, and programming options, will be discussed.

Areas of Eligibility

A longstanding and heated debate within special education has centered on the use of labels or categories for determining eligibility for special services. Some believe that categorization is a demeaning process that contributes to stigmatization as well as social and educational isolation of students with disabilities (Reynolds, 1991) and lack educational relevance (Gargiulo, 2003). Others, however, argue that the use of technical and diagnostic terms and categories is necessary for appropriate placement in programs, distribution of funding, tracking of prevalence data, and promoting political and social awareness of disability issues through advocacy groups (Kuther, 1994). Regardless of the relative merits and pitfalls, the use of special education categories is the current practice, and school administrators at all levels must be aware of their general definition and personnel implications. The federal government, through IDEA, has provided states with guidance on the categories of eligibility for special education services and definitions of disabling conditions that, in turn, drive evaluation processes.

Note the explicit requirement within the definition of each category that the condition must adversely affect educational performance. Students who manifest one or more disabling conditions but whose academic performance is unaffected would not be eligible for special education services. However, this does not mean the child must be failing in school to receive special education and related services. IDEIA specifies that states must make a free, appropriate public education available to any student with a disability who needs special education and related services, even if the child has not failed or been retained in a grade or course, and is progressing from grade to grade (National Dissemination Center for Children with Disabilities, 2013).

Although states have the option of developing their own categories and definitions based on federal requirements, most states adhere to the definitions set forth through the IDEA legislation (Gargiulo, 2003). Table 3.1 lists the federal categories of special education eligibility along with their definitions. There are variations between and even within states, however, as to the specific criteria that are used to determine whether students meet eligibility under the various categories. Therefore,

Table 3.1. Federally Recognized Categories of Special Education Eligibility.

Category	Federal Definition
Autism	A developmental disability significantly affecting verbal and non-verbal communication and social interaction, generally evident before age three, that adversely affects a child's educational performance. Other characteristics often associated with autism are engagement in repetitive activities and stereotyped movements, resistance to environmental change or change in daily routines, and unusual responses to sensory experiences. The term does not apply if a child's educational performance is adversely affected primarily because the child has an emotional disturbance as defined below.
Deaf-Blindness	Concomitant hearing and visual impairments, the combination of which causes such severe communication and other developmental and educational needs that they cannot be accommodated in special education programs solely for children with deafness or with blindness.
Deafness	A hearing impairment that is so severe that the child is impaired in processing linguistic information through hearing, with or without amplification, that adversely affects educational performance.
Developmental Delay	For children from birth to age three (under IDEA Part C) and children from ages three through nine (under IDEA Part B), a delay in one or more of the following areas: physical development; cognitive development; communication; social or emotional development; or adaptive (behavioral) development.
Emotional Disturbance	A condition exhibiting one or more of the following characteristics over a long period of time and to a marked degree that adversely affects a child's educational performance: A. An inability to learn that cannot be explained by intellectual, sensory, or health factors B. An inability to build or maintain satisfactory interpersonal relationships with peers and teachers C. Inappropriate types of behaviors or feelings under normal circumstances D. A general pervasive mood of unhappiness or depression E. A tendency to develop physical symptoms or fears associated with personal or school problems The term includes schizophrenia. The term does not apply to children who are socially maladjusted, unless it is determined that they have an emotional disturbance.
Hearing Impairment	An impairment in hearing, whether permanent or fluctuating, that adversely affects a child's educational performance but that is not included under the definition of deafness.
Intellectual Disability	Significantly subaverage general intellectual functioning, existing concurrently with deficits in adaptive behavior and manifested during the developmental period, which adversely affects a child's educational performance.
Multiple Disabilities	Concomitant impairments (such intellectual disability-blindness, intellectual disability-orthopedic impairment, etc.), the combination of which causes such severe educational needs that they cannot be accommodated in special education programs solely for one of the impairments. The term does not include deaf-blindness.

(continued)

Table 3.1 (continued). Federally Recognized Categories of Special Education Eligibility.

Category	Federal Definition
Orthopedic Impairment	Severe orthopedic impairment that adversely affects a child's educational performance. The term includes impairments caused by congenital anomaly (e.g., clubfoot, absence of some member, etc.), impairments caused by disease (e.g., poliomyelitis, bone tuberculosis, etc.), and impairments from other causes (e.g., cerebral palsy, amputations, and fractures or burns that cause contractures).
Other Health Impairment	Having limited strength, vitality, or alertness, including a heightened alertness to environmental stimuli, that results in a limited alertness with respect to the educational environment that: i. is due to chronic or acute health problems such as asthma, attention deficit disorder or attention deficit hyperactivity disorder, diabetes, epilepsy, a heart condition, hemophilia, lead poisoning, leukemia, nephritis, rheumatic fever, sickle cell anemia, and Tourette Syndrome; AND ii. adversely affects a child's educational performance
Specific Learning Disability	A disorder in one or more of the basic psychological processes involved in understanding or in using language, spoken or written, that may manifest itself in an imperfect ability to listen, think, speak, read, write, spell, or to do mathematical calculations. The term includes such conditions as perceptual disabilities, brain injury, minimal brain dysfunction, dyslexia, and developmental aphasia. The term does not include learning problems that are primarily the result of visual, hearing, or motor disabilities; of intellectual disability; of emotional disturbance; or of environmental, cultural, or economic disadvantage.
Speech or Language Impairment	A communication disorder, such as stuttering, impaired articulation, a language impairment, or a voice impairment, that adversely affects a child's educational performance.
Traumatic Brain Injury	An acquired injury to the brain caused by an external physical force, resulting in total or partial functional disability or psychosocial impairment, or both, that adversely affects a child's educational performance. The term applies to open- or closed-head injuries resulting in impairments in one or more areas such as: cognition; language; memory; attention; reasoning; abstract thinking; judgment; problem-solving; sensory, perceptual, and motor abilities; psychosocial behavior; physical functions; information processing; and speech. The term does not apply to brain injuries that are congenital or degenerative, or to brain injuries induced by birth trauma.
Visual Impairment	An impairment of vision that, even with correction, adversely affects a child's educational performance. The term includes both partial sight and blindness.

Source: Individuals with Disabilities Education Act, 34 CFR 300.8

administrators are cautioned to become familiar with the definitions and requirements outlined within the special education rules and regulations published by their state board of education.

The Referral Process

Eligibility for special education services is contingent upon the presence of a disabling condition that falls within a recognized category of special education eligibility and that adversely affects educational performance. Therefore, comprehensive evaluation and decision-making processes must be in place that draw not only upon the expertise of a variety of professionals within and outside the school setting, but also allow for the involvement of parents and, where appropriate, the student. Students are sometimes referred for special education services due to socio-cultural differences, linguistic background, limited English proficiency, lack of educational exposure, and even inappropriate expectations from teachers. Thus, the process often, but not always, begins with some form of pre-referral intervention plan (Carter & Sugai, 1989). Although there are a variety of formats for pre-referral interventions, they often take the form of a pre-referral team, which usually comprised general education teachers, special education teachers, related services personnel, evaluation specialists, and the school administrators who collaborate to develop accommodations, modifications, and alternative instructional or management strategies available through general education that will meet the needs of an individual learner. The preliminary referral process serves several purposes: (1) reduction of unwarranted or unnecessary referrals; (2) proactive, collaborative instructional problem-solving for individual students within the general education setting in order to prevent declines in academic functioning; and (3) in cases where the pre-referral interventions ultimately prove unsuccessful in helping the student attain satisfactory academic progress, justification for a formal referral for special education services.

Currently, there is an increasing emphasis on understanding and adjusting the student's educational environment (rather than looking for deficits within the individual student) prior to considering whether special education services are necessary. With this shift in thinking, a Response to Intervention (RtI) approach has been widely advocated (National Center on Response to Intervention). Using this approach, schools identify students who are at risk for poor learning outcomes and monitor the progress of these students. Evidence-based interventions are then put into place, and continued monitoring of progress takes place. During this time, the nature and intensity of the intervention is adjusted, based on the student's responsiveness. Interventions typically are grouped into three tiers: Tier I interventions may be implemented for small groups of students or even for an entire class, and typically last between 6–8 weeks. Tier II interventions are targeted toward students whose response to the Tier I interventions was less than adequate, and are normally geared toward small groups of students or individual students. Tier II interventions routinely last longer than Tier I interventions, and student response is again monitored. For those students who still have not responded adequately to Tier II interventions, Tier III interventions are designed and implemented for an individual student, and often represent intensive interventions. If the student continues to demonstrate inadequate response to this level of intervention s/he is referred for an individual evaluation to determine eligibility for special education services (National Dissemination Center for Children with Disabilities, August 2012). This approach has been widely advocated as a means of addressing and reducing the disproportionate representation of students receiving special education services who are racial/ethnic minorities, English language learners, from low socio-economic backgrounds, and / or who have not been exposed to appropriate instruction (Hosp, n.d.). However, it should be noted that IDEA specifies that RtI may not be used as a means of delaying or refusing to conduct an individual evaluation for eligibility for special education services if the school suspects that a child has a disability or if the parents request such an evaluation (National Dissemination Center for Children with Disabilities, August 2012).

Once it has been determined by a pre-referral intervention team that the intervention plan was not successful, the next step is often a formal referral for special education services. As stated above, however, a pre-referral intervention is not always in place prior to special education referral. In fact, referral for special education services may be initiated as a result of a child-find effort, an IDEA-mandated process intended to screen for and identify students needing special services. Or it may be requested by individuals outside the school setting, such as a parent or physician who is justifiably concerned with the academic progress of an individual student. Nonetheless, it is important to understand that the purpose of special education evaluations is not to identify disabling conditions per se unless the student's educational performance is adversely affected.

Determining Eligibility

Once a child is formally referred for special education services, the referral process itself follows a fairly standard format. However, the specific assessments that are conducted and the involvement of professionals within and outside the school setting vary tremendously, depending upon the nature of the suspected disabling condition(s). Before any formal evaluation for determining eligibility for special education services can begin, the parent(s) or legal guardian(s) of the student must receive written notification. This notification, in general, should explain in the parents' or guardians' native language the reasons for and nature of the evaluation as well as the types of special education programs and services currently available within the district for which the student might qualify. The parent(s) or legal guardian(s) must in turn provide the school or agency with written consent for the evaluation before the referral can proceed further. Once parental consent has been obtained, a multidisciplinary evaluation team, sometimes referred to as the MET, evaluates the student. This team is typically designated by state board special education rules and regulations and is intended to ensure that appropriate professionals evaluate and provide input on the status of individual children who may require special education or related services. Table 3.2 provides a brief description of the various roles and responsibilities of members of METs, although it should be remembered that these roles and functions will vary across states. Furthermore, the roles and responsibilities of teachers of special education are not described since these also vary significantly across states and even across programs within states. When in doubt, school administrators and personnel should consult current special education rules and regulations issued by the state.

Members of the MET will compile individual reports or collaborate on a single evaluation report which makes a recommendation of eligibility and describes the student's strengths and weaknesses. The MET must consider information from a variety of sources rather than just one, and they must make recommendations for educational services and placement consistent with the least restrictive environment in which the child can reasonably be expected to succeed (Fiedler, 2000). These findings are then reported to a committee frequently known as the Individual Education Plan Team (IEPT). This committee is known, however, by various names such as the Admission Review Dismissal Committee (ARD) in Texas (Texas Education Agency, 2002) or the Child Study Team in other states. It is important to understand, however, that the members of the MET, individually and collectively, make recommendations as to eligibility but do not make the decision *per se*. The decision is made by the IEPT, which may include the following members:

- A representative of the educational agency (school or district), usually an administrator or administrative designee.
- Appropriate representatives of both general and regular education that must include a teacher or teachers with whom the student has had direct instructional contact.
- The student's parent(s) or legal guardian(s).

Table 3.1. Multidisciplinary Evaluation Team Roles and Responsibilities.

Professional Role	Involvement in Evaluation of Disability	Provision of Related Services
School Counselor	Where available, may serve as the coordinator of the initial referral process; often is responsible for initial collection of information from parents and teachers, and may conduct formal observations or interview students; is often a participant of the MET and IEPT.	Typically not involved in related service delivery although may help coordinate service delivery efforts
School Psychologist	Increasingly responsible in many states for the coordination of the initial and re-evaluation referral processes for all disability areas; play key role in the evaluation of learning disabilities, cognitive impairments, emotional impairments, and autistic spectrum disorders.	May provide related services such as special education counseling, transition services, and assistive technology services in addition to consulting with parents, teachers, and school administrators on a variety of issues related to special education needs.
Educational Diagnostician	Although this role has increasingly been subsumed by the school psychologist position, it nevertheless continues in some states. Responsible for the coordination of the initial and re-evaluation referral processes for all disability areas and for the evaluation of learning disabilities, cognitive impairments, and autistic spectrum disorders. Participates in the MET of all other referrals, conducting evaluation and providing input regarding academic functioning as well as academic strengths and weaknesses related to the disabling condition.	May play a role in providing transition services and assistive technology services. Consultation with parents, teachers, and school administrators is a key function of the educational diagnostician.
Teacher Consultant	Evaluates the academic and instructional needs of students referred for special education services. May conduct individualized normative assessments, although assessments conducted by teacher consultants are more frequently criterion- or curriculum-based assessments.	Provides consultation to education personnel on behalf of students with disabilities and provides instructional services in support of both general and special education teachers who teach students with disabilities.
Speech and Language Pathologist/Therapist	Provides evaluation for students for whom a specific speech and/or language impairment or autistic spectrum disorder is suspected. Evaluation focuses on language development, articulation, voice, and fluency.	Provides individual and group speech/language therapy services and instructional support for students using augmentative communication devices. May provide consultative services to parents and teachers regarding language development in the home and class room.
School Social Worker	Where available, primarily responsible for evaluating the social history and social / emotional needs of students suspected of having an emotional impairment or autistic spectrum disorder.	Special education counseling for individual students and groups; often serves as a liaison between the school and outside agencies in which students with disabilities are involved (e.g., juvenile courts, mental health agencies, foster homes); may conduct home visits.

(continued)

50

Table 3.1 (continued). Multidisciplinary Evaluation Team Roles and Responsibilities.

Professional Role	Involvement in Evaluation of Disability	Provision of Related Services
School Nurse	Where available, is responsible for ruling out possible defects of vision or hearing prior to referral for special education services; may service as a member of the MET or IEPT when there are medical considerations.	Usually does not provide any related services but may administer necessary medications and routine medical procedures for both special and general education students.
Audiologist	Must be involved in the evaluation of students suspected of having a hearing impairment.	None
Orientation and Mobility Specialist	May be involved in the evaluation of functional, adaptive, and mobility skill students with visual impairments.	Assist students with visual impairments to achieve maximum independence through instruction in safe, efficient travel within the home, school, and community.
Medical Practitioner	A medical doctor such as a family physician, pediatrician, or neurologist, or a nurse-practitioner must be involved in the evaluation of students suspected of having a health impairment or orthopedic impairment. An ophthalmologist must be involved in the evaluation of students suspected of having a visual impairment.	None
Physical Therapist	Usually involved in the evaluation of students suspected of having an orthopedic impairment or other disability that would require some form of physical therapy.	Provision of direct physical therapy as it relates to movement such as gross motor control, balance, and basic motility necessary for educational performance.
Occupational Therapist	Often provides consultative evaluation for students suspected of having a variety of disabling conditions, particularly those that involve fine motor /or perceptual and impairments.	Provision of direct occupational therapy to improve visual-motor and fine-motor and perceptual functioning; consultation to parents, teachers, and school administrators.

Source: Individuals with Disabilities Education Act, 34 CFR 300.8

51

- At least one person who is trained to interpret the instructional implications of the evaluation results.
- The student whenever appropriate.
- Related services personnel.
- Other persons at the discretion of the parents or education agency.
  (34 C.F.R. Sec. 300.344(A)(1)-(3)).

Although the school must make every effort to involve parents or guardians in the decision-making process, the IEPT may be conducted in the absence of a parent or guardian if these efforts fail. School administrators should carefully document any and all attempts to arrange for mutually convenient meetings including records of telephone calls, correspondence to and from the parent/guardian, and home visits or other direct personal encounters with the parent/guardian (Fiedler, 2000).

Once a student is placed in a special education program, the IEP and placement are reviewed at least once per year and more often as need arises or is requested by any member of the IEPT or the parent/guardian. Furthermore, the student is re-evaluated once every three years to re-determine eligibility and update information on the student's academic strengths, weaknesses, and needs. Although in the past, the three-year re-evaluation often took the form of an abbreviated version of the initial evaluation, there has been increasing flexibility in the approach to this component of the special education process. Currently, there is an increased emphasis on a process called the Review of Existing Evaluation Data (REED) for three year re-evaluations and even, to some extent, for initial evaluations. This tendency has largely been the result of increased emphasis on the systematic collection of formative assessment data based on core curriculum content standards for all students, and the process must include evaluation data from previous evaluations, information (including any additional evaluations) offered by the parent(s), information from and observations by the student's classroom teacher(s), and classroom-based, local, and state assessments. Once these data are collected, it may be determined that no further data are needed to determine continued eligibility for special education services (IDEA, 2004). The re-evaluation process can be used to improve or ensure continuation of the effectiveness of the student's educational placement and programming and can provide a forum for collaborative consultation between various professionals, teachers, and the parent(s)/guardian(s). Finally, before a student is dismissed from special education services, the IEPT must evaluate and document that extra services are no longer necessary for educational success. Most school districts also build in at least a year of monitoring by special education personnel to ensure a smooth transition from special to general education.

Procedural Safeguards and Due Process

Procedural safeguards ensure that parents are informed and involved in the special education process from beginning to end. Of particular importance are issues of notice and consent, access to student records, appointment of surrogate parents, independent evaluations, voluntary mediation, and due process hearings. In addition to written notification for initial multidisciplinary team evaluations and re-evaluations, IDEA requires that written notice be provided to parents prior to the initiation, change, or discontinuation of any special education or related services. Furthermore, voluntary and informed parental consent must be obtained under all of the above-mentioned conditions. If a school attempts but fails to secure parental consent, a mediation or due process hearing may be initiated that will enable the school to conduct necessary evaluations or make educational placements without such consent.

In keeping with the Family Educational Rights and Privacy Act (FERPA) (20 U.S.C. Sec. 1232g; 34 C.F.R. part 99), schools must provide parents with access to their child's educational records within 45 days of initial request, and must provide interpretation or explanation of such records when requested. Parents are entitled to copies of their child's educational records, and the schools must provide such copies if the parent is unable to make or pay for copies. An interesting conflict has arisen under FERPA. Test protocols, which fall under the category of educational records, must be provided and even copied for parents, which results in a direct violation of copyright law and the obligation of school psychologists and teacher consultants to maintain test security (Jacob-Timm & Hartshorne, 1998). Parents should also receive, without specific request, copies of all multidisciplinary evaluation team reports, individualized education plans, and committee meeting notes or minutes. Another provision of FERPA is that a parent may request amendments to any educational record they believe to contain misleading or inaccurate information and may request a due process hearing in the event that the school refuses to make such an amendment. Finally, FERPA requires that educational records on students are kept confidential and, thus, only personnel who work with a student with a disability may have access.

If a student with a disability or suspected of having a disabling condition does not have a parent, if the parent cannot be found, or if the child is a ward of the state, IDEA requires that a surrogate parent be appointed. The surrogate parent serves as the child's educational advocate and assumes all the rights and responsibilities delegated by IDEA to natural parents or legal guardians. The surrogate parent must not have any conflicts of interest with the assumed role, may not be employed by the education agency through which the child is receiving a free appropriate public education, and must have the knowledge and skills to appropriately advocate for the student's educational rights and needs. Schools may not appoint a surrogate parent when natural parents or legal guardians are known but refuse to participate in the child's education (Fiedler, 2000).

When parents disagree with a school's evaluation, they may request an independent educational evaluation (IEE). Education agencies must provide parents not only with information on where and how to obtain an IEE but must also pay for the evaluation within an established reasonable cost structure. If the education agency maintains that its evaluation is appropriate and that an IEE is thus unnecessary, a due process hearing may be requested. Once an IEE has been obtained, the results must be considered by the education agency in its decision making, although this does not imply an obligation to agree with or accept the IEE findings or recommendations. It should be noted that a school or education agency is not obligated to pay for an IEE if it is obtained by a parent or guardian outside of formal request procedures (Jacob-Timm & Hartshorne, 1998). Disputes between parents/guardians and education agencies over issues of special education evaluation, placement, and programming may be settled through voluntary mediation, which is an option that both parties must agree to. Mediation, led by an impartial mediator, is an attempt to reach a non-adversarial resolution of a dispute by engaging both parties directly in a collaborative problem-solving process (Dobbs, Primm, & Primm, 1991). The most recent reauthorization of IDEA specifies that parents/guardians and schools must now attempt to resolve conflicts before a lawsuit can be filed on behalf of a student receiving special education services. Parents/guardians must file a clear and specific complaint to the school. Within 15 days of the filing of the complaint, a meeting must take place where all appropriate parties are present and the school then has an additional 15 days to react and offer a resolution. It is only after this point, if the resolution is unacceptable to the party filing the complaint, that a lawsuit may be filed. Furthermore, if the lawsuit is found to be frivolous by the courts, the prosecuting attorney will be held accountable for all costs of the lawsuit including all costs to the school district and school personnel (IDEA, 2004).

Disciplinary Action and Students with Disabilities

When students with and without disabilities face suspension or expulsion from school for disciplinary reasons, they have protections under the due process clauses of the Fifth and Fourteenth Amendments to the U.S. Constitution. According to Fiedler (2000, p. 74), for short-term suspensions (fewer than 10 days), schools must give written or oral notice of the charges against a student and must provide an opportunity for the student to respond to the charges in either an informal or formal setting. If a student faces long-term suspension or expulsion, the school must go further and provide the following:

- Written notice specifying the charges.
- Notice of the evidence, witnesses, and substance of their testimony.
- Advance notices of the time, place, and procedures to be followed in a formal hearing, usually conducted by the school board.
- The right to confront witnesses and present one's own witnesses.
- A written or taped record of the hearing proceedings.
- The right of appeal.

Such protections do not apply to brief in-school sanctions such as detention or in-school suspension. This holds true for students with disabilities if: (1) the disciplinary procedure is minor, (2) is part of the school district's discipline plan, (3) is commonly used with all students, and (4) does not result in any change of educational placement. In addition, these protections can be temporarily overridden when students, with and without disabilities, pose a clear and present danger to themselves or others. In such a situation, the student may be removed from school, with the due process procedures retroactively put into place. Furthermore, a student with a disability may be suspended or expelled from school if he or she is in possession of a gun or weapon, knowingly possesses or sells illegal drugs, or causes serious bodily injury to others, as long as the disabling condition is not the primary cause of the incident.

However, there are additional considerations for students with disabilities when long-term suspension or expulsion is considered for disciplinary reasons. Because such sanctions constitute essentially a change in educational placement, an IEP (or ARD, etc.) meeting must be convened prior to any action. During this IEP meeting, which should include the parent(s) or legal guardian(s), a "manifestation determination" review will take place. The purpose of this process is to determine whether or not a school policy violation by a student receiving special education services is related to his or her disability. A student may not be denied a free appropriate public education due to behavior that is a direct result of a disabling condition. If the behavior or school policy violation was found to be unrelated to the student's disability, then the student may be disciplined under the general code of conduct of the school. Any resultant changes of educational placement, however, must include continuation of any and all special education services (Fiedler, 2000; Meloy, 1999). In other words, short-term suspensions that result in more than 10 days of absence from school, long-term suspensions, and expulsions of students with disabilities are viewed as a change in placement in terms of the location of service delivery (e.g., home-bound services rather than school-based services).

Although it has been argued that there are no valid procedures for making such a determination (Katsiyannis & Maag, 1998), there are some questions that should be addressed. A careful and thorough review of previous and current records including psychological and educational evaluations, observations of the student, input from teachers and parents regarding current and past behavior, and the student's IEP should be undertaken in order to address the following questions:

- Is the student's IEP appropriate?
- Is the IEP being implemented as written?
- Did the disability prevent the student from understanding the impact and consequences of his/her behavior?
- Did the disability prevent the student from controlling the behavior?

Of particular importance is whether the IEP included a specific plan for behavior management and crisis intervention procedures. Although not required for every IEP, these components should be included and frequently reviewed for any student receiving special education services and for whom behavior is a potential concern (Malloy, 1999). A behavioral intervention plan should be based on a functional behavioral assessment including proactive positive behavior supports and interventions and must state behavior goals and objectives.

A student may not be suspended or expelled if the manifestation determination reveals any of following circumstances: (1) the IEP is considered to be inadequate or inappropriate for addressing the student's cognitive, emotional, and behavioral needs; (2) the student's disability impairs his or her ability to understand school policy; (3) he student's disability impairs his or her ability to understand the impact and consequences of his or her behavior; (4) the student could not control his or her behavior due to the disabling condition. However, the school may then take steps to change the student's educational placement or programming, including movement to a more restrictive environment, if such a change is needed to ensure improved outcomes for the student.

Students who have not yet been found to be eligible for special education services can invoke the same protections afforded to students with disabilities under IDEA if school district personnel had knowledge that the student had a disability before the policy violation occurred. Thus, IDEA extends equal protection to students who are in the referral process (e.g., a request for special education evaluation was made by the parents or teacher) or whose behavior indicates a need for special education services (Fiedler, 2000).

Section 504

Section 504 of the Rehabilitation Act of 1974 is designed to prevent discrimination against individuals with disabilities in programs receiving federal financial assistance (29 U.S.C. Sec. 794). This statute applies not only to students in the public school setting but also to individuals in post-secondary settings, employment settings, and includes parents and school employees who are disabled (Fiedler, 2000). More broadly defined than special education eligibility categories specified through IDEA, Section 504 defines a "handicapped person" as one who has a physical or mental impairment that substantially limits one or more of his or her major life activities. Physical impairments in this context means any physiological disorder or condition affecting one or more body systems. Mental impairment in this context means any mental or psychological disorder such as emotional or mental illness, or a specific learning disability. Major life activities include caring for one's self, performing manual tasks, walking, seeing, hearing, speaking, breathing, learning, and working. Handicapped refers to individuals with a history of impairment as well as those perceived to have an impairment who may, in fact, have no actual impairment (Jacob-Timm & Hartshorne, 1998). While this statement may be confusing, one need not look far to see examples of individuals who were denied access to educational and recreational programs or employment on the basis of a perception of disability. Students who are considered to have a disabling condition under IDEA are protected by Section 504, but students who are not eligible for special education services under IDEA may, nevertheless, be considered to have a disabling condition under Section 504 and have protected status. Some common categories of disabling conditions that often do not warrant special education but that would invoke special accommodations and modifications through Section 504 include:

- Individuals with ADD/ADHD but whose academic performance is not adversely affected enough to warrant special education services.
- Individuals who have learning disabilities but do not meet the IDEA definition due to a lack of a severe discrepancy between aptitude and achievement.
- Individuals who have graduated from a special education program.

- Individuals who are socially maladjusted.
- Individuals with drug or alcohol dependency.
- Individuals with health needs.
- Individuals with communicable diseases.

Section 504 is not as specific in its language regarding identification of individuals and documentation of a plan for reasonable accommodations, modifications, and services (Fiedler, 2000). Nevertheless, these must be in place for each student within a school who is considered to have a disabling condition according to the above definitions (Jacob-Timm & Hartshorne, 1998). Although section 504 has been a source of confusion and debate in both educational and legal circles, the intent of the statute is to protect all individuals from discrimination based on a real or perceived disability and to afford equal opportunity for access to education, employment, and recreation.

Personnel Issues

Special education services delivery has become increasingly inclusive, often provided within the general education setting, resulting in a blending of special and general education functions and roles. This blending of roles and responsibilities has brought to the forefront a host of personnel issues, particularly pre-service education and training as well as subsequent professional development. Below is a brief introduction to some of the personnel issues facing school administrators as they grapple with the changing landscape of special education.

The Changing Roles and Responsibilities of Special and General Education Teachers

As the concepts of normalization (Wolfensberger, 1972) and least restrictive environment began to make their way into the structure of special education service delivery, there was a trend away from custodial, institutional care and toward education for individuals with disabilities in basic self-care skills, socialization, and recreation within standard environments. Regional and cluster programs within the public school setting allowed for students with low-incidence disabilities (for example, severe and profound levels of cognitive impairment) to be educated together by a teacher with specialized training designed to meet the unique learning needs of such individuals (Fisher, Frey, & Thousand, 2003). Even for students with high-incidence disabilities (such as learning disabilities), the general perception within education (and one that continues to some extent) was that all students with disabilities required specialized instructional techniques and methods that general education teachers did not possess.

However, as decentralization of programs gained momentum and an emphasis on inclusive educational practices increased in the late 1980s and early 1990s, the logistics of providing specialized programming based on disability classification became difficult to maintain. Teachers certified to provide educational services to students with low-incidence disabilities became, out of necessity, itinerant or traveling personnel, often working in multiple locations within a district or even in multiple districts. Instead of direct service provision, a consultation model was increasingly utilized. Under this model, cross-categorical teachers of special education became responsible for all students with IEPs, while itinerant teachers with specialized training in specific disability categories provide consultation and indirect services on a regular but sometimes infrequent basis.

Trends in Teacher Education and Professional Development

The blending of general and special education roles and functions resulted in a need for a shift in the training and professional development needs of both special and general education teachers (Sindelar, Ross, Brownell, Griffin, & Rennels, 1997). Formative training and education along with continued professional development in consultation skills, inclusive practices, methods of collaboration, greater content knowledge, leadership skills, and generalized instruction are among the needs most frequently cited by special education teachers (Wigle & Wilcox, 2003). Special education teachers, however, must demonstrate that they are highly qualified as stipulated under the *No Child Left Behind* (NCLB) legislation (see chapter 2). New special education teachers who teach multiple subject areas and who are "highly qualified" in math, language arts, or science have two years to demonstrate proficiency in any additional subject areas for which they are responsible (NASP, 2004). Furthermore, general education teachers, given their increasing role in the education of students with all classifications of special education eligibility, have also called for increased professional development and training in addition to administrative and collegial support. In particular, knowledge of the characteristics of specific disabling conditions, an understanding of classification procedures, and skills in developing and implementing appropriate adaptations and accommodations to the curriculum are the most pressing. General education teachers need time to meet the needs of students with increasingly diverse abilities, time to collaborate with other professionals, and time to seek information necessary for effective instruction (Kamens, Loprete, & Slostad, 2003).

Qualification and Training of Paraeducators

In addition to certified teachers, administrators must also be aware of issues related to paraeducators (also known as teacher aides, instructional assistants, paraprofessionals, etc.), who contribute significantly to the delivery of special education services to students at all levels and within all eligibility classifications. While paraeducators have for a long time filled an essential role in special education, continued use of the collaborative model of special education service delivery as well as teacher shortages, expanding numbers of English Language Learners, higher emphasis on differentiated instruction, specialized job roles, and increased accountability for public schools have substantially increased the need for appropriately trained paraeducators (NEA, 2013; Villareal, 2010; York & Tundidor, 1995). In fact, the National Clearinghouse for Professions in Special Education reports that the number of paraeducators providing special education services to children aged 3–21 increased by 60% between the years 1992 and 1999 (NCPSE, 2001), and it is estimated there are currently 1,288,300 paraeducators serving special and general education students across the K–12 national landscape (Bureau of Labor Statistics, 2012). And as the role of paraeducator has become more complex and demanding, the Elementary and Secondary Education Act (ESEA) now requires that paraeducators who work in Title 1 schools have a high-school diploma plus an associate's degree, or two years of college, or a passing score on a state or local assessment that demonstrates their ability to assist in with instruction in reading, writing, and mathematics. Furthermore, as states and local districts have realized the impact of paraeducators on student achievement outcomes, many have come to recognize the need for staff development and continuing education for these professionals, and have implemented a variety of programs to assist paraeducators in seeking additional training and education (NEA, 2013; Villareal, 2010).

In their research on the perceptions of paraeducators regarding areas of satisfaction and dissatisfaction with their positions, Tillery, Werts, Roark, & Harris (2003) identified several trends. Reasons frequently cited for becoming a paraeducator and/or staying in the position included the following:

- having a love of children,
- wanting to satisfy unfulfilled dreams of becoming a teacher,

- being able to enjoy teaching and working with children without the additional duties and responsibilities outside of school hours,
- the convenience of working that revolves around the school calendar and hours.

In fact, according to the National Education Association (NEA, 2013), nearly half of paraeducators who belong to the organization aspire to become fully certified educators at some point in the future. Despite these generally positive perceptions, however, there were also several areas of dissatisfaction cited by paraeducators. First and foremost among the concerns most frequently mentioned was low pay. Paraeducators, according to these authors, typically earn anywhere from one- half to one- third the salary of classroom teachers (p. 118), with a median yearly salary for full-time work in 2010 of $23,220 (Bureau of Labor Statistics, 2012). Additionally, dissatisfaction with workload, level of respect, constant program changes, and the introduction of additional competencies as a condition of continued employment (typing, driving buses, etc.) were mentioned along with high levels of stress caused by student discipline and administrative issues. Finally, issues beyond the paraeducator's control, such as being asked to perform duties that were unsafe, tasks for which they were untrained, or that went beyond reasonable expectations for the position level, were significant sources of dissatisfaction. Ultimately, while level of pay is out of the control of most school administrators, other areas of dissatisfaction listed above can and should be addressed at the administrative level in order to improve the retention of paraeducators. Systematic efforts to improve the job satisfaction among paraeducators might include: improving the clarity of the job description, on-going training and professional development, and greater involvement in site-based decision making.

Funding Special Education Programming and Services

Since the Individuals with Disabilities Act (IDEA) was enacted, states and local school districts have always assumed primary responsibility for funding and providing special education programs and services to eligible children with disabilities. While IDEA authorizes the federal government to fund up to 40% of the average per pupil expenditure (APPE) for all students in public elementary and secondary schools, federal funding has never reached this level, despite the fact that special education funding comprises the second largest federal K–12 program behind Title 1 grants for economically disadvantaged students. And while federal support for special education programs has increased from 5.1% of the APPE in 1977–1978 to 17.7% in 2006, states and local school districts ultimately bear the majority of responsibility for funding special education programming and services (IDEA Funding Coalition, 2006). Federal funding for IDEA is distributed to states according to a formula that factors in fiscal year 1999 levels of funding, the proportion of children aged 3–21, and the proportion of those children living in poverty. States then divide this funding across school districts using a variety of formulas (McCann, 2013).

Spending for special education services varies tremendously across states, and data sources that accurately report the total expenditure for special education services in public schools across the United States are lacking (Chambers, Parrish, Lieberman, & Wolman, 1998; Verstegan, 2011). Generally, states report paying for special education programming and services using one of four major methods: (1) per pupil funding—either pupil weighted systems or a flat grant; (2) cost reimbursement; (3) instruction / teacher units; and (4) census. States may also provide funding through intermediate units rather than directly to the local education agency. At the time of her research, Verstegan found that 21 states reported providing per pupil funding for special education through weights that recognize the excess cost of special education programs and services beyond the regular education program amount. States sometimes may set limits on the percent of students funded under weighted systems, and can include multiple or single weights for different categories of special education eligibility, instructional arrangements (e.g., resource room, self-contained, mainstreamed, etc.), broad categories of exceptionality, or needed support levels. Other states (10) reported using cost reimbursement to support special education. This method usually defines eligible cost categories and the percentage of these costs that will be reimbursed by the state. Additionally, six states reported using an instructional unit method that pays for teachers based on the number of students served. Finally, five states reported using census-based funding, which account for costs based on the total number of students in the school district rather than on the basis of the number of students with disabilities. Verstegen asserted that this model of funding provides no fiscal incentive for districts to classify students as eligible for special education services in order to receive additional funding, yet still allocates funds for students in need of such services.

The increasing cost of special education has become a topic of heated debate and conflict within education and amid the public in general. Educational funding must be distributed among general education, special education, and other entitlement programs such as Title 1, bilingual education, and school improvement. The proportion of funding allocated to special education, therefore, is necessarily inversely proportional to funding allocated for other programs. Furthermore, the general trend toward inclusive models of service delivery has not diminished the financial burden of such programming. In fact, according to Ysseldyke, Algozzine, and Thurlow (2000), approximately eighty percent of the funds for special education are used to pay for teachers and other direct-service personnel. In general, the costs associated with special education services are directly proportional to the nature and severity of the disability, with more complex and severe disabilities requiring much more extensive and costly services and equipment. Some policymakers have suggested that increasing costs of special education services can be directly linked to increased numbers of children being served through special education. It has been argued, for example, that increases in special education enrollment is a result of efforts to solve instructional and behavioral problems within the general education classroom and of intensified advocacy on the part of parents and physicians (Berman & Urion, 2003). However, there is little evidence of significant increases in enrollment in special education programs. Instead, Berman & Urion (2003) argue the rising financial cost is due to increases in the severity of needs of students determined to be eligible for services. In particular, advances in medical technology have reduced infant mortality and as a result have multiplied the incidence of low-birth weight babies and infants with severe medical complications that result in cognitive, behavioral, and learning difficulties by the time they reach school age. In addition, deinstitutionalization has shifted service provision and its financial costs to departments of education and away from other state agencies. There has also been a concomitant rise in privatization of services, which arguably results in increased financial burdens for school districts. Finally, increasing numbers of children are living in poverty, and this can serve to limit the cognitive and learning experiences to which children are exposed and often results in social and economic stress within the family, increasing the risk for child abuse and neglect, substance abuse, and dysfunctional home environments. These factors heighten the risk of cognitive, behavioral, and learning difficulties among students, and thus the probability in a student population of eligibility for special education services (Berman & Urion, 2003).

Higher special education costs are ultimately borne by states and local school districts. Further complicating the funding issue is a legislative provision within IDEA that requires states to meet maintenance of effort (MOE) to continue to receive federal education funding. MOE requires states to provide levels of special education funding that are at least equal to the previous year's spending level, unless they are granted a waiver from the U.S. Department of Education. States that fail to comply will have their federal special education allocations diminished by the amount they failed to provide at the state level. However, this reduction will affect the state only in the year(s) in which they are out of compliance and not permanently as earlier language stated. In addition, funding that is withheld from non-compliant states is reallocated to states that are in compliance with the MOE requirements (McCann, 2013).

Parrish & Wolman (2004) made specific recommendations to school leaders for dealing with the increased financial burden to local school districts in the provision of special education services. First, they recommend pooling funding to service all students with special educational needs. Flexibility in allocation of funding sources such as Title 1, IDEA, and state compensatory education funds can create opportunities to blend funds to establish a broader range of prevention and remedial programs, which may, in turn, reduce the number of referrals for special education and also improve student achievement. Parrish & Wolman encourage school leaders to embrace accountability for all, moving away from the idea of different outcome expectations for regular vs. special education students. In addition, they recommend local district and regional cooperation and collaboration in order to create more cost-effective and efficient provision of services for students, particularly those with low-incidence disabilities who require intensive and costly services. Furthermore, these authors advocate lobbying state and federal policymakers for additional funding and/or a hiatus in new requirements for special education services and programming.

While states, local education agencies, and the general public may have deep concerns about the costs of special education services in accordance with IDEA and other federal mandates, there are no simple answers to the question of whether we are spending too much or too little. Few rigorous cost-benefit program evaluations of special education have been undertaken. To begin with, such analyses are fairly new approaches to policy and decision-making in public education. Perhaps of more significance, however, is the difficulty inherent in determining costs beyond hard dollars and identifying benefits or outcomes. For example, should program evaluators analyze the efficiency and productivity of special education services in terms of academic indicators, personal/social/affective indicators, quality-of-life indicators, or some combination of all of these (Ysseldyke, Algozzine, Thurlow, 2000)? How are the costs to society from the absence of such programming to be determined since all public education agencies are required by federal mandate to provide such services? There is no basis for comparison. The complexity and variability of special education programs and services and the individuals they serve further complicate the matter. Issues of equity versus equality in funding for educational programs will continue to foster both productive dialogue and heated debate among educators and the general public.

Some Current Controversies and Future Directions

Beyond financing, many components within special education have become or remain controversial, including current definitions of specific eligibility categories, use of standardized testing in student assessment, racial disparities, and methods of special education placement. These controversial issues have become the target of much discussion, dialogue, and debate within and outside special education and, along with other factors, have served as the driving forces behind current policy and anticipated future trends in special education.

Definitions of Disabling Conditions

The purpose of definitions in special education is to create a conceptual model for explaining and classifying various conditions and to make placement and instructional decisions based upon the academic, functional, and social needs associated with a given condition. However, many conditions, as so defined, are merely constructs, i.e., qualities or traits that are not directly observable or objectively measurable. Many disabling conditions, which cannot be measured directly, give rise to associated measurable phenomena (Reber, 1985). A cognitive impairment, for example, cannot be seen, felt, or otherwise directly observed but is generally associated with observable deficits in social skills, adaptive behavior, language development, and reasoning ability. According to Ysseldyke (2000, p. 95), definitions created to describe individuals with special learning needs generally fall into one of two groups:

1. Definitions based on sensory deficits with an associated functional disability (e.g., blindness, deafness, etc.)
2. Definitions based on psychometric deficits with an associated disability assigned to them (e.g., learning disability, cognitive impairment, etc.)

Disability categories are hypothetical abstractions, and special education definitions are operational in nature. Therefore, there are often disagreements as to exactly which associated features, especially those based on psychometric deficits, are most descriptive, predictive, and explanatory. Furthermore, the definitional term itself is often descriptively immaterial in a technical or scientific sense. For example, the terms "imbecile," "idiot," "mentally retarded," and "cognitively impaired," have all been used at one time or another to describe the same condition. Furthermore, the psychometric deficits used as markers to identify such a "condition" have been considered by some (e.g., Bogdan & Taylor, 1976) to be based on a relatively arbitrary distinction between normal and abnormal, a position with historical support.

In 1959, the definition of mental retardation adopted by the American Association on Mental Retardation (in Biasini, Grupe, Huffman, & Bray, 1999) included three components: impaired adaptive functioning, intellectual functioning greater than one standard deviation below the mean (that is, an IQ < 85), and onset before age 16. A change in the definition issued in 1973 kept the three components but modified the level of intellectual functioning to greater than two standard deviations below the mean (IQ < 70). This change significantly reduced the number of individuals identified (or misidentified) as mentally retarded. A further revision in 1992 focused on the functional status of the individual with mental retardation and the impact of environmental influences on adaptive skill development. The 1992 revision also eliminated the severity level classification scheme (mild, moderate, severe, profound) in favor of one that addresses the type and intensity of support needed by the individual (intermittent, limited, extensive, or pervasive).

Another, more recent, example of the arbitrary nature of psychometrically-based definitions is that of "learning disability." Berninger and Abbott (2000) summed up the essence of this problem in the following statements:

> Since Samuel Kirk coined the term *learning disability* in 1963 to capture the concept of children who cannot learn academic skills despite having normal intelligence, we still have not reached a consensus on the definition of learning disabilities. However, until recently a common thread among most definitions of learning disability, whether for the purpose of service delivery or research, was the notion that students with learning disabilities show a discrepancy between aptitude (as measured by IQ) and achievement (p. 163).

Yet, research has generally shown that discrepancy models fail to differentiate students with specific learning disabilities from other students who struggle academically- so-called slow learners, underachievers, or generally poor readers. In addition, the use of discrepancy models often resulted in an over-identification of certain groups of students, while simultaneously failing to correctly identify specific learning disabilities in other groups of students, such as those who are learning English as a second language and students from impoverished backgrounds. The reauthorization of IDEA in 2004 specifically prohibits the use of IQ-achievement discrepancy formulas and, instead, requires states to have a process for determining a child's response to scientific, research-based intervention (U. S. Department of Education) and/or demonstration of a pattern of strengths and weaknesses (PSW). Determining a pattern of strengths and weaknesses depends on deploying several models based on different theories of cognitive processing, and states that allow or require this approach usually specify the model to be used (Hanson, Sharman, and Esparza-Brown, 2009). With both the child-response and PSW approaches, the emphasis has shifted from identifying a deficit within the individual student to, instead, providing the student with differentiated, research-based interventions designed to improve achievement outcomes.

These two examples of changes in conceptualization of disabling conditions, evolving over time and due to a variety of factors, demonstrate the seemingly arbitrary nature of categorical definitions that impact eligibility for special education services for entire groups of individuals. A related issue that continues to be controversial in special education, and is primarily a function of definitions of disabilities based on psychometric deficits, is the use of variable assessment instruments and methods in the evaluation process.

Issues in Assessment

Central to the placement of students in special education is the multidisciplinary team evaluation process. This process usually consists of several information-gathering approaches, including observation of the student in one or more settings, interviews with the student, parent, and others regarding the areas of difficulty, formal assessment techniques, and careful review of records and work samples (Ysseldyke, Algozzine, & Thurlow). Of these four methods, formal assessment techniques or psychometric testing causes the most controversy. To begin with, the validity of norm-referenced, standardized tests such as those thought to measure intelligence has been questioned for specific groups of students. Of particular concern is that the language and cultural background of individual students taking the test may differ significantly from that of the group on which the test was normed, rendering the use of such tests for decision-making purposes questionable at best.

In addition, it has been argued that the majority of students who are referred and ultimately tested are then placed in special education (Algozzine, Christenson, & Ysseldyke, 1982; Ysseldyke, Vanderwood, & Shriner, 1997). This has led many researchers and practitioners to suspect that tests are often chosen on the basis of their ability to provide the scores necessary for eligibility (Johnson, 1998), leaving open the question as to whether the testing process contributes anything to the decision-making process. Finally, the relevance of standardized test results for instructional planning has been cited as a major reason for assessment reform in special education (Christenson & Ysseldyke, 1987; Heller, Holtzman, & Messick, 1982) and in general education.

Within the past decade or so, shifts in philosophy regarding the practice of testing for special education eligibility have resulted in a broader scope of assessment options. Curriculum-based measurement (Deno, Fuchs, Marston, & Shin, 2001), performance assessment (Elliott & Fuchs, 1997), portfolio assessment (Hager & Slocum, 2002), and functional behavior analysis (Landrum, 2001) are examples of alternatives to traditional standardized testing. Even with continued use of standardized tests for eligibility and placement decisions, increasing numbers of school psychologists are utilizing a cross-battery approach to assessment in an effort to improve the validity of results and relevance of information for instructional planning (Flanagan, 2000; Plank, 2001).

Racial Disparities Within Special Education

One of the most contentious issues facing special education is that of disparities among students referred to and placed in special education programs for high-incidence categories such as learning disabled, mild cognitively impaired, speech/language impaired, and emotionally disturbed. At issue is the disproportionate numbers of minority students who are so categorized and placed, especially African-American and Latino students, which has led many educators and researchers to question not only the methods of referral and identification procedures as potentially biased, but also to investigate a host of other factors that are or may be contributing to the problem. Cultural and language differences, which render many currently-used standardized assessment methods questionable at best and potentially invalid, have been considered by some to be at the root of the observed disparities. In addition, due to economic disadvantages that pervade many cities and neighborhoods populated by minorities, the schools attended by these students often lack the resources and qualified personnel that more economically-stable schools enjoy. Other variables, such as faculty racial composition and minority administrative power have been cited as explanatory factors for the disproportionate minority representation in special education (Herrera, 1998).

If one considers the somewhat artificial and arbitrary nature of categorical definitions, combined with limitations of many assessment methods currently in use, the fact of racial disparity within the special education population is not surprising. Minnow (1990), for example, points out that the dilemma of difference. Differences in behavior, language, learning, and cognitive abilities exist because they rest on the assumption that difference is linked to abnormality, even deviance. This is supported by Herrera's (1998) analysis of special education placements in ten cities across the United States, which demonstrated that cities with higher percentages of African American teachers and administrators had lower percentages of African American male students placed in special education. Thus, normative comparisons such as those used in classification schemes and standardized testing are based on what is considered to be natural, normal, or nearly universal behaviors, abilities, and traits, and those individuals falling outside this norm are viewed as deficient in some way (Gould, 1995). And, to the extent that special education placements are sometimes seen as a way to remove problems from the general education environment, racial disparities arising from the current system perpetuate educational and social inequity.

In their comprehensive meta-analysis of work investigating the existence and causes of racial disparities within special education, Hosp and Reschly (2003) point out there is currently a relative lack of research that identifies strategies to address the issue. They conclude that, in order to reverse and prevent such disparities, all stages in special education eligibility, beginning with the referral process, must be examined. Macmillan and Reschly (1998) caution that

> Discrimination is a two-edged sword. Although we must remain vigilant in scrutinizing placement practices in order to prevent the qualification of any children for services for which they do not qualify and from which they will not benefit, we must be equally on guard to prevent the denial of access to services for which children do qualify and from which they are likely to benefit because of their ethnicity. Efforts to "correct" overrepresentation by denying services to children of a particular ethnic group that is "at quota" when one of those children needs the services and supports provided are equally repugnant and constitute educational malpractice (p. 24).

Additionally, Artiles (1998) recommends that addressing the existence of racial disparities in special education requires an understanding of the socio-historical context out of which such disparities have grown and the application of social justice and multicultural perspectives to any attempt to rectify the situation.

Placement Issues

Controversies within special education do not end with the referral and eligibility issues discussed above. Debates about placement decisions and instructional practices abound as well. Because categories of special education eligibility were ostensibly created solely for the purpose of identifying individuals with disabling conditions who are expected to require different or additional educational and related services, the eligibility category of an individual student should not drive the actual educational placement decision. Two students with the same eligibility classification (mild cognitive impairment, for example) may, in fact, need and benefit from very different educational placements depending upon the exact nature of the underlying disability, their individual strengths and weaknesses, as well as a host of other social, personality, and historical factors. Unfortunately, all too often, students are placed in specific programs or classrooms based solely on the basis of the eligibility label. An example of this type of thinking was in evidence in a small suburban school district in Texas. A school psychologist, hired on a temporary basis, noticed that there were no students in the district with an "emotional disturbance" eligibility classification. When she asked about this apparent discrepancy, she was told the district never used that label because it did not have an "emotionally disturbed classroom"!

The most pressing issue at hand, however, is the controversy surrounding the most effective placements for students with high-incidence disabilities. Ideally, each individual student's needs are considered carefully and placement along a continuum of options ranging from the regular education setting all the way through home-bound services is made, with provisions for the least restrictive environment taken into consideration. In reality, however, the philosophical orientation of the individuals and institution involved are often the primary driving force in such decision-making processes. According to Ysseldyke, Algozzine, & Thurlow (2000), special education began as a way to ensure that students with disabilities received some form of education and was originally conceived as a somewhat separate education system with its own curricula, teaching methods, staff, and administration. However, as the concept of mild disabilities expanded, the practice of separate educational systems was questioned, resulting in what came to be known as the regular education initiative. This initiative ultimately paved the way for the practice of inclusion, which continues to be a topic of heated debate to this day. Some argue with zealous insistence that it is the right of all students and the responsibility of society to foster an attitude of acceptance of and active involvement by individuals in all aspects of the community including educational settings (York & Tundidor, 1995). On the other side of the coin are those who are equally passionate in their insistence that inclusion is poorly disguised attempt to reduce the costs of special education and that it undermines the right of students with disabilities to an appropriate education (Cohen, 1995). Regardless of the stance, one fact remains certain: more research is needed in order to ascertain the cost-effectiveness and learning outcomes associated with special education placements from inclusive settings to homebound and residential placements. Finally, Tucker (1989) cautions that when making placement decisions, the least restrictive environment refers not to the physical location of the person but to the conditions surrounding the person; thus, placement should never be confused with program.

Future Trends in Special Education

There is no general consensus regarding the future of special education. It is suggested by some that in order to know where one is going, one must know where one is and has been, and that is the crux of the problem. Since the mid-1980s, special education seems to have suffered an identity crisis of sorts, stemming from controversies surrounding its common practices and the very philosophical and ethical foundation on which it is based. In response to the changing focus of legislation and policy away from access to special education and toward access to regular education, Zigmond (2001) suggests that the profession begin by reclaiming and reaffirming the core values and professional responsibilities of teaching to the special needs of students with disabilities. There are also strong admonishments to base future special education policy and practice on valid research rather than on values and special interests.

Paul *et al.* (1997) have identified four themes important to the future of special education: collaboration, diversity, accountability, and ethics. They maintain that collaboration is essential to "reduce fragmentation of service delivery, discontinuities in perspectives on care, territoriality among care providers, and the deep cultural and political divides that separate general from special education, schools from universities, and schools from communities and families" (p. 243). Increasing diversity within the public school setting will require special educators to re-think a variety of educational practices ranging from assessment and programming to behavior management and discipline policies. Also critical to the future of special education is greater accountability for teacher education programs, student performance, and program outcomes and how success or failure for each will be determined. Finally, the ethics of care and community are suggested as the foundation for schools of the future, with a caution that the value of pluralism not lead to ethical relativism.

Administrative Issues

The role of the school leader in the administration of special education programs has become more complex and multifaceted. School principals must perform the following: make arrange-ments for appropriate resources and facilities, actively participate in special education deci-sion-making through consultation and attendance at IEP committee meetings, supervise spe-cial education personnel including teachers and paraeducators, and deal effectively with the wide range of instructional, behavioral, and disciplinary needs of students receiving special services. In addition, school principals should be well-versed in both conceptual understanding of special education practice as well as the legal and ethical requirements of such program-ming, and must continue to update their knowledge as special education requirements evolve (Littleton & Schroth, 2001). Fostering a climate of care (Pazey, 1993) for students with special needs, from the initiation of a pre-referral intervention all the way through delivery of services and, potentially, dismissal from special education is an important element of successful leader-ship in the integration of special education services into the neighborhood school. Additional-ly, school leaders should strive to ensure all students are challenged, appropriately placed, and assessed regularly using valid and reliable techniques.

Finally, school principals must foster strong, positive relationships between central office staff, school personnel, students, and families based on cooperation and mutual respect. This can be particularly difficult since conflict can arise due to differing opinions as to what is in the best interest of a particular child. In addition, the heightened vigilance for possible breaches of legal and ethical principles that often is part of the fabric of the special education environment can create a climate of distrust between school staff and families, and among school personnel as a whole. Furthermore, philosophical rifts stemming from various orientations regarding the de-livery of special education services (e.g., full inclusion versus pull-out programs, consultation versus direct-service) can engender hostility among these groups. Thus, the school principal must also be skilled in relationship-building techniques and conflict resolution. Perhaps one of the most crucial elements of successful building leadership regarding special education services is having an understanding of when to defer to the expertise of other professionals and knowing when to seek additional information and counsel from outside.

Summary

Special education has existed for a relatively short period of time in American schools and yet has undergone tremendous philosophical and conceptual shifts that are reflected in the historical changes in policy and legislation. More so than with perhaps any other aspect of public educa-tion, controversies surrounding special education tend to reflect the political, philosophical, and social biases of society as a whole. Issues of social justice, civil rights, and even human dignity have fueled debates about a broad spectrum of practices within special education. The idea of special education services for individuals with disabilities, once heralded as a progressive movement within education, is now seen by many as a system of stigmatization and segregation. And yet, there are educators for whom the mission of special education is as valid and noble as it has always been. In its current state, successful special education programs require informed administrative involvement and support, quality teacher education and professional development, and improved practices based on research rather than values and special interest. As special education moves into the future, there must be increased attention to issues central to education in the 21st century: acceptance of diversity, family-school-community collaboration, improved accountability, and development of core values and professional ethics.

Questions for Consideration

1. Should general and special education become more fully integrated? If so, how can this be achieved?
2. What are some potential conflicts between special education policy and current educational reform efforts such as the *No Child Left Behind Act* and accountability movements?
3. How do funding formulas impact the numbers of students receiving special education services and the types of programs offered?
4. What are some of the legal and ethical implications of enacting broad policy changes with regard to special education placement options?

Case Study

Parental and Student Rights vs. School Responsibility

Sue Strong is the mother of three children at Kennedy Elementary School. Mrs. Strong has been a very active parent at the school, involved in PTA and volunteering on a regular basis. Two of the Strong children, Kim in the fifth grade and Brian in the third grade, have done well and have been actively involved in clubs and extracurricular activities. The youngest child, Matthew, was diagnosed with autism when he was three years old, and he attended the district's preschool and primary program for children with impairments.

Although Matthew appears bright in many ways and he has language skills, his ability to communicate effectively with adults and peers alike is significantly impaired. In addition, Matthew has a lot of difficulty with transitions and generally seems to perform much better when there are a limited number of children, adults and settings with which he must work. Matthew has a history of severe behavioral episodes and currently has a behavior plan and crisis intervention plan as part of his IEP. During kindergarten and first grade, Matthew spent most of his school day in a self-contained classroom that serves primarily students with developmental disabilities including students with mild to moderate cognitive impairments. Matthew is only one of two children in the program with autism. Although Mrs. Strong participated actively in the development of the IEP and appeared to agree with the placement, she has, over the past year, increasingly become involved with an autism advocacy group. As Matthew begins his second grade year, she has come to you, the school administrator, with the request that Matthew be placed in a regular second grade classroom.

Mrs. Strong is concerned that Matthew's language and social skills will not fully develop unless he has regular contact with students without disabilities. In addition, there is no evidence that Matthew has a cognitive impairment and she is concerned that his level of academic achievement will be limited if he remains in his current special education placement. Matthew's teachers, however, insist that his current placement is appropriate and that he is working on first and second grade material in addition to receiving specialized communication and social skills instruction that he would not get in a regular second grade classroom. Furthermore, Matthew's teachers have significant concerns about his ability to deal with transitions. The regular second grade classrooms have as many as 28 children and have different teachers for reading, math, music, art, physical education, and science lab. His current classroom serves only 8 students, and there is a regular full-time paraeducator in addition to the teacher. The teacher and paraeducator remain in the classroom during music, art, adaptive physical education, and speech therapy services, which are delivered in the classroom by specially trained personnel.

At this point, the school administrator feels caught between a rock and a hard place. She can see both sides of the issue and, while the decision will be a committee decision and not hers alone, she feels pressure to avoid any potential litigation. In addition, she knows that the teachers expect to have her support as their educational leader, but she also does not want to alienate this parent, who has contributed so much to the school.

Questions for Discussion

1. What are the legal issues involved?
2. Are there any ethical considerations? If so, what are they?
3. What should be the first step taken by the school administrator?
4. What are some options that the IEP Team could consider?

References

Algozzine, B., Christenson, S., & Ysseldyke, J. E. (1982). Probabilities associated with the referral to placement process. *Teacher Education and Special Education, 5*(3), 19–23.

Artiles, A. J. (1998). The dilemma of difference: Enriching the disproportionality discourse with theory and context. *The Journal of Special Education, 32*(1), 32–36.

Berman, S. H. & Urion, D. K. (2003). The misdiagnosis of special education costs. *School Administrator, 60*(3), 6–10.

Biasini, F. J., Grupe, L., Huffman, L., & Bray, N. W. (1999). Mental retardation: a symptom and a syndrome. In S. D. Netherton, D. Holmes, & Walker, C. E. (Eds.). *Child and adolescent psychological disorders: A comprehensive textbook.* New York: Oxford University Press.

Bogdan, R. & Taylor, S. (1976). The judged, not the judges: An insider's view of mental retardation. *American Psychologist, 31*, 47–52.

Bureau of Labor Statistics (2012). *Occupational outlook handbook: Teacher assistants.* Retrieved from http://www.bls.gov/ooh/Education-Training-and-Library/Teacher-assistants.htm.

Carter, J. & Sugai, G. (1989). Survey on prereferral practices: Responses from state departments of education. *Exceptional Children, 55*(4), 298–302.

Chambers, J. G., Parrish, T. B., Lieberman, J. C., & Wolman, J. M. (1998). *What are we spending on special education in the U.S.?* CSEF Brief No. 8. Palo Alto, CA: Center for Special Education Finance, American Institutes for Research.

Christenson, S. L. & Ysseldyke, J. E. (1989). Assessing student performance: An important change is needed. *Journal of School Psychology, 27*, 409–426.

Cohen, O. P. (1995). *The adverse implication of inclusion for deaf students.* US: New York. (ERIC Document Reproduction Service No. ED389106).

Deno, S. L., Fuchs, L. S., Marston, D., & Shin, J. (2001). Using curriculum-based measurement to establish growth standards for students with learning disabilities. *School Psychology Review, 30*(4), 507–524.

Dobbs, R. F., Primm, E. B., & Primm, B. (1991). Mediation: A common sense approach for resolving conflicts in special education. *Focus on Exceptional Children, 24*, 1–11.

Elliott, S. N. & Fuchs, L. S. (1997). The utility of curriculum-based measurement and performance assessment as alternatives to traditional intelligence and achievement tests. *The School Psychology Review, 26*(2), 224–233.

Fiedler, C. R. (2000). *Making a difference: Advocacy competencies for special education professionals.* Boston: Allyn & Bacon.

Fisher, D., Frey, N. & Thousand, J. (2003). What do special educators need to know and be prepared to do for inclusive schooling to work? *Teachers Education and Special Education, 26*(1), 42–50.

Flanagan, D. P. (2000). Wechsler-based CHC cross-battery assessment and reading achievement: Strengthening the validity of interpretations drawn from Wechsler test scores. *School Psychology Quarterly, 15*(3), 295–329.

Garguilo, R. M. (2003). *Special education in contemporary society: An introduction to exceptionality.* Belmont, CA: Wadsworth Publishing.

Gould, S. J. (1995). *The mismeasure of man (Rev. ed.).* New York: Norton.

Hager, K. D. & Slocum, T. A. (2002). Alternate assessment: No child left behind during statewide testing. *Annual National Conference Proceedings of the American Council on Rural Special Education. Reno, Nevada, 22.*

Hanson, J., Sharman, L. A., & Esparza-Brown, J. (2009). *Pattern of strengths and weaknesses in specific learning disabilities: What's it all about?* Oregon School Psychologists Association. Retrieved from http://ospa.wildapricot.org/Default.aspx?pageId=417777

Heller, K. A., Holtzman, W., & Messick, S. (1982). *Placing children in special education: A strategy for equity.* Washington, DC: National Academy Press.

Herrera, J. (1998). *The disproportionate placement of African Americans in special education: An analysis of ten cities.* US: Wisconsin. (ERIC Document Reproduction Service No. ED423324).

Heward, W. L. (2006). *Legal challenges based on IDEA.* Retrieved from www.education.com/reference/article/legal-challenges-IDEA/

Hosp, J. L., & Reschly, D. J. (2003). Referral rates for intervention or assessment: A meta-analysis of racial differences. *Journal of Special Education, 37*(2), 67–80.

Hosp, J. L. (n.d.). Response to intervention and the disproportionate representation of culturally and linguistically diverse students in special education. *RTI Action Network.* Retrieved from http://www.rtinetwork.org/learn/diversity/disproportionaterepresentation.

IDEA Funding Coalition (2006). *IDEA funding: Time for congress to live up to the commitment.* Retrieved from http://www.nassp.org/Portals/0/Content/53654.pdf.

Individuals with Disabilities Education Act (Pub. L. No. 101-476), 20 U.S.C. Chapter 33. Ammended by Pub. L. No. 105-17 in June, 1997. 34 CFR part 300.

Itard, E.M. (1962). *The wild boy of Aveyron.* (G. Humphries & M. Humphries, Trans.). New York: Appleton-Century-Crofts.

Jacob-Timm, S. & Hartshorne, T. S. (1998). *Ethics and law for school psychologists, 3rd edition.* New York: John Wiley & Sons, Inc.

Johnson, E. S. (1998). *Are mathematical applications and intelligence separate or related constructs?* Unpublished manuscript, University of Houston.

Kamens, M. W., Loprete, S. J., & Slostad, F. A. (2003). Inclusive classrooms: What practicing teachers want to know. *Action in Teacher Education, 25*(1), 20–26.

Katsiyannis, A. & Maag, J. (1998). Disciplining students with disabilities: Issues and considerations for implementing IDEA '97. *Behavioral Disorders, 23,* 276–289.

Kauffman, J. M. (2003). Reflections on the field. *Education and Treatment of Children, 26*(4), 325–329.

Kleinhammer-Tramill, J. & Fiore, T. A. (2003). A history of federal support for preparing special educators and related services personnel to serve children and youth with disabilities. *Teacher Education and Special Education, 26*(3), 217–229.

Kuther, T. L. (1994). *Diagnostic classification of children within the educational system: Should it be eliminated?* New York. (ERIC Document Reproduction Service NO. ED393259).

Landrum, T. J. (2001). Assessment for eligibility: Issues in identifying students with emotional or behavioral disorders. *Assessment for Effective Intervention, 26*(1), 41–49.

Littleton, M. & Schroth, G. (2001). Special Education. In G. Schroth & M Littleton (Eds.). *The administration and supervision of special programs in education*, 1–22. Dubuque, IA: Kendall/Hunt Publishing Co.

MacMillan, D. L., & Reschly, D. J. (1998). Overrepresentation of minority students: The case for greater specificity or reconsideration of the variables examined. *Journal of Special Education, 32*(1), 15–24.

McCann, C. (2013). *Individuals with disabilities education act (IDEA)*. New America Foundation. Retrieved from http://edmoney.newamerica.net/taxonomy/term/1900

Meloy, L.L. (1999). Manifestation determination. NASP Communique', 28(4), 8.

Minnow, M. (1990). *Making all the difference: Inclusion, exclusion, and American law*. Ithaca, NY: Cornell University Press.

National Association of School Psychologists (2004). *NASP Legislative Update: IDEA Conference Report Passes*. Retrieved from http://www.nasponline.org/advocacy/legisup111904.html#item1.

National Center of Response to Intervention (n.d.). Retrieved from http://www.rti4success.org/.

National Clearinghouse for Professions in Special Education (2001). *Paraeducator resources*. Retrieved from http://www.special-ed-careers.org/educator_resources/para_resources.html.

National Commission on Excellence (1983). *A nation at risk: The imperative for educational reform*. Washington, DC: U.S. Government Printing Office.

National Dissemination Center for Children with Disabilities (2013). *Categories of disabilities under IDEA*. Retrieved from http://nichcy.org/disability/categories.

National Dissemination Center for Children with Disabilities (2012). *Response to intervention*. Retrieved from http://nichcy.org/schools-administrators/rti.

National Education Association (2013). *Getting educated: Paraeducators*. Retrieved from http://www.nea.org/home/18605.htm.

Neal, A. (2001). *Phillipe Pinel, 1745–1826*. Retrieved from http://websrv.utica.edu/faculty/tbrown/times/obits/pinel.htm

Nelson, M. C. (2003). Through a glass darkly: Reflections on our field and its nature. *Education and Treatment of Children, 26*(4), 330–336.

Parrish, T. B. (1996). *Special education finance: Past, present, and future*. Policy Paper No. 8. Palo Alto, CA: Center for Special Education Finance, American Institutes for Research.

Parrish, T. B., O'Reilly, F., Duenas, I. E., & Wolman, J. (1997). *State special education finance systems, 1994–95*. Palo Alto, CA: Center for Special Education Finance, American Institutes for Research. Retrieved from http://www.csef-air.org/publications/csef/state/statsped.pdf.

Paul, J. L. & Morse, W. C. (1997). Creating and using knowledge for special education practice: The conundrum and the promise. In J. L. Paul, M. Churton, W. C. Morse, A. J. Duchnowski, B. Epanchin, P. G. Osnes, & R. L. Smith (Eds.), *Special education practice: Applying the knowledge, affirming the values and creating the future*, pp. 10–25. Pacific Grove, CA: Brooks/Cole Publishing.

Paul, J. L., Duchnowski, A., Morse, W. C., Christenson, L., & Martinez, Y.G. (1997). Values, knowledge, and action: Issues facing the profession. In J. L. Paul, M. Churton, W. C. Morse, A. J. Duchnowski, B. Epanchin, P. G. Osnes, & R. L. Smith (Eds.), *Special education practice: Applying the knowledge, affirming the values and creating the future*, pp. 241–249. Pacific Grove, CA: Brooks/Cole Publishing.

Pazey, B. (1993). *The missing link for the administration of special education: The ethic of care*. Paper presented at the Conference of the University Council of Educational Administration, Houston, TX.

Plank, G. A. (2001). Application of the cross-battery approach in the assessment of Native American children: A viable alternative. *American Indian and Alaskan Native Mental Health Research, 10*(1), 21–33.

Plucker, J. (2003). *Jean-Marc Gaspard Itard*. Retrieved from http://www.indiana.edu/%7Eintell/itard.shtml.

Polsgrove, L. (2003). Reflections on the past and future. *Education and Treatment of Children, 26*(4), 337–344.

Reber, A. S. (1985). *The Penguin dictionary of psychology.* London: Penguin Books.

Rozicki, E. G. (2002). The practice of special education: Definitely immoral, potentially illegal. *Educational Horizons, 81*(1), 8–9.

Scruggs, T. E. & Mastropieri, M. A. (2002). On babies and bathwater: Addressing the problems of identification of learning disabilities. *Learning Disabilities Quarterly, 25,* 155–168.

Sindelar, P. T., Ross, D. D., Brownell, M. T., Griffin, C. G., & Rennels, M. S. (1997). Teacher education for Florida's 21st century. In J. L. Paul, M. Churton, W. C. Morse, A. J. Duchnowski, B. Epanchin, P. G. Osnes, & R. L. Smith (Eds.), *Special education practice: Applying the knowledge, affirming the values, and creating the future,* pp. 192–208. Pacific Grove, CA: Brookes/Cole Publishing.

Shonkoff, J. & Meisels, S. (1990). Early childhood intervention: The evolution of a concept. In S. Meisels & J. Shonkoff (Eds.), *Handbook of early childhood intervention* (pp. 3–31). Cambridge, England: Cambridge University Press.

Texas Education Agency (2002). Special education in Texas: A guide to the admission, review, and dismissal process. Austin, TX: TEA Division of Special Education.

Tillery, C. Y., Werts, M. G., Roark, R., & Harris, S. (2003). Perceptions of paraeducators on job retention. *Teacher Education and Special Education, 25*(2), 118–127.

Tucker, J. A. (1989). Less required energy: A response to Danielson and Bellamy. *Exceptional Children, 55,* 456–458.

U.S. Department of Education (1974). *Family Education Rights and Privacy Act.* 20 U.S.C. Sec. 1232g; 34 C.F.R. Part 99.

U.S. Department of Education (1974). *Rehabilitation Act of 1974* (Pub. L. No. 93-112), 29 U.S.C. Part 794.

U.S. Department of Education (1992). *Individuals with Disabilities Education Act Part B Regulations,* 34 C.F.R. Sections 300.660-662.

U.S. Department of Education (2013). *Individuals with Disabilities Education Improvement Act.* Sec. 614(b). Retrieved from http://www2.ed.gov/policy/speced/guid/idea/idea2004.html.

U.S. Department of Education (1995). Archived special education funding in the states. *Seventeenth Annual Report to Congress on the Implementation of the Individuals with Disabilities Act.* Retrieved from http://www.ed.gov/pubs/OSEP95AnlRpt/ch5b.html.

Varin, R. (1998). Mental retardation. Retrieved from http://home.earthlink.net/~varin/teaching/te01002.htm.

Verstegan, D. A. (2011). Public education finance systems in the United States and funding policies for populations with special education needs. *Education Policy Analysis Archives 19*(21).

Villareal, D. A. (2010). A case study of instructional paraeducators' staff development needs. University of Houston). ProQuest Dissertations and Theses, 179. Retrieved from http://search.proquest.com/docview/519055011?accountid=12924. (519055011).

Wigle, S. E. & Wilcox, D. J. (2003). Changing roles and responsibilities of special educators; implications for teacher education. *Action in Teacher Education, 25*(1), 27–37.

Wolfensberger, W. (1972). *The principle of normalization in human services.* Toronto: National Institute on Mental Retardation.

Wright, P. W. D. (2006). *Summary of major chances in IDEA regulations.* Retrieved from www.wrightslaw.com/idea/law/htm.

York, J. & Tundidor, M. (1995). Issues raised in the name of inclusion: Perspectives of educators, parents, and students. *Journal of the Association for Persons with Severe Handicaps, 20*(1), 31–44.

Young, I. M. (2001). Justice and the politics of difference. In S. Seidman & J. C. Alexander (Eds.), *The new social theory reader,* pp. 203–211. London: Routledge.

Ysseldyke, J. E., Vanderwood, M. L., & Shriner, J. G. (1997). Changes over the past decade in special education referral to placement probability. *Diagnostique, 23*(1), 193–201.

Ysseldyke, J. E., Algozzine, B. & Thurlow, M. L. (2000). *Critical issues in special education.* Boston: Houghton Mifflin.

Zigmond, N. (2001). Special education at a crossroad. *Preventing School Failure, 45*(2), 70–74.

CHAPTER 4

Programs for Students with Gifts and Talents

Introduction

WITH current educational trends emphasizing differentiated instruction, fully inclusive educational programming, and standards-based outcomes, there is a growing push toward providing all instruction to nearly all students within the regular education classroom. Yet, there has been a resistance to the idea of inclusion for some segments of the population of students with special or exceptional needs, including students with gifts and talents. Controversy abounds as to the most appropriate programming options for such students, the very definition of "gifted" and "talented," methods of identifying such students, prevalence estimates, the veracity of concurrent giftedness and disability, and differences in manifestation of gifts and talents among linguistically and culturally diverse students. This chapter will examine the history, current trends, legal implications, funding and personnel issues of gifted programs, and the impact of such programs on society in general.

Historical Overview

Although there is no clear point during which schools in the United States began to recognize and plan specialized programming for students with gifts and talents, there are certain historical events and developments in the fields of psychology and education that contributed. Indeed, one can reach as far back as Plato to see that there has long been a tendency to perceive youth of promise as requiring and deserving special educational treatment (Burt, 1975). Most often, within the United States, specialized treatment of academically advanced and intellectually gifted students took the form of acceleration through the curriculum, and until the educational reforms led by Horace Mann and Henry Bernard, which led to the common practice of same-age groupings, it was not uncommon for such students to enter academies and universities at a relatively young age (Sayler, 1999). This approach, however, was unsystematic, widely scattered, and the outcome of grade acceleration was seldom evaluated. The period from 1900 to 1950 is known as the "psychological and scientific movement in gifted education" and was dominated by a fixed view of intelligence (For a more detailed review of this period, see Boschee, Beyer, Engelking, & Boschee, 1997, pp. 51–59.) This trend came at a time when calls for restrictions on immigration into the United States were being made, and newly developed tests of intelligence were thought to be a scientific means to sort and classify students into tracks based on intellectual merit. E.

L. Thorndike proclaimed, around this period, that "the role of the school is to select individuals for their places in the meritocracy and to provide an education that prepares individuals to live in a society ruled by merit and intelligence" (Spring, 2011). Unfortunately, the emphasis on psychological testing and the supposedly scientific methods of classifying students served to benefit Caucasian students from middle to upper class backgrounds while relegating students of other racial classifications—and certainly those who lacked fluency in English—to less academically oriented educational programs.

In 1868, William Torrey Harris, Superintendent of St. Louis Public Schools, instituted one of the earliest efforts to identify and educate gifted students, and in 1901, the first school for gifted students opened in Worcester, Massachusetts. In 1918, schools in Louisville, Kentucky began to systematically identify gifted students, accelerate these students through the curriculum, and monitor the outcome. Other school systems followed suit, and within a few decades, the efficacy of the increasingly common practice of pushing students through the standard program without enrichment and attention to individual needs was questioned. Leta Hollingworth (1926), in particular, questioned this practice and was instrumental in developing innovative programs that emphasized a deeper understanding of core content areas through enrichment and specialized instruction.

Along with a virtual explosion of intelligence and aptitude tests developed during the First and Second World Wars, the demands for educated young men who were suited to officer training and the increasing need for accomplished mathematicians and scientists in the workforce resulted in a renewed interest in programs to develop academic talent. However, interest waned as the post-war economy grew and jobs became plentiful. Furthermore, the stock and somewhat narrow definition of giftedness, which carried with it a connotation of intellectual elitism, along with a growing trend toward pragmatics and competence-based programs over intellectually and academically rigorous curricula further lessened the interest in, and development of, such programs. However, in the 1950s, J. P. Guilford proposed a new approach to the understanding and measurement of intelligence to include, among other factors, acculturation knowledge, reasoning, visualization and spatial orientation, listening, and speed of processing. In addition, he encouraged educators and psychologists alike to broaden their view of giftedness to include multiple abilities as well as creativity. A short time later, in 1957, the Russian launch of Sputnik brought an immediate change of focus in education in the United States, and efforts to develop and strengthen programs for gifted students were renewed.

In 1969, an amendment to PL91-230 added provisions for gifted children to the Title III and Title IV programs. A report by then-Commissioner of Education, Sydney Marland (1972), indicated that very few gifted students were receiving any special services due to lack of funding, trained teachers, and appropriate curricular materials necessary for such programming. In 1974, the Federal Office of Gifted Education was established and, as a result, funding for programs increased, along with attention to research on gifted individuals, educational programs, and the development of a wide variety of approaches and models. The office was closed under the Reagan administration in 1982, but in 1988, the Jacob K. Javits Gifted and Talented Students Education Act (P.L. 100-297), was passed. This act, currently re-authorized under part B of Title X of the Elementary and Secondary Education Act (ESEA), articulates the need to identify and provide appropriate services for individuals with potential for outstanding achievement who are in environments where their aptitude may not be recognized or nurtured, including students with disabilities, limited English proficiency, or from economically disadvantaged backgrounds. Through this act, interest in and funding for research, development, and evaluation of programs has continued with the establishment of The National Research Center on the Gifted and Talented, a consortium of research universities, collaborative school districts, consulting scholars, and state and territorial departments of education.

Definitions of Giftedness

Over the years, federal definitions of giftedness have changed as terminology has been added and deleted. After the formation of a federal task force to study gifted education under former Commissioner of Education Stanley Marland in 1972, the following definition was developed:

Gifted and Talented children are those identified by professionally qualified persons who, by virtue of outstanding abilities, are capable of high performance. These are children who require differentiated educational programs and / or services beyond those normally provided by the regular school program in order to realize their contribution to self and society. Children capable of high performance include those with demonstrated achievement and / or potential ability in any of the following areas, singly or in combination:

1. general intellectual ability
2. specific academic aptitude
3. creative or productive thinking
4. leadership ability
5. visual and performing arts
6. psychomotor ability

Although this definition has undergone several revisions throughout the years, including the elimination of reference to psychomotor ability and visual / performing arts with the passage of the Javits act of 1988, it nevertheless remains the basis for most identification procedures today. Ultimately, the term "gifted" was eliminated altogether in light of research findings regarding the interaction between potential and environmental factors. Thus, the current definition identifies gifted students as:

Students, children, or youth who give evidence of high achievement capability in areas such as intellectual, creative, artistic, or leadership capacity, or in specific academic fields, and who need services and activities not ordinarily provided by the school in order to fully develop those capabilities (NAGC, 2008).

These definitions have provided over time a foundation for most state definitions of giftedness and talent, and, thus, have served as a basis for identifying students for participation in special programs. Alternative definitions of giftedness have been proposed as a means to drive theory and research. For example, Sternberg conceived of giftedness as developing expertise (2000); Clark (1997) defined giftedness in terms of accelerated development of functions within the brain; and Renzulli (1978) described giftedness as a three-ring confluence of task commitment, above-average ability, and creativity. Still others have identified traits and characteristics thought to be associated with gifted and talented individuals such as curiosity, persistence, perceptiveness, critical thinking, ability to see relationships, divergent thinking, and high verbal ability (Tuttle, 1988). Ideas of giftedness have evolved from an instrumental definition that presupposes the fixed nature and primary importance of IQ (e.g., Terman's 1925 definition of giftedness as performance within the first percentile rank on the Stanford-Binet Intelligence Scale) (Stephens & Karnes, 2000) to one that recognizes the cultural and contextual relevance of various forms of ability, and differentiates between the expression of and potential for outstanding talent. As definitions of giftedness changed, methods for identifying gifts and talents also evolved.

Methods of Identifying Gifts and Talents

Current methods of identifying students with gifts and talents rely less on formal measures of general intelligence than before; however, these tests are still used. The traditional measures of achievement and intelligence are considered static due to their focus on individual performance on standardized tasks at a specific moment in time without attempts to change or improve performance. Tests of this type also tend to reflect what an individual knows as a result of prior experiences (Haywood, Brown, & Wingenfeld, 1990). Of particular concern is that such tests underestimate the intellectual potential of students from diverse cultural and linguistic backgrounds as well as of students who are socio-economically disadvantaged (Skuy, Kaniel, & Turziel, 1988; Tellegen & Laros, 1993; Frasier & Passow, 1994; Ford & Harris, 1999).

Instead, there is growing interest in the validity and applicability of various forms of dynamic assessment for identification purposes. In contrast to static measures of ability, dynamic assessment is a methodology that is derived, in part, from the work of Vygotsky, especially his construct known as the zone of proximal development or ZPD (1978). The ZPD is defined as "the distance between the actual developmental level as determined by independent problem solving and the level of potential development as determined through problem solving under adult guidance or in collaboration with more capable peers" (p. 86). Thus, dynamic assessment methods attempt to assess learning-in-process by activating the complex relationship among teaching, learning, and assessment, thereby providing information about a student's learning potential rather than past experience (Kanevsky, 2000).

Regardless of the assessment methodology employed, the process used to identify students with gifts and talents should encompass a wide variety of techniques and sources of information about the student, should take into account the individual's cultural and social background, and should continue over time through multiple phases (Pfleger, 1977; Renzulli & Smith, 1977; Borland & Wright, 1994). Techniques that have been used in the identification of students with gifts, talents, and latent potential include the following: individualized standardized tests; group administered ability tests; dynamic assessment methods; biographical inventories; recommendations from teachers, parents, and peers; ratings by past and current teachers; parent and self-ratings; observations of and interviews with the student; portfolios; performance-based assessment; and evaluations of specific areas of talent or giftedness (e.g., creativity, leadership, musical ability, etc.).

In an effort to improve identification efforts and foster equitable access to programs for students with gifts and talents among culturally, linguistically, and economically diverse student populations, Frasier & Passow (1994) have proposed a "new paradigm for identifying talent potential." This paradigm enjoins educators to recognize new constructs of giftedness that reflect multicultural, multidimensional perspectives and that are defined by traits, aptitudes, and behaviors that are nurtured rather than by static test performance. In addition, the new paradigm differentiates between absolute attributes of giftedness, traits, and behaviors that characterize high performance cross-culturally, and specific attributes and behaviors that manifest themselves in particular cultural contexts or settings. Furthermore, educators are encouraged to develop an increased understanding of and sensitivity to culturally and contextually determined behaviors in order to recognize and interpret performance indicators of talent potential. Finally, the emerging paradigm advocates for more varied and authentic assessment techniques, and for the opportunity for children to display gifts and talent potential through rich learning experiences provided to all students.

Programs and Service Delivery Models for Students with Gifts and Talents

Throughout the years, a variety of educational programs and services have been developed to meet the needs of students with gifts and talents. However, Eby & Smutney (1990) cautioned educators that shopping for existing programs and attempting to duplicate a prior model is unwise and unlikely to meet the needs of a school district or its learners. Instead, they advocated that "a well-reasoned educational philosophy and clear objectives are essential for an effective program.

If a program is to thrive, its design must not only reflect an educational philosophy and objectives but also creatively address the district's limitations" (p. 142). Nevertheless, they outlined several models commonly found in the public school setting and reflective of traditional approaches to programming for students with gifts and talents.

One of the most frequently encountered is the pull-out model through which identified students spend most of their instructional time in heterogeneous, regular education classrooms but are "pulled out" to attend special classes with other identified students. The popularity of this model is not an indication of its effectiveness but, rather, of its relative ease of implementation and logistical simplicity. A number of disadvantages have been identified with this model, including potential stigmatization or, conversely, an attitude of elitism among the participants, discontinuity between educational experiences and expectations for participants, and a failure to fully address the needs of the participants (Eby & Smutny, 1990). Similar to the pull-out model is the cluster program in which a small group of gifted or talented students are clustered together within a heterogeneous classroom. The classroom teacher, program coordinator, or consultant provides enrichment and additional instruction to the cluster, and similar advantages and disadvantages have been identified for this type of program as for pull-out programs.

Representing an increased commitment of resources are special class and special school models. These models have advantages over pull-out and cluster models in that they are more suited to the complex needs of selected participants and provide for integrated and interdisciplinary curricula. Special schools have additional advantages including the ability to structure the school to meet the unique needs of its students (e.g., flexible scheduling, non-graded courses, interdisciplinary class blocks), extended programming options (e.g., sophisticated science lab, unique fine-arts program) due to pooling of district funds for gifted and talented education, and increased opportunity for stimulating and challenging interaction and collaboration among students (Eby & Smutny, 1990).

In addition to these program models, Eby & Smutny identify three curriculum categories including acceleration, enrichment, and individualized curriculum models (1990). Acceleration is based on the assumption that students identified as gifted or talented learn more rapidly and, thus, need to move quickly through a subject. Examples of acceleration include early entrance to educational programs such as kindergarten or college, skipping grades through double promotion, and taking higher levels of specific courses (e.g., a second-grade student who is assigned to a fifth-grade reading class or a high school student who leaves three afternoons per week to attend a college chemistry course). While concerns with achievement gaps and poor social/emotional outcomes are frequently associated with this type of programming, several research studies have concluded these concerns are largely unfounded (Sayler & Brookshire, 1993; Gross, 1994; Lynch, 1994; White, 1995). Rather, failure to provide accelerated curricular options to gifted students for whom it would have been appropriate often resulted in under-achievement, maladjustment, and social isolation (Gross, 1994).

Curriculum enrichment programs are founded on the assumption that students identified as gifted or talented benefit from learning experiences of greater depth or breadth. Curriculum compacting, in which the regular curriculum is fit into a shorter time frame or limited in its original content in order to allow for additional time to be spent on supplemental content or deeper levels of remaining content, is one example. Other examples of curriculum enrichment programs include topic-related activities such as field trips or special projects, collaborative or competitive problem-solving teams, programs to develop higher-order and critical thinking skills, and development of gifted behaviors such as leadership, visual-spatial skills, etc. (Eby, 1984).

Implicit in the development of individualized curriculum models is the assumption that students identified as gifted have special interests or extraordinary abilities that require individualization of the curriculum and independent study of self-selected topics (Eby & Smutny, 1990). Examples of individualized curriculum models include Treffinger's (1975) Self-Directed Learning, which uses learning contracts to guide student learning to successively more independent levels, and Renzulli's (1977) Enrichment Triad, which seeks to develop individual ability to identify, research, investigate, and solve real problems.

Efforts have been made to develop curricula and programs to meet the challenge for gifted and talented programming outlined in the Javits Act of 1988 and described in the historical overview of this chapter. Tomlinson, Kaplan, Renzulli, Purcell, Leppein, and Burns (2002) propose a "parallel curriculum" model that seeks to address changes in society, changes in views of intelligence and giftedness, and the need to explore similarities and differences in curricula for all learners versus those intended for gifted learners. As society becomes increasingly consumer-oriented and pluralistic in its views, and demands greater amounts of specialization and adaptability, curricula must be developed to prepare all students at multiple levels for a variety of roles and functions. Furthermore, whereas intelligence was once viewed as a relatively fixed trait, contemporary conceptualizations of intelligence include assumptions of fluidity, multidimensionality, and the importance of context. Thus, a curriculum for all learners should provide rich opportunities for exploration and expansion of a wide range of abilities and human endeavors, allow for identification and development of potential across these abilities and endeavors, and address variability in manifestations of high ability as well as talent development over time in a broad range of learners (p. 3).

The proposed parallel curriculum has as its theoretical underpinnings the need to respect the unique characteristics of the learner and epistemological findings, including levels of knowing and levels of involvement. Fundamental to the parallel curriculum is the need to "ensure a basic curriculum for all learners focused on making sense of and applying the seminal ideas and skills of the disciplines but adapted to address learner variability evident in the student population" Tominson et al., 2002 (p. 13). In order to effectively address variability in cognitive development, readiness, interest, and motivation, an ascending intellectual demand is built into the parallel curriculum such that learner advances in knowledge, understanding, and skill within a domain are met with increasing levels of challenge.

The four parallels of the curriculum include: (1) a core or basic curriculum through which learners develop a framework for knowledge, understanding, and skill of the discipline; (2) a curriculum of connections through which learners discover the interconnectedness of knowledge within and across disciplines, and across time, locations, and cultures; (3) a curriculum of practice, through which learners extend their knowledge, understanding, and skill of a discipline via real-world application, disciplinary problem-solving, and professional role-taking; and (4) a curriculum of identity through which learners think about themselves, their goals, and their opportunities to make a contribution to the world through the lens of a particular discipline.

Several attempts have been made within the last decade to develop, implement, and evaluate programs designed specifically for culturally and linguistically diverse students with gifts and talents. Aguirre & Hernandez (2002) described in detail three programs that have been successful over time. Project GOTCHA (Galaxies of Thinking and Creative Heights of Achievements) is a former Title VII Academic Excellence Program that identifies and serves gifted, creative, and talented English-language learners in grades 1–8. The program is highly acclaimed for its promotion of critical thinking skills and gifted strategies within integrated and interdisciplinary curriculum units, and the utilization of performance-based outcomes and portfolio assessment for students with limited English proficiency.

Another program highlighted by Aguirre & Hernandez (2002) is the Milwaukee Public Schools Bilingual Gifted/Talented Program, which seeks to "create a stimulating environment in which the potential of every student is challenged through a variety of intensive learning experiences" (p. 211). The program serves students in grades 3–5 and is organized into self-contained classrooms that are action-oriented and involve small- and large-group work as well as individualization. Finally, Project EXCEL, a K–2, self-contained program offered through San Diego City Schools is cited (Aguirre & Hernandez, 2002). The focus of this program is on early identification and differentiated curriculum and emphasizes student readiness, professional development for teachers, and parent involvement. Project EXCEL is among the longest running programs of its kind and has had a direct and significant impact on the number of Hispanic students now participating in the district's main gifted and talented education program (GATE).

Although there is no consensus regarding the best approach to programming for students identified as gifted and talented, Smutney (2003) identified four principles that should guide the development and implementation of any such program:

1. Offer not just enrichment but a cohesive, rigorous, creative, and in-depth course of study.
2. Use the best possible teachers in the subjects offered.
3. Accommodate children with different learning styles, cultural and socioeconomic backgrounds.
4. Counsel children and families who need help with emotional, social, and other problems commonly associated with giftedness.

Additionally, Moon & Rosselli (2000) urge gifted and talented program developers to focus on local context and the implications for program design. Consideration should be given to contextual issues including theoretical conceptions of giftedness and critical appraisals of gifted education. Cultural beliefs regarding gifts, talents, and the purpose of education must be examined closely, and local values concerning family, conformity vs. independence, and differential weighing of talent domains should be taken into consideration in the development of educational programming. In addition, local politics including educational policy, the interface between general and gifted education, the attitudes of stakeholders toward gifted education, principles of educational change, and the legal rights of gifted students ultimately shape the design and development of programs as well.

Administrative and Personnel Issues

Moon and Rosselli (2000) have discussed in-depth the process of planning and implementing programs for students with gifts and talents from a situated program development perspective, indicating that, "Because theoretical, cultural, and political issues pervade the design process, program design is most effective when it is contextualized" (p. 506). In addition to emphasizing the need for situated program development, these authors delineate key steps in the planning and implementation phase. To begin with, advocacy for a proposed program and the students it is intended to serve is a crucial element in paving the way for a viable and effective program even if the contextual and political factors are favorable to the development and implementation of such a program. Advocacy can be seen as a process of problem solving, through which a problem is conceptualized, redefined, and analyzed, and strategic plans to bring about necessary educational changes are forged as related concerns, issues, and options emerge (Maier, 1993).

Any new gifted and talented program, if it is to be effective in meeting the local contextual needs, is inherently innovative in nature. Therefore, once the stage has been set through advocacy, strong leadership in the form of a broad-based advisory group is recommended in order to provide diversified input into the planning process and to increase ownership in the new program. This advisory group may comprise administrators, teachers, parents, students, ancillary personnel (e.g., school psychologist, school counselor, curriculum coordinator, etc.), community members (business, arts, and professional), university professors, and possibly representatives from regional, state, or national education offices. The role of leadership in the development process is crucial, since it is through leadership that the cause of the program will be championed, and the existing system, beliefs, and structure will be changed (Moon & Rosselli, 2000).

Effective program planning requires that all steps be carefully undertaken in a systematic manner. First, a comprehensive needs assessment must be undertaken to ascertain the nature of existing policy, attitudes of stakeholders toward gifted and talented education, local prevalence or incidence of giftedness and the types of gifts and talents recognized, existing educational practices, and human, material, and financial resource availability and constraints. Once these needs have been determined, a shared philosophy of gifted education can be developed that is based on and reflects the theoretical, cultural, and political contexts previously identified. This philosophy then forms the basis of an action plan through which a specific program will be proposed. This action plan should include: goals of the program, practical means of achieving the goals including major tasks and individuals responsible for each, timelines for development and implementation, projected budget, and evaluation procedures. Embedded within the action plan and derived from the program philosophy are many issues such as the following: the nature or definition of the gifts and talents to be addressed; methods for identifying students with these types of gifts and talents; characteristics and qualifications of teachers and other staff responsible for program implementation; the design, facilitation, and evaluation of staff development to support the program over time; plans for family and community involvement; and plans for evaluation and restructuring (Moon & Rosselli, 2000).

Bernal (2002) spoke directly to the issue of characteristics and qualifications of teachers of students with gifts and talents, especially for instructors serving under-represented groups of students. His recommendations for teacher recruitment and retention begin with active identification of creative and proficient teachers with expertise and training in GT instruction and/or bilingual education. Selected teachers must then be invited to participate in shaping the program, and there must be a demonstration of strong commitment of support on the part of the school and the district with resources and ongoing professional development. Finally, provisions for collaboration between the program teachers, gifted/talented and bilingual program coordinators, and school principals in the implementation and eventual evolution of the program should be in place. Although states vary in their requirements for teacher preparation in the area of gifted and talented education, Smutney (2003) notes that most studies of successful teachers of the gifted have focused on characteristics and behavior rather than on specific preparation. Kaplan (1989) identified five basic competencies necessary for successful teaching in programs designed for students with gifts and talents. These include an appreciation of scholarship and intellectualism, the ability to create an atmosphere of productivity and independence, the capacity to stimulate awe and wonder, the willingness to develop an awareness of intellectual stamina, and the ability to serve as an intellectual leader. Finally, additional personnel such as counselors, school psychologists, and home-school-community coordinators should also be considered in the planning, implementation, and evaluation of gifted and talented education programs.

Funding Issues

Currently in the United States, programs for gifted and talented education have been developed without federal funding. Most programs are supported through state and district funding, and the largest portion of funds are used to support personnel (Moon & Rosselli, 2000). However, federal funds earmarked for gifted education are available through a grant from the Jacob K. Javits Gifted and Talented Students Education Program, and funds from Title I. Challenge technology grants may be directed in part to support such programs as well. Other sources of funding for these programs include grants from various agencies and organizations with interest in gifted and talented education and gifts from private foundations such as the Davidson Foundation and Davidson Institute for Talent Development. Many local, regional, state, and national gifted and talented organizations and advocacy groups also provide funding opportunities for individual students, and there is financial support available for individual participation in summer institutes and scholar programs. Finally, because many programs for gifted and talented education rely at least in part on private donations and fundraising programs, financial resources and constraints should be taken into consideration at the very beginning stages of program development.

Legal Issues

Currently, gifted preschool, elementary, and secondary students have very limited protection under federal law, and legislative responsibility for educational programming rests with the state. According to the Council of State Directors of Programs for the Gifted and the National Council for Gifted Children (2009), thirty-two states have mandates for gifted education, either for identification or services or both. Fifteen states have no mandate at all, and five states do not provide any funding for their mandates. Legislation ranges from full mandates for gifted education through which identification, programming, and personnel for gifted programs are required. Partial mandates range from identification only, to minimal services at the discretion of the Local Educational Agency, to merely recognizing the educational needs of students with gifts and talents. Moon & Rosselli (2002) note, however, that the Office of Civil Rights within the US Department of Education has investigated cases of discrimination involving gifted students as members of protected groups including those of ethnic minority status or those with disabilities. These cases have typically involved four areas of gifted education: admission to gifted programs, methods used for identification of students with gifts and talents, placement in gifted programs, and procedures involving notification, communication, or testing of gifted students (Karnes, Troxclair, & Marquandt, 1997). Thus, extreme care must be taken to consider local culture and context in the conceptualization and definition of the types and levels of gifts and talents a program is designed to enhance and to create a valid, ethical, and defensible means of identifying potential students for participation. Finally, the program itself must provide a logical and consistent format for the development and expression of the gifts and talents it is designed to support, and families and members of the community should be encouraged and empowered to contribute to continued program development.

Impact of Gifted and Talented Education Programs

Opinions regarding the efficacy and usefulness of gifted and talented programs often seem to use as a starting point Lewis Terman's landmark longitudinal study in which 1500 gifted children were studied from childhood through adulthood (Terman & Oden, 1959). Certain researchers interpret these findings to indicate that, in general, participants failed to achieve eminence or otherwise make significant contributions despite superior intelligence (e.g., Worcester, 1956; Zepeda & Langenback, 1999) and, therefore, that the concept of giftedness and talent is flawed as are the programs designed to educate such students. A multitude of similar studies conducted across several countries and using a variety of methodology (Trost, 2000) have produced confusing and sometimes contradictory findings regarding the factors which are most likely to lead to outstanding achievement.

Critics of gifted and talented education programs in the United States frequently question the degree to which the programs benefit the students who are selected for participation, and even suggest they are developed for political rather than educational reasons. Others critics point to insufficient evidence that other students would not benefit equally from the programs and services offered to students identified as gifted or talented. It is clear from such criticism that systematic program evaluation which, when planned and executed thoughtfully, would provide data not only on outcomes of the program, but also provide documentation and justification for the existing need, program goals, identification methods, and program format, structure, and instructional methods. (Callahan, 2000).

Increasingly, we are seeing attention given to the contextual and cultural relativity of new conceptualizations of gifts and talents and a subsequent variability in methods of identification and programming efforts. Furthermore, Moon & Rosselli (2000) assert that most effective and valid gifted and talented education programs are developed within a situated context to meet a local need that is defined within theoretical, contextual, and political parameters. Therefore, broad attempts to study the outcome or impact of gifted and talented programs in general are, at best, misguided, and likely to result in untenable conclusions. Instead, efforts to assess the impact of gifted and talented programs are perhaps most effectively accomplished at the level of program implementation (e.g., local, regional, or state level programming), and best conceived as an integral part of the overall program development plan.

Summary

Over the years, there have been substantial changes in the way gifted and talented programs have been developed and implemented, and changes in the definitions of gifts and talents reflect changes in the prevailing values and beliefs of society in general. Although controversy over the efficacy and validity of gifted and talented programs continues, this has served as an impetus for increased communication and collaboration between researchers and practitioners and has spawned a multitude of alternative approaches to education for students with gifts and talents. Some alternatives, such as parallel curriculum design and bilingual gifted programs have revolutionized the way in which children are both identified and served, thus increasing access to challenging and stimulating educational opportunities for traditionally under-represented students. There is a need, however, for continued research on the nature of gifts and talents, approaches to identification and service delivery, and innovations in the evaluation of programs. As stated by Callahan (1996),

> If we truly believe in the importance of serving the diverse needs of gifted children, then we cannot risk being dinosaurs in the field of education. Whatever we do, the highly able students will still be there in schools. Hence, we need to do our best to ensure that we don't jeopardize their welfare through lack of knowledge, inappropriate actions, or neglect (p. 149).

Questions for Consideration

1. What are some reasons for the disparities within and across states in programming for students with gifts and talents?
2. List several of the problems faced by school leaders in determining the "best" method for identifying students with gifts and talents?
3. In what ways can school leaders take an active role in the development and implementation of programs for students with gifts and talents in order to ensure their success?
4. What are some potential funding sources for gifted and talented programs? Are there ways to combine programs and resources within a school or district to maximize program efficacy?
5. What do you believe is the future of programs for students with gifts and talents at the federal level? State level? Local level?

Case Study

Educational Need or Special Privilege?

Dr. Cavenaugh is the gifted and talented program coordinator of a small, suburban school district on the outskirts of a major mid-western city. She was promoted to program coordinator from middle school science teacher in 1991 after earning her doctorate in child development. She has served in this capacity on a continuous basis, and is proud of the program she has built. The program serves students in second through twelfth grade, is focused mainly on academic and intellectual giftedness, and is primarily enrichment-based. For several years, the selection criteria for program participation were limited to results of a group-administered intelligence test and a personal interview conducted by Dr. Cavenaugh, with students being selected on an annual basis.

Over the years, the selection criteria expanded to include observations by Dr. Cavenaugh of small groups of students engaging in a problem-solving situation within the classroom plus the recommendations of teachers, in addition to intelligence test results and a personal interview. Furthermore, students began participating for two consecutive years, so the selection process only takes place during the even-numbered grades. However, the program itself has changed very little. Between the two program divisions of elementary and secondary, approximately one-hundred students participate from six elementary schools, two middle schools, and one high school.

Within each division, students engage in special bi-weekly field trips to local museums, businesses, libraries, and other community locations, and weekly half-day seminars that take place in a classroom in the central administration building. Students who attend the six schools that are beyond walking distance to the administration building for these seminars are transported using a district school bus. The half-day seminars center on special projects that involve creative problem-solving, mathematics, science, technology, and higher cognitive processes such as analysis, synthesis, and evaluation. Dr. Cavenaugh assumes the primary responsibility for instruction during the seminars and field trips with the help of two paraeducators and several parent volunteers. In general, students involved in the program have reported a high level of engagement with the activities and have had positive experiences with participation.

Although certain teachers over the years have complained about students missing significant amounts of class time and the elitist attitude the program seems to carry with it, Dr. Cavenaugh has always been able to defend her approach with strong backing from the district administrators and some of the most vocal and involved parents. However, the district and surrounding community, which remained relatively small and insular over the past several decades, is beginning to see rapid changes. To begin with, many of the district's top administrators have recently retired, and are being replaced with younger administrators who hold different opinions about educational programming. In addition, the district is beginning to see changes in the size and demographics of the student population. In the past twenty years, only two elementary schools and one middle school were added. Now, however, this district is facing the prospect of building two new elementary schools within the next three years, and a middle school and high school within the next five years. And while the student population had been comprised middle-class Caucasian students, there has been a large influx of Hmong students who have recently arrived in the United States and African American students who have moved from nearby inner-city school districts. What was once Dr. Cavenaugh's undisputed domain and a source of pride for the district is increasingly being questioned.

To begin with, more and more teachers are complaining about the participating students missing class, and with the district increasingly utilizing hands-on, cross-curricular instructional approaches, students can no longer simply make up missing assignments on their own. In addition, both the elementary and secondary curriculum coordinators, both hired within the past two years, are questioning the gifted and talented program's lack of integration with the standard curriculum. Funding for the program has also begun to cause controversy; although Dr. Cavenaugh has consistently been able to obtain state funding and private foundation grants, a significant portion of the program's expenses, including travel and personnel, are paid through the district's discretionary program funding. In the shifting atmosphere within the district, Dr. Cavenaugh is being asked to respond to more questions. Is the enrichment-based pull-out program the best way to provide for gifted and talented students? Wouldn't all students benefit from the resource-rich seminars and field trips currently offered only to students identified as gifted? Why has the number of students served by the program remained relatively steady despite increases in enrollment across the district? Why does the academic content of the program seem to focus on math and science? In fact, why does the program focus on academic and intellectual giftedness and not other forms of giftedness such as artistic or leadership ability? Is the program cost-effective in terms of long-term benefits? Who is it that benefits from the program and in what ways? Finally, there are serious concerns increasingly being voiced regarding the under-representation of minority and English-language-learning students selected for program participation, and the selection process has been sharply criticized by both parents and teachers. Of particular concern is the continued use of group-administered intelligence tests, which lack validity for certain groups of students, and the weight of Dr. Cavenaugh's own judgment about student ability in the selection of participants. Dr. Cavenaugh has been asked by the new superintendent to submit a comprehensive plan for restructuring the program by the end of the school year and she has heard rumors within the district that there are unofficial plans to eliminate all district funding for the program in order to redirect it to a much-needed program for English-language-learners.

Questions for Discussion

1. What are some of the reasons Dr. Cavenaugh's program was viewed as successful and effective when it was first developed in the 1980s but is now unacceptable to many parents and teachers?

2. How would you recommend beginning the task of restructuring the program? Who should be involved and what factors should be considered?

3. In restructuring the program, how should "gifted" and "talented" be defined? What should the selection or identification process include?

4. How should the program format be restructured so that it is better integrated with the standard curriculum? Is there a way to combine programs and resources at the district level so that utilization of available funding is maximized?

References

Aguirre, N. & Hernandez, N. E. (2002). Portraits of success: Programs that work. In J. A. Castellano & E. I. Diaz (Eds.) *Reaching new horizons: Gifted and talented education for culturally and linguistically diverse students.* Boston: Allyn & Bacon.

Bernal, E. M. (2002). Recruiting teachers for bilingual gifted and talented programs. In J. A. Castellano & E. I. Diaz (Eds.), *Reaching new horizons: Gifted and talented education for culturally and linguistically diverse students.* Boston: Allyn & Bacon.

Borland, J. H. & Wright, L. (1994). Identifying young, potentially gifted, economically disadvantaged students. *Gifted Child Quarterly, 38*(4), 164–171.

Boschee, F., Beyer, B. M., Engleking, J. L. & Boschee, M. A. (1997). *Special and compensatory programs: The administrator's role.* Lancaster, PA: Technomic Publishing Co., Inc.

Burt, C. (1975). *The gifted child.* New York: John Wiley & Sons.

Callahan, C. M. (1996). A critical self-study of gifted education: Healthy practice, necessary evil, or sedition? *Journal for the Education of the Gifted, 19*(2), 148–163.

Callahan, C. M. (2000). Evaluation as a critical component of program development and implementation. In K. A. Heller, F. J. Monks, R. J. Sternberg, and R. F. Subotnik (Eds.), *International handbook of giftedness and talent, second edition.* Oxford: Elsevier Science Ltd.

Clark, B. (1997). *Growing up gifted (5th ed.)*. Columbus, OH: Macmillan.

Council of State Directors of Programs for the Gifted (2009). Retrieved from http://www.nagc.org/upload-edFiles/Information_and_Resources/State_of_the_States_2008-2009/2008-09%20State%20of%20the%20States%20Report%20%28full%29.pdf.

Eby, J. W. (1984). Developing gifted behavior. *Educational Leadership, 1*(7), 35–43.

Eby, J. W. & Smutny, J. F. (1990). *A thoughtful overview of gifted education.* New York: Longman.

Ford, D. Y. & Harris, J. J. (1999). *Multicultural gifted education.* New York:Teachers College Press.

Frasier, M. M., & Passow. A. H. (1994). *Toward a new paradigm for identifying talent potential* (Research Monograph 94112). Storrs, CT: The National Research Center on the Gifted and Talented, University of Connecticut.

Gross, M. U. M. (1994). Radical acceleration: Responding to academic and social needs of extremely gifted adolescents. *Journal of Secondary Gifted Education, 5*(4), 27–34.

Guilford, J. P. (1956). The structure of intellect. *Psychological Bulletin, 53*, 267–293.

Guilford, J. P. (1950). Creativity. *Academic Psychologist, 5*, 444–454.

Haywood, H. C., Brown, A. L., & Wingenfeld, S. (1990). Dynamic approaches to psycho-educational assessment. *School Psychology Review, 19*(4), 411–422.

Hollingworth, L. S. (1926). *Gifted children: Their nature and nurture.* New York: Macmillan Publishing Company.

Jacob K. Javits Gifted and Talented Students Education Act. (1988). P.L. 100-297, Title IV, Part B, Sec.1101.

Kanevsky, L. (2000). Dynamic assessment of gifted students. In K. A. Heller, F. J. Monks, R. J. Sternberg, & R. F. Subotnik (Eds.). *International handbook of giftedness and talent, second edition* (pp. 283–295). Oxford: Elsevier Science, Ltd.

Kaplan, S. (1989). Competency cluster for the teachers of the gifted. *CAG Communicator, 19*(4), 13–14.

Karnes, F. A., Troxclair, D. A., & Marquandt, R. G. (1997). The Office of Civil Rights and the gifted: An update. *The Roeper Review, 19*(3), 162–165.

Lynch, S. J. (1994). *Should gifted students be grade-advanced?* Reston, VA: Council for Exceptional Children. EDO-EC-93-9.

Maier, N. (1993). Advocacy as a force in the education of the gifted and talented. *Gifted International, 8*(1), 20–26.

Marland, S. (1972). Education of the gifted and talented: Report to the Congress of the United States by the U.S. Commissioner of Education. Washington, DC: U.S. Government Printing Office.

Moon, S. M. & Rosselli, H. C. (2000). Developing gifted programs. In K. A. Heller, F. J. Monks, R. J. Sternberg, and R. F. Subotnik (Eds.), *International handbook of giftedness and talent, second edition.* Oxford: Elsevier Science Ltd.

National Association for Gifted Children (2008). Retrieved from http://www.nagc.org/.

National Research Center on the Gifted and Talented (n.d.). Retrieved from http://www.gifted.uconn.edu/nrcgt.html

Pfleger, L. R. (1977). *Research and guidance laboratory practices: Identifying and programming gifted and talented students.* Madison, WI: University of Wisconsin ED 138 001.

Renzulli, J. (1977). *The Enrichment Triad Model: A guide for developing defensible programs for the gifted and talented.* Mansfield Center, CT: Creative Learning Press.

Renzulli, J. & Smith, L. H. (1977). Two approaches to identification of gifted students. *Exceptional Children, 43*, 512–518.

Renzulli, J. (1978). What makes giftedness? Re-examining a definition. *Phi Beta Kappan, 261*, 180–184.

Sayler, M. F. (1999). American gifted education at the millennium: 150 years of experience. *Understanding Our Gifted, 12*(1), 11–15.

Sayler, M. F. & Brookshire, W. K. (1993). Social, emotional, and behavioral adjustment of accelerated students, students in gifted classes, and regular students in eighth grade. *Gifted Child Quarterly, 37*(4), 150–154.

Skuy, M., Kaniel, S. & Tzuriel, D. (1988). Dynamic assessment of intellectually superior Israeli children in a low socio-economic status community. Gifted Education International, 5, 90–96.

Smutney, J. F. (2003). *Designing and developing programs for gifted students.* Thousand Oaks, CA: Corwin Press, Inc.

Spring, J. (2011). *The American school: A global context from the puritans to the Obama era.* New York, NY: McGraw-Hill.

Stephens, K. R. & Karnes, F. A. (2000). State definitions for the gifted and talented revisited. *Exceptional Children, 66*(2), 219–238.

Sternberg, R. J. (2000). Giftedness as developing expertise. In K. A. Heller, F. J. Monks, R. J. Sternberg, and R. F. Subotnik (Eds.), International handbook of giftedness and talent, second edition. Oxford: Elsevier Science Ltd.

Tellegen, P. J. & Laros, J. A. (1993). The Snijders-Oomen non-verbal intelligence tests: General intelligence tests or tests for learning potential? In J. H. M. Hammers, K. Sijtsma, & A. J. J. M. Ruijssenaars, (Eds.) *Learning potential assessment: Theoretical, methodological, and practical issues* (pp. 267–283). Berwyn, PA: Swets & Zeitlinger.

Terman, L. M. & Oden, M. H. (1959). *The gifted group at midlife: Thirty-five years' follow-up of the superior child.* Stanford, CA: Stanford University Press.

Tomlinson, C. A., Kaplan, S. N., Renzulli, J. S., Purcell, J., Leppien, J., & Burns, D. (2002). *The parallel curriculum: A design to develop high potential and challenge high-ability learners.* Thousand Oaks, CA: Corwin Press, Inc.

Treffinger, D. J. (1975). Teaching for self-directed learning: A priority for the gifted and talented. *Gifted Child Quarterly, 19*(1), 46–59.

Trost, G. (2000). *Prediction of excellence in school, higher education, and work.* In K. Heller, F. J. Monks, R. J. Sternberg, and R. F. Subotnik (Eds.), International handbook of giftedness and talent, second edition. Oxford: Elsevier Science Ltd.

Tuttle, F. B. (1988). *Characteristics and identification of gifted and talented students.* Washington, DC: National Education Association.

Vygotsky, L. S. (1978). *Mind in society: The development of higher psychological processes.* Cambridge, MA: Harvard University Press.

White, L. A. (1995). *Acceleration: A viable option for gifted children.* Ontario, Canada: ED387992.

Worcester, D. A. (1956). *The education of children of above-average mentality.* Lincoln, NE: University of Nebraska Press.

Zepeda, S. J. & Langenback, M. (1999). *Special programs in regular schools: Historical foundations, standards, and contemporary issues.* Boston: Allyn & Bacon.

CHAPTER 5

Programs for English Language Learners

Introduction

INCREASES in numbers of English language learners in schools during the last century have created a greater awareness of instructional methodologies and curriculum development related to the needs of non-native English speakers in schools, who speak a variety of world languages and bring with them a wide variety of cultural values and norms associated with the countries from which they emigrate. Immigration policies of the United States over the past century have had a direct influence on the increased numbers of people entering the United States and on the development of multicultural classrooms throughout U.S. schools (Steward, 1994). The cultural heritages and languages of ELL students differ from that of their native English-speaking peers in schools and have a direct effect on the academic performance of these students in schools, often resulting in academic failure (Beyer-Houda, 1995). Not all teachers have been prepared to provide quality instruction in the academic content areas that also addresses the needs of English language learners in regular education classrooms. As a result, the instructional and academic needs of many English language learners are never met. It has been observed that

(the) recent increase in immigration accounts for rapid and substantial demographic changes in the United States' school-aged population. An estimated 25 percent—one-in-four—children in America are from immigrant families and live in households where a language other than English is spoken. This has significant implications for schools and the current discourse about the role of teacher quality and effectiveness in improving outcomes (Samson & Collins, 2012).

In the early 20th century immigrants coming to the United States arrived mainly from European countries, along with Middle Eastern and Asian populations. Many of these groups arrived seeking employment, and often they settled in urban areas and in communities reflecting their own language and cultural heritage. Neighborhood schools both private and public were established in which students were offered or required to attend classes in their native language and were thus provided the opportunity to maintain both the culture and language of their native heritage and at the same time to become proficient in two languages—English and their native tongue. In more recent times, immigrant populations in the United States have come from across the globe—Asia, Africa, the Middle East, India, the Russian Federation, Central America, South America, Central Asia, and others. These groups have not only settled in ethnic communities but have also migrated to and settled in previously less integrated communities across the United

States, which has resulted in school districts being unprepared to meet both the language and academic needs of non-native English speakers in classrooms.

> Currently, more than one out of four of all children in the United States are from immigrant families, and in most cases these children speak a language other than English at home. In the decade between the 1997–98 and 2008–09 school years, the number of English-language learners in public schools increased by 51 percent while the general population of students grew by just 7 percent (National Center for English Language Acquisition, 2011)

The Civil Rights Act of 1964 and the Equal Education Opportunities Act of 1974 addressed the rights of students pointing to the obligation of schools to develop and offer educational programs addressing the specific needs of non-English-speaking students in schools. The Bilingual Education Act of 1974 made bilingual education in schools mandatory for all schools receiving federal funding.

Historical Overview

Many assume that ESL instruction has a relatively recent history in American schooling, and there is a prevalent myth that previous generations of immigrants were eager to assimilate into American culture by abandoning their native languages and customs. However, historical records demonstrate that language of instruction has long been controversial in American public schools. According to Spring (2011), the diverse populations settling into the New York (New Amsterdam) area in the late 1600s resulted in a system of private schools that offered a broad range of subjects and served the particular needs of the various religious, cultural and linguistic groups. Between the 18th and early 20th centuries, large numbers of German-speaking immigrants resulted in over 30 German language newspapers and journals published in the colonies and United States, and German was the language of instruction in some public schools, especially in the Pennsylvania and Ohio regions. However, in contrast to the relative tolerance of cultural diversity seen in the New York region, the clash between German and English settlers over language use resulted in a policy of Anglicization that attempted to prohibit publication and instruction in German, forcing instead the use of English as the official language in schools and the press.

According to Spring (2011), the conflict between German and English settlers over language and culture foreshadowed conflicts over language in the schools that would endure into the 21st century. While other groups of immigrants, primarily from Europe, were supposedly being inculcated into a democratic society through the common schools, African, Mexican, Native American, Asian, and Puerto Rican Americans were increasingly segregated and denied linguistic and cultural rights in the public schools. For example, after the United States acquired territories previously belonging to Mexico, persons of Mexican descent found themselves without a nationality, as the government of the United States denied them U.S. citizenship. Minority groups were often relegated to segregated schools designed to rid them of their native language and customs. In 1855, the California Bureau of Instruction mandated English as the language of instruction in all public schools in an attempt to eradicate the use of Spanish, and in 1870 Texas followed suit. Going even further, in 1918 Texas passed legislation that made it a criminal offense to use any language except English in the schools, and required all school personnel, including teachers, principals, and even custodians to use only English when on school premises. Native American children were famously separated from parents and community groups, and sent to boarding schools that operated on a paramilitary model and were designed to strip children of their Native American languages, customs, and even their Native American identity through name reassignment (Bear, 2008).

During the late 19th and early 20th centuries, large numbers of immigrants from Asia, particularly Japan, came to the United States as laborers. In order to preserve their Japanese language and culture, local Japanese communities often operated private schools that Japanese children would attend after school and on weekends. In an attempt to eradicate this trend toward Japanese cultural and linguistic preservation and to instill a "100% Americanism" mentality, the territorial government in 1923 passed a law severely limiting the operation of such private schools. However, the U.S. Supreme Court overturned the law in 1927, finding no adequate reason for bringing these language and culture schools under government control. The struggle over language control in the public schools continues to this day. Throughout the late 20th century and into the current era, the issue of language instruction, especially Spanish, has caused conflict, although other languages are also causing similar conflict within public schools. For example, in 2009, Dearborn Public Schools, located in Dearborn, Michigan, considered banning Arabic language in its schools, in which as many as 90% of students come from homes where Arabic is the primary language. The recommendation, which was made based on a study commissioned by the regional education agency, cited not only concern that bilingual instruction would "slow the assimilation of Arabic students into the school and American society in general," but also cited fears that the use of Arabic language, even informally among students in non-classroom settings, "fosters suspicion among students and teachers who do not speak the language" (Ali, 2009).

Thus, throughout the history of public schooling in the United States, much of the conflict about language in the schools has and continues to center on ideals of "Americanization" and embracing the dominant culture and language instead of seeking to value and retain multiple cultures and languages despite strong evidence that bilingual instruction can be effective in preparing English language learners for success in school and in the greater community (Arce, 2004).

The Elementary and Secondary Education Act of 2001, NCLB

Title III of the Elementary and Secondary Education Act of 2001, referred to as NCLB, addresses Language Instruction for Limited English Proficient and Immigrant Students. Historically, since the first authorization of the Act, a separate title has been designated to provide assistance to English language learners. The title programs have utilized a variety of designations over the years, most often as a reflection of current research and instructional methodologies related to serving English learners in schools. These designations have included immigrant students, bilingual education, English as a Second Language (ESL), Limited English Proficient (LEP), English Language Learner (ELL), and most recently English Learners (ELs). Each reauthorization of this section of the Elementary and Secondary Education Act has stressed rationale, programming, instruction, funding, and parental involvement. The goals of the programs have been to foster proficiency in the English language through a variety of instructional methodologies and discretionary grant support for program development. The ultimate goal has been to bring English Language Learners to a level of proficiency in English to learn and interact with their peers in regular education classrooms with native English speakers, and more recently to score at a designated percentile on mandated academic proficiency tests. Under NCLB, LEP students are required to move to a level of academic proficiency required of all students in all schools in meeting standards and benchmarks set forth by NCLB.

As discussed in the next section, in the recently published Blueprint for Reform: Reauthorization of the Elementary and Secondary Education Act, that bilingual, ESL, and LEP students have been renamed as English Learners (ELs) and grouped together with prior separate ESEA categories designated for Native American, Native Hawaiian, and Alaskan Native students; migrant and rural students; students with disabilities; and homeless and neglected or delinquent students under the category of diverse student needs (U.S. Department of Education, 2010a). Since the Blueprint is a proposal for reauthorization of the Elementary and Secondary Education Act, it will be interesting to see the final product once the reauthorization has passed through both houses of Congress and to the President's desk for signature and implementation. Readers may refer to Chapters 1, 2, and 6 for additional information related to programs, services, and funding for Limited English Proficient (LEP) students.

Blueprint for Reform: Reauthorization of the Elementary and Secondary Education Act

In a move from prior title categories of the Elementary and Secondary Act from its inception in 1964 through its most recent reauthorization of No Child Left Behind in 2001, in 2010 the federal government, through the Office of the Secretary of Education, developed and publicized a Blueprint for Reform: Reauthorization of the Elementary and Secondary Education Act (subsequently referred to as the Blueprint). The Blueprint states in a section entitled Meeting the Needs of English Learners and Other Diverse Learners that,

> Schools must support all students, including by providing appropriate instruction and access to a challenging curriculum along with additional supports and attention where needed. From English Learners and students with disabilities to Native American students, homeless students, migrant students, rural students, and neglected or delinquent students, our proposal will continue to support and strengthen programs for these students and ensure that schools are helping them meet college- and career-ready standards (U.S. Department of Education, 2010b).

The Blueprint combines the current Title III program for English Language Learners with educational programs found in other title categories such as: Title I: Improving the Academic Achievement of the Disadvantaged which addresses the needs of migratory children, children and youth who are neglected, delinquent, or at-risk, and school dropout prevention; Title V: Promoting Informed Parental Choice addressing Foreign Language Assistance, and the educational, cultural, apprenticeship, and exchange programs for Alaska Natives, Native Hawaiians, and their historical whaling partners in Massachusetts; Title VI: Rural education initiatives for small, rural school achievement, and initiatives for rural and low-income schools; and Title VII: Indian, Native Hawaiian, and Alaskan Indian Education. Specifically, programs for Native American students, homeless students, students with disabilities, migrant students, and rural students are combined into a newly proposed category under the heading, Meeting the Needs of English Learners and Other Diverse Students. The Blueprint states,

> In each of these areas the Administration's ESEA reauthorization proposal will continue and strengthen the federal commitment to serving all students, and improve each program to ensure that federal funds are used more effectively to meet the needs of the students they serve.
>
> • Improving programs for English Learners and encouraging innovative programs and practices to support English Learners' success and build the knowledge base about what works.
> • Maintaining the strengthening formula grant programs for Native American students, homeless students, migrant students, and neglected or delinquent students; as well as for districts that are in rural areas or that are affected by federal property and activities.
> • Meeting the need of students with disabilities through ESEA and through the Individuals with Disabilities Education Act (U.S. Department of Education, 2010c).

The Blueprint goes on to state that ESEA should be responsible for providing funding and resources to support the educational needs of diverse learners to ensure that all students are college- and career-ready.

> America's schools are responsible for meeting the educational needs of an increasingly diverse student population, and ESEA programs must provide a wide range of resources and support to ensure

that all students have the opportunity to succeed in college and in a career. ESEA includes programs that help schools meet the special educational needs of children working to learn the English language, students with disabilities, Native American students, homeless students, the children of migrant workers, and neglected or delinquent students. In addition, the federal government has a responsibility to provide assistance to certain high-need regions and areas, including rural districts and districts that are affected by federal property and activities. (U.S. Department of Education, 2010a)

Legal and Legislative Background

Programs for English language learners have transitioned over time and been supported by each reauthorization of the Elementary and Secondary Education Act (ESEA) since its inception in 1965. The first title designation of the ESEA referred to programs supporting student acquisition of the English language as bilingual education, and has subsequently been referred to and known through the years as English language learners (ELL), limited English proficient (LEP) students, and English as a second language (ESL) programs. As stated in the first edition of this text, the U.S. government "influences public education through legal action, such the 1964 Supreme Court decision in *Brown v. the Board of Education of Topeka*, or through programs that offer funds or funding grants for educational purposes (Beyer & Johnson, 2005, p. 1). Funding has been regularly available through each reauthorization of the Elementary and Secondary Education Act to support English language acquisition in the schools and legal action has regularly been brought to the courts to help define these programs. Table 5.1 demonstrates the regularity of legislation passed to help define programs serving English language learners. Beginning with *Brown v. the Board of Education of Topeka* and the Civil Rights Act of 1964 calling for equal education opportunities for all children and youth in schools and followed by the Bilingual Education Act of 1968, numerous cases and federal actions have worked to reinforce the importance of instruction in schools to support the specific needs of English Language Learners. *Cisneros V. Corpus Christi* (1973) was based on the rationale that the equal education opportunities and Civil Rights Act of 1964 applied equally to Mexican-American students. This was followed closely by cases related to the same rights for American Indian students in *Geraud v. Schrader* (1975) and *Natonabah v. Board of Education of Gallup-McKinley County School District* (1975). The landmark Supreme Court case of *Lau v. Nichols* affirmed Chinese-American student rights to bilingual education opportunities under both the Fourteenth Amendment to the Constitution and Title VI of the Civil Rights Act of 1964. The Court stated,

> . . . there is no equality of treatment merely by providing students the same facilities, textbooks, teachers, and curriculum; for students who do not understand English are effectively foreclosed from any meaningful education (Alexander & Alexander, 1998).

Title VI Language Discrimination Guidelines were established in 1980 stating the Lau v. Nichols guidelines for non-English or limited English speaking students to include assessment, program assignment, and exit criteria. The 1974 Equal Educational Opportunities Act (EEOA) requiring school systems to develop programs for limited English proficiency students states in part,

> . . . no state shall deny educational opportunity to an individual on account of his or her race, color, sex, or national origin, by…the failure of an educational agency to take appropriate action to overcome language barriers that impede equal participation by its students in its instructional programs (Alexander & Alexander, 1998; EEOC, 1974),

The case of *Morgan v. Kerrigan* (1981) brought to light and rectified the fact that the City of Boston provided bilingual education programs for multiple linguistic groups including Chinese, French-Haitian, Greek, Italian, and Portuguese students but not for over 32,600 Hispanic speak-

Table 5.1. Legislation Related to Programs for English Language Learners.

1954 *Brown v. Board of Education of Topeka*
1964 Title VI of the Civil Rights Act of 1964
1965 Title V of the Elementary and Secondary Education Act of 1965;
1968 Bilingual Education Act of 1968
1970 *Cisneros v. Corpus Christi* (Mexican-American)
1973 *Natonabah v. Board of Education of Gallup-McKinley County School District* (American Indian)
1974 *Lau v. Nichols* (Chinese-American); Equal Educational Opportunity Act: Bilingual Education Act of 1974
1975 *Geraud v. Schrader* (American Indian)
1978 Bilingual Education Act of 1978: Revisions to The Elementary and Secondary Education Act
1980 Title VI Language Discrimination Guidelines
1981 *Morgan v. Kerrigan* (Hispanic)
1988 Bilingual Education Act of 1988
1995 Bilingual Education Act of 1994 (Title VII, Part A of Improving America's Schools Act of 1994: Reauthorizing the Elementary and Secondary Education Act of 1965)
2001 Title III of the No Child Left Behind Act of 2001: Reauthorization of the Elementary and Secondary Education Act of 1965
2010 Blueprint for Reform: Reauthorization of the Elementary and Secondary Education Act. Proposal by the U.S. Department of Education.

ing students. Table 5.1 outlines legislation related to programs for English learners including some key court cases related to language programming for Mexican-American, American Indian, Chinese-American, and Hispanic students beginning in 1964 up to the 2010 proposal Blueprint for Reform: Redesignation of the Elementary and Secondary Education Act.

Indian, Native Hawaiian, and Alaska Native Education

The Elementary and Secondary Education Act has long recognized the need and demand for specialized programs related to Indian, Native Hawaiian, and Alaska Native educational programs. The current ESEA recognizes this need through Title VII of the No Child Left Behind Act of 2001, which addresses the specific needs of these individual groups. The variety of grants available under this section of the Act is demonstrated in Table 5.2.

The Blueprint for Reform includes the education of these specific groups into a larger program proposed for diverse learners. As stated in the Blueprint,

> Our proposal will continue strong support—through formula and competitive grants to states; districts; Indian tribes; Indian institutions of higher education; Indian, Native Hawaiian, and Alaska Native educational and community-based organizations; and nonprofit organizations, agencies, and institutions—to help meet the unique needs of Indian students, Native Hawaiian students, and Alaska Native students. Grantees under the Indian education program will have greater flexibility to use funds to carry out programs that meet the needs of Indian students, including Native language immersion and Native language restoration programs, and develop tribal specific standards and assessments. Our proposal will improve access to funds for Indian tribes under other ESEA programs, and recognize and strengthen the role of tribal education departments in coordinating and implementing services and programs for Indian students within their jurisdiction. To ensure that programs reflect the academic, language, and cultural needs of Indian students, we will continue to require the participation of the parents of Indian children in the design of programs. To support effective programs, we will expand eligibility to school districts and public charter schools under the Native Hawaiian and Alaska Native programs (U.S. Department of Education, 2010a)

Instructional Programming

There has been disagreement among educators as to which type of program is best suited to serve the needs of English Language Learners. Some states have adopted a specific pedagogy and others have left it to the local school districts to make decisions related to English learner student needs. There is crossover in program philosophies and individual student needs resulting in an adaptation of both bilingual education and ESL instructional techniques. Looking beyond philosophical differences, as stated by Samson and Collins, a report released by the Center for American Progress outlines promising practices that all teachers can employ in teaching and program development serving the growing population of English language learners in schools. As noted above:

> The recent increase in immigration accounts for rapid and substantial demographic changes in the United States' school-aged population. An estimated 25 percent—one-in-four—children in America are from immigrant families and live in households where a language other than English is spoken. This has significant implications for schools and the current discourse about the role of teacher quality and effectiveness in improving outcomes (Samson & Collins, 2012).

Bilingual and ESL Programs

There has been controversy over the effectiveness of bilingual education and English as a Second Language (ESL) instruction and whether one instructional program is more effective than the other. The basic difference in instructional program philosophies is that bilingual programs offer education to students in their native language with the intent of developing not only proficiency in English, but to also gain expertise in both English and their native language. This view has been supported by the rationale that for living in a global society and for academic and career readiness it is important to have and maintain fluency in more than one language. ESL programs are directed toward proficiency in the English language with the goal of gaining proficiency in the English language and being mainstreamed into the regular education classroom as quickly as possible. Confusion over the differences in bilingual and ESL programs has often resulted in hiring and assigning ESL or bilingual certified teachers to programs that do not reflect their instructional expertise. Additionally, English language-learning (ELL) students are often transitioned to regular education classrooms without the language program support to perform cognitively and with English language proficiency at a rate equal to their native English language peers. This problem is exacerbated further by the fact that most regular education teachers have not been trained in ELL instructional techniques and do not know how to work with ELLs in their classrooms.

> English language learners, or ELLs, require special attention particularly because of their growing numbers and low performance relative to their non-ELL peers. While educational specialists such as English as a second language and bilingual teachers have expertise in supporting ELLs, many teachers do not. Yet the reality is that most, if not all, teachers have or can expect to have ELL students in their classroom and therefore must be prepared to best support these children (Samson & Collins, 2012).

Table 5.2. NCLB Program Grants.

- Program Development and Implementation
- Supplemental Instruction Programs
- Comprehensive School-wide Programs
- System-wide Projects
- Native Language Support
- Paraprofessional and Instructional Aides
- Professional Development for Teachers, Administrators, and Paraprofessionals

Current bilingual and ESL programs use paraprofessionals in the classroom to support the instruction of the regular education classroom teacher. Programs have been developed to serve students from early childhood through high school and all programs have as their goal the proficiency of students in the English language and their ability to compete academically with native English-speaking students. The Blueprint for Reform recognizes there are currently multiple instructional programs serving English learners by stating,

> Our proposal will continue to provide significant formula grants to help states and school districts implement high-quality language instruction educational programs to improve the education of English Learners. Grantees may provide dual-language programs, transitional bilingual education, sheltered English immersion, newcomer programs for late-entrant English Learners, or other language instruction educational programs. Grantees may also provide effective professional development for all teachers of English Learners, including teachers of academic content areas, that is responsive to demonstrated needs identified by evaluations (Department of Education, 2010b).

Bilingual Education

Bilingual education programs generally fall into the categories of transitional or early-exit, maintenance or late-exit, and two-way or dual-language. The goal of transitional or early-exit bilingual programs is to develop proficiency in English by using two languages in instruction, English and the native language of the student. Opponents of the program contend this instructional model does not take into consideration how long it takes to develop both the cognitive ability and academic language proficiency needed for school success and students are moved out of the programs too soon to successfully compete with regular education students in the regular education classroom. Maintenance or late-exit and two-way or dual-language bilingual programs recognize that it takes longer to develop proficiency in two languages and supports development of both language proficiency in the native language and English, along with cultural awareness (Adler, 2005; Bouchee, Beyer, Engelking, & Boschee, 1997).

English as a Second Language (ESL)

ESL classes require the expertise of a trained ESL teacher. ESL programs have been offered in monolingual English classrooms with students of multiple languages taught in the same classroom. English language classes emphasize vocabulary and grammar "not in isolation, but in meaningful contexts relevant to the students' learning experiences as members of linguistically and culturally diverse communities" (Bouchee, *et al.*, 1997). Both pull-out and self-contained classrooms have been used when teaching the core content areas (e.g., math, science, social studies) often utilizing visual aids and simplified English to encourage and support understanding of academic content. Pull-out programs generally have been conducted with individual and small group instruction in the English language. As has been recognized over the years with Title I programming and instruction, pull-out programs are not the most successful because students too often miss out on core content area instruction in regular education classrooms. There has been a switch to pull-in programs with specially certified ESL teachers often with the assistance of paraprofessionals working with teachers and students in the regular education classroom. ESL instruction has also been provided to students of mixed language groups in the same classroom setting particularly in the core content areas. In pull-in programs instruction is often supported by paraprofessionals fluent in native languages and ESL professionals working in the classroom with regular education teachers to encourage and support student understanding of course content.

Common Core State Standards and English Language Learners

When attempting to determine how English language learners (ELLs) in schools relate to the Common Core State Standards (CCSS), it is important to examine the number of current and future ELL students currently in the schools and projections for the future. The TESOL International Association, including demographic information published by the National Education Association, states,

> ELLs are the fastest growing population in U.S. public schools. Close to 6 million ELLs are enrolled in public schools—an increase of more than 100% since 1991, when there were 2.4 million ELLs enrolled. Today, 1 in 10 students is an ELL; by 2025 it is predicted that ELLs will make up 25% of the student population (National Education Association). This is a dramatic increase; no other student population has experienced this amount of growth. The increasing number of ELLs in the U.S. public school system today—along with the attendant questions on educational achievement—will have an impact on every school as it implements the CCSS (TESOL International Association, 2013).

To address the academic needs of the anticipated number of ELL students and meet required learning assessment standards, it becomes apparent that curriculum and program development, particularly as they relate to attaining Common Core State Standards, are of utmost importance. When discussing curriculum development and alignment with the Common Core, it is important to note at this point that the Common Core State Standards were developed by the Council of Chief State School Officers (CCSSO) and this organization has had a prominent role in development of assessment of learning protocols related to the Common Core. The U.S. Government is not allowed to develop and implement a national curriculum; hence the current U.S. Department of Education has incorporated support for curriculum development and achievement standards through grants related to Race to the Top. In the words of TESOL,

> Under U.S. law, the federal government cannot institute a national curriculum or national standards. The administration embedded support for such standards in the guidelines for states applying for grants under the federal Race to the Top Fund (RTTT). Specifically, states that chose to adopt "college- and career-ready" standards were eligible to compete for RTTT funds (TESOL International Association, 2013).

The Council of Chief State School Officers published an English language proficiency development (ELPD) framework in 2012 to assist states in the development of standards for English language learners to meet Common Core State Standards and Next Generation Science Standards. This framework does not outline specific standards or issues related to assessment of learning, but rather outlines how language instruction in listening, speaking, reading, and writing can be utilized to help ELL students prepare for and meet Common Core requirements (CCSSO, 2012; TESOL International Association, 2013).

Assessment of Learning

Recognizing that English language learners will be required to meet Common Core State Standards, the U.S. Government has provided development grants for state consortia to align English language development assessments with Common Core assessments. Under the guidelines of the grants, the English language proficiency development assessments were required to correspond to the college- and career-ready standards in English language arts and mathematics. Developed assessment results are to be valid and reliable and must meet the following criteria. Specifically, the assessments must:

- Be based on a common definition of English language learner adopted by all consortium states;
- include diagnostic (e.g., screener, placement) and summative assessments;
- assess English language proficiency across the four language domains (reading, writing, speaking, and listening) for each grade level from kindergarten through Grade 12;
- produce results that indicate whether individual students have attained a level and complexity of English language proficiency that is necessary to participate fully in academic instruction in English;
- be accessible to all ELLs with the exception of those who are eligible for alternate assessment based on alternate academic standards;
- use technology to the maximum extent appropriate to develop, administer, and score assessments (CCSSO, 2012; TESOL International Association, 2013).

These assessments guidelines for ELLs have been written by English language learner experts and CCSSO writers and many states have already begun to redevelop their English language proficiency development assessments to correspond to the Common Core State Standards.

Issues in Assessment of ELL Students

Difficulties with State-mandated Testing and ELL Students

According to Monty Neill, Executive Director of Fair Test (2005), several problems have cropped up in assessing of ELL students under NCLB. First, ELL students disproportionately come from low-income backgrounds and are more likely to attend lower-resourced schools. Unequal funding affects all students who attend under-resourced schools but particularly impacts ELL students since these students are unlikely to progress as rapidly as native English speakers in content areas that are taught in English. This problem is further exacerbated by the shortage of bilingual teachers and paraprofessionals and the increasing difficulties in obtaining and maintaining certification as highly qualified under provisions of NCLB (Hanna & Allen, 2012). In addition, as Zacarian (2013) pointed out, to be successful in school, students must possess an appropriate degree of academic language that includes deep cultural knowledge, the ability to listen, speak, and write, academic knowledge, and the ability to think to learn. Academic language may be presented to children in English or in their native language, in the case of ELLs, but children from low-income backgrounds, whether ELL or native English speakers, tend to have less exposure to, and therefore an increased need to develop, academic language. English language learners from low- income backgrounds tend, therefore, to have a dual deficit: a lack of exposure to academic language and a lack of proficiency in English. This issue is further compounded by the trend in several states away from bilingual education to full-language immersion approaches. Artiles and Ortiz (2002) note that English language learners with the least amount of language support are most likely to be referred to special education, and ELLs receiving all instruction in English are nearly three times as likely to be certified as a special education student than those receiving some educational support in their native language.

Another issue is that schools with large numbers of ELL students, who are often more ethnically and culturally diverse and tend to come from low-income backgrounds, typically start already behind in the achievement indicators used to determine adequately yearly progress (AYP). Under the provisions of AYP, these students are expected not only to catch up to their peers, but to maintain the same level of academic growth. This problem is further compounded by the definition of ELL as a "subgroup" to be counted in the evaluation of AYP. As students gain proficiency in English, they no longer count in the Limited English Proficiency subgroup (after two years).

Potentially high-scoring students leave the subgroup and are replaced by incoming students, who may have very limited proficiency in English. Thus, for many schools with high numbers of ELLs, it is impossible to show AYP for this subgroup of students since it is not a stable group and, by its very nature, cannot reach 100% proficiency. The problem is further compounded by unrealistic expectations contained within the NCLB legislation; research consistently demonstrates that it takes anywhere from 4–7 years or longer to attain proficiency in academic English (CAPELL, 2011; Hakuta, Butler, & Witt, 2000), much longer than the three years allowed by provisions contained within NCLB (Neill, 2005). Adding to the complexity is the fact that older language proficiency tests have been found to exhibit low reliability for determining language proficiency. Further, correlations between LEP classification codes and scores on instruments such as the Language Assessment Scales, Stanford 9, and ITBS have been particularly weak, especially at the higher end (Abedi, 2004). Thus, there is a lack of validity and consistency across states in classifying ELLs, which potentially affects not only instructional outcomes for the individual student but of the entire school in terms of AYP expectations.

To address these issues, Neill (2005) has made several recommendations. Common standards for definitions of Limited English Proficiency and "proficient" that are rooted in valid, current research need to be developed and used across all states. Valid and reliable tests of English language proficiency need to be made widely available, and standardized achievement tests should be revised to simplify the language and to ensure the recognizability of embedded cultural and social references. These tests must also be re-normed to include a statistically representative sample of ELLs at various levels of proficiency. Furthermore, multiple measures of language proficiency and academic achievement should be used not only for formative, instructional decision-making but to address the attainment of AYP. Neill suggests that the AYP formula itself must be revisited to address the unequal starting points and inevitably changing composition of the ELL subgroup within a school or district. Finally, adequate and equitable resources, including appropriate numbers of bilingual teachers and paraprofessionals, must be available for students who need language support.

Special Education Eligibility and ELL Students

There are several difficulties with evaluating ELL students for special education eligibility, and ELL students are over-represented in special education referrals and eligibility. According to Artiles and Ortiz (2002), there are three categories of English language learners who experience academic difficulties: those who have insufficient support or ineffective learning environments that do not support their language and cultural needs; those who experience difficulties due to interrupted schooling, limited exposure to formal schooling, low attendance, high transiency rates, etc.; and those who truly have an intellectual, learning, emotional, sensory, or physical impairment that requires specialized services. It can often be very difficult to ascertain whether a student who is learning English as a second (or third) language into any one (or none) of these categories because ELL students often lag behind their native English-speaking peers. It is therefore critical for school administrators to ensure that ELL students receive appropriate instruction and support for their unique learning needs and to ensure that appropriate assessment practices are followed when a referral for special education seems appropriate. In this context several issues must be considered.

Understanding the Impact of Second Language Acquisition and Cultural Norms

The rate at which students become proficient in a second language depends on several factors, including age, level of acculturation, attitude and motivation, learning style, level of proficiency in the native language, and the influence of family and community (Orosco & Hoover, 2009). In general, the younger the student is when the process of learning a second language begins, the more successful the student will be in reaching proficiency. However, Krashen & Terrill (1983) were among the first researchers to identify stages of second language acquisition. During the first six months, the ELL student has minimal comprehension and limited ability to verbalize in the second language. Between six and 12 months, the ELL student is in the Early Production phase, characterized by limited comprehension and the ability to verbalize using primarily key words and familiar phrases. The Speech Emergence phase, which typically takes place between the first and third years of second language acquisition, is characterized by improved comprehension and verbalizing in simple sentences with frequent errors in grammar and pronunciation. It is not until most ELL students have been exposed to the second language for more than three years that Intermediate Fluency is reached. This stage is characterized by good comprehension and reduced errors in speech production. Finally, after approximately 5–7 years, ELL students reach Advanced Fluency, which is characterized by native-language level proficiency. Too often, however, students who are in the stages of second language acquisition are dismissed prematurely from ESL and bilingual programs and are then mistakenly suspected of having a disability. This is often due to a failure to distinguish between basic interpersonal communication skills (BICS) and cognitive academic language proficiency (CALP) (Cummins, 1979), or more informally "playground" language and "classroom" language. Further compounding the issue is the fact that the communication difficulties experienced by many ELL students can lead to feelings of frustration, isolation, and poor self-esteem, which in turn, may lead to behavior problems that may be misunderstood and not attributed to the root linguistic communication cause.

Culture also plays a significant role in how well ELL students fare in school. Immigrant families with different cultural backgrounds often hold beliefs about education and schooling that differ from that of the dominant cultural group. Cultural differences exist in conceptions of time, the role of gender, individualism vs. collectivism, styles of learning and approaches to teaching, and even communication styles (direct versus indirect) (National Institute for Urban School Improvement, n.d.). These cultural differences can lead educators to misinterpret student and behavior and attitudes, and to inappropriate referrals for special education. Assessments can be further complicated by cultural differences noted by Artiles and Ortiz (2002) regarding participation in education by parents from diverse cultural backgrounds. For example, differences include: decision-making roles, where the parent who is in contact with the school may or may not be in a position to make decisions about the student's schooling. The expectation that parents have a right to disagree with the school may conflict directly with cultural beliefs about harmony trumping individual rights, or beliefs about power and authority, thus creating an apparent and misleading consensus between school and parent. Some cultural groups nod to demonstrate understanding, not agreement, while other cultural groups consider it impolite to contradict someone. Additionally, cultural groups have divergent attitudes and beliefs about public and private information such as health, illness, disability, family history, etc., and upholding the honor of the family is sometimes considered more important than providing accurate information. Finally, there are cultural differences in beliefs and attitudes about normality and disability that may differ from legal definitions. Many cultural differences can lead to misunderstanding and miscommunication between schools and families, especially when ELL students are referred for special education.

Use of Standardized, Norm-referenced Tests

Using nationally standardized, norm-referenced test scores to determine eligibility of ELL students for special education causes several problems. Ample evidence implies that psychometric tests lack reliability and validity for ELL students due to language and cultural content embedded within the tests. Blatchley & Lau, 2010 suggest that when ELL students are referred for special education, specific tasks from these tests can be beneficial in determining what skills a given student does and does not have, but that standardized scores should not be considered if a student's background experience and level of language proficiency differs from that of the norm group. And while IDEA specifies that children must be evaluated in their native language, this is also problematic in that ELL students often lack proficiency in both languages since they may not have been exposed to cognitive academic learning language in their native language. The use of interpreters does not mitigate this problem. Employing interpreters ipso facto renders the test procedures not standardized, and some tests items simply cannot be translated from English to another language without distorting the meaning of the item or providing clues as to the correct response. In addition, interpreters may or may not provide the correct instructions or the actual responses, instead filling in or omitting information. And use of family or community members as interpreters may compromise confidentiality. Finally, the content of standardized tests, even nonverbal ones, is often culturally biased. As a result, a student's ability to perform or respond to items on such tests is affected by his or her level of acculturation in addition to language proficiency. This remains true even of the few existing bilingual test instruments. Instead, Blatchley & Lau suggest that descriptive information from a variety of sources and methods collected over an appropriate length of time along with close monitoring of effective learning supports and interventions is needed to determine whether a student has a true disabling condition instead of difficulties with learning due to lack of proficiency in English or other mitigating cultural factors. Thus, while the Response to Intervention (RtI) model for determining the existence of a learning disability has become the preferred method for all school populations, it is particularly important for ELL students. School personnel face particular challenges when ELL students are suspected of having a language or behavioral impairment, since the role of language acquisition and proficiency in both languages and the impact of culture must be carefully investigated and considered before any determination of eligibility can be made. When ELL students are found to be eligible for special education services, Cloud (1988) suggested that the special education services and programs in which these students are placed must still consider the need for native-language support in addition to continued ESL support, and that stronger pre-referral programs and supports will reduce the number of inappropriate referrals of ELL students.

Funding: ESEA and the Blueprint for Reform

ESEA provides multiple funding opportunities for the development, implementation, and support of programs serving English learners. The Bilingual Education Act of 1968 and subsequent reauthorizations created discretionary grant programs to local school districts to develop programs serving limited English speaking students. Table 5.3 provides a list of some of the funding opportunities supporting programs for English language learners.

Title VII of Improving America's Schools Act of 1994 offered financial assistance to institu-

Table 5.3. ELL Program Development Funding Opportunities.

- K–12 curriculum development
- Instructional programs based on scientific research
- Early childhood programs
- Alternative instructional programs
- Family education programs
- Cultural enrichment activities
- Academic counseling
- Gifted and talented programs
- Professional development for teachers, administrators, and support personnel

tions of higher education, community-based organizations, and local education agencies to de-velop and enhance programs that provide high quality instruction through bilingual education or special alternative instructional programs for students of limited English proficiency, to assist students in developing proficiency in English and to assist LEP students in meeting the same level of academic achievement and state content standards expected of all children and youth in schools (Improving America's Schools Act of 1994). No Child Left Behind continues to support these funding initiatives and requires states to establish standards and benchmarks, as well as annual achievement objectives for LEP students.

The Blueprint for Reform proposes to continue the availability of formula grants to states, school districts, and nonprofit agencies to improve the education of English Learners. To ensure that grant assistance supports the conditions needed to foster English Learners' success, the proposal would require states to:

- Establish new criteria to ensure consistent statewide identification of students as English Learners, and to determine eligibility, placement, and duration of programs and services, based on the states' valid and reliable English language proficiency assessment.
- Implement a system to evaluate the effectiveness of language instruction educational programs, and to provide information on the achievement of subgroups of English Learners, to drive better decisions by school districts for program improvement, and to support districts in selection of effective programs.

Districts that are not improving the performance of English Learners will lose flexibility around the use of funds under this program, and must work with the state to implement more effective strategies (U.S. Department of Education, 2010).

The proposal for ESEA reauthorization will continue to support competitive grants to states; districts; Indian tribes; Indian institutions of higher education; Indian, Native Hawaiian, and Alaska Native educational and community based organizations; and nonprofit organizations, agencies, and institutions—to help meet the unique need of Indian students, Native Hawaiian students, and Alaska Native students (U.S. Department of Education, 2010a).

Please refer to Chapters 1, 2, and 6 for additional information on funding sources for English Language Learners (ELL) and Limited English Proficient (LEP) students and programs.

The Role of Teachers and Administrators as Instructional Leaders

Programs for English learners present a unique opportunity for the school administrator to work with faculty, parents, and community groups in the development of programs serving students at a variety of levels of limited English proficiency and in fostering not only English language speaking, listening, and writing skills, but knowledge in the academic content areas.

Given the current demographic shifts in the U.S. population, it is likely that all teachers at some point in their careers will encounter students who do not yet have sufficient proficiency in English to fully access academic content in traditional classrooms. Many teachers do not have preparation to provide high-quality instruction to this population of students (Ballantyne, Sanderman, & Levy, 2008).

Mainstream teacher training and ongoing professional development in ELL instructional knowledge and skills is needed to close the achievement gap between limited English proficient students and native English speakers. It is important that all teachers be able to distinguish between oral abilities and cognitive abilities in the language acquisition process of English language learners.

The National Staff Development Council (NSDC, 2001) developed a set of guidelines that have a direct relationship to content area teachers and their students. The first part of the report addresses guidelines for mainstream teachers of English language learners. The guidelines are specific to the content area courses--English/language arts, math, science, and social studies. Each guideline presents curricular and instructional strategies for teachers working with ELL students and contains content area, vocabulary, and contextual information on the factors relevant to specific disciplines. The guidelines advocate ongoing training rather than one time workshops and stress standards development in the areas of context, process, and content standards. Specifically, context standards should be addressed in learning communities, leadership development, and the acquisition and equitable distribution of resources. Process standards should be collaborative in design and learning goals, research based, and data driven. Content standards should be equitable for all students based on quality teaching and family involvement (Ballantyne, Sanderman, & Levy, 2008).

In 2012 the NSDC changed its name to Learning Forward. Learning Forward continues to advocate for ongoing training, particularly in the form of learning communities in which teachers, administrators, and paraprofessionals work together in advocating and developing new strategies for working with students. The strategies encourage schools to work together to solve the problems of curricular and instructional strategies not simply for ELL students in isolation, but for all students with diverse needs in schools (Learning Forward, 2012).

School administrators at the school and district levels still maintain the primary responsibility for budgeting, acquiring funding resources, acting as school/community advocates, evaluating programs and instructional staff, and advocating for the development of innovative instructional programs to serve student needs. The Blueprint for Reform proposes funding to support programs for English language learners.

> Our proposal will also provide new competitive grants to states, districts, and nonprofit partners to support the development of innovative programs, build the knowledge base about promising practices, and scale up effective practices to improve instruction for English Learners, including funding for graduate fellowships to support research and leadership in developing effective practices to improve English Learner outcomes, as well as state or district partnerships with colleges and universities for developing effective teachers. In addition, under the College- and Career-Ready Students program, states will be required to adopt and implement statewide grade-by-grade English language proficiency standards that are linked to the state's college- and career-ready academic content standards (U.S. Department of Education, 2010d).

Attention to instructional programming and the professional development of all teachers and administrators, particularly as a part of learning community activities in schools, are essential elements to the improvement and advancement of services to ELL students and closing the achievement gap between English language learners and regular education students. As pointed out by Learning Forward (2012) ongoing training is essential for all educational professionals in schools. This ongoing training and dialogue among educators is a necessity particularly in light of implementation of the Common Core State Standards and the goal to ensure that all students are college- and career-ready when graduating from school. Emphasis needs to be placed on training of regular education teachers, who are integrating English language learners into mainstreamed classrooms and for the paraprofessionals offering instructional support within regular education classroom settings. Funding sources for curriculum and instructional development along with teacher and administrator training at the state, school, and school district levels are currently available under No Child Left Behind. Support for professional learning is also proposed to continue under the Blueprint for Reform.

Summary

The historical overview of programs for English language learners demonstrates the differences of opinions both in the past and present related to the education of English language learners. Such differences have had both positive and negative results on the education of students not proficient in the English language. Controversy still remains between advocates of bilingual and ESL instructional programs. The current and anticipated increase of ELL students in classrooms across the nation points to the need for more research, funding, and learning activities for paraprofessionals, teachers, and school administrators. ELL student performance on mandated testing and placement in special education classes must be investigated and reforms implemented that address inequalities.

Questions for Consideration

1. What changes to the *Elementary and Secondary Education Act of 2001: No Child Left Behind* related to English Language Learners have been proposed in *The Blueprint for Reform: Reauthorization of the Elementary and Secondary Education Act?* What is the rationale for these proposals? Do you agree or disagree with the proposals? Explain why.

2. What role can parents play in the education of English Language Learners? What are the roles of teachers and school administrators related to parental involvement?

3. What role do paraprofessionals play in the education of English Language Learners? Are paraprofessionals an essential component of classroom instruction and program support? Explain why or why not.

4. What are the suggestions that have been made to prepare regular education teachers serving the needs of English Language Learners in the regular education classroom? Do you have suggestions of your own?

5. Which instructional methodology do you support for English Language Learners—Bilingual Education, English as a Second Language, or mainstreaming into a regular education classroom? Explain the rationale for your preference.

6. What roles do teachers and administrators play in relationship to programs and services for English Language Learners in schools?

Case Study

Changing Demographics at Newbrook Elementary School

Susan Criner is the principal of Newbrook Elementary School, located in a relatively small district on the outskirts of a large urban center in the southwest United States. While most of the district enrolls predominantly white, middle-class students, it has experienced a sudden and rapid shift in demographics, especially in the geographic area surrounding Newbrook Elementary. The student population in that vicinity is approximately 46% African American, 28% Latino, 17% Asian, 6% Caucasian, and 3% other. The school is in its first year of operation and Susan is one of the first principals to be recruited from outside the district in several years. Susan was recruited in part due to her experience and success in maintaining high academic standards and performance in an urban elementary school that enrolled primarily minority students from low SES backgrounds. One of the most challenging aspects of her new position is dealing with the diverse linguistic backgrounds of the families of students who will attend Newbrook. In her previous position, the percentage of students who were English Language Learners was negligible. At Newbrook, on the other hand, home language surveys filled out by parents at enrollment indicate that over 30 languages and dialects are spoken as primary or secondary languages in the homes of enrolled students. In addition, the number of students entering Newbrook with minimal exposure to English is higher than expected. Susan anticipated that finding ways to effectively communicate with parents and families would be her primary challenge. However, as the school year progressed, she has been dismayed to find that many teachers in the building are unprepared to differentiate their instruction for ELL students to the degree necessary for student success, and the two ELL teachers are overwhelmed with the numbers of students they are assigned.

By mid-October, Susan has become concerned about the number ELL students who are being referred to the Student Intervention Team for evaluation. The district has adopted a Response to Intervention model for student referrals, but the intervention tiers that have been successful in other schools in the district are proving inadequate for Newbrook, according to the teachers and school psychologist. One typical example is that of Miguel Delgado. Jennifer Jones, a highly respected 5th grade teacher who followed Susan to the new school, has referred Miguel for special education for a suspected learning disability. Miguel is 10 years old and has attended school in the district since 2nd grade. His family immigrated to the United States from El Salvador when Miguel was 7, and he had not attended school regularly until his family arrived in the district. He was placed in 2nd grade, as was age-appropriate, with ESL level I support. He reached ESL level III by the end of 3rd grade, the last level of ESL support before a student is exited from the program, and was exited from ESL at the end of 4th grade, having achieved mastery of English. Although his accent is still very noticeable, he can communicate easily with teachers, peers, and other staff in the building, and even translates for his mother when she tries to speak to the teacher. He is generally good-natured and gets along well with others but increasingly seems moody and irritable to his teachers. Miguel, as expected, performs much better in math than other academic areas that require greater proficiency in English, but his teacher is especially concerned about his writing. She has come to suspect that he has a learning disability based on the relative strengths of his well-developed oral communication and math skills and adequate performance in other subjects compared to his writing, which is often filled with spelling, punctuation, and grammatical errors and appears more like the writing expected in late first grade or early second grade. Jennifer is concerned that Miguel might "slip through the cracks" and have significant difficulty in middle school if he does not receive the special education services she believes he needs. She firmly believes that Miguel has received adequate ESL support and has had appropriate instructional interventions to address his difficulty with writing, but he is still not progressing as she thinks he should. Furthermore, she is concerned about how Miguel will fare on the state-mandated writing exam, which is conducted in 5th grade. Susan feels pressure, on the one hand, to respect the professional opinion of the teacher. Furthermore, Susan feels a significant amount of pressure to ensure that student performance on the state-mandated exams meet district and state-level expectations, and she is overwhelmed by the unexpectedly low levels of achievement demonstrated by many of the students. If Miguel qualifies as a student with a learning disability, he can be assessed using alternative measures provided by the state. On the other hand, Susan knows that exiting ESL does not necessarily indicate that a student is fully proficient in English or that he has the academic language necessary to be successful in all subject areas. Furthermore, Susan is concerned that Miguel's moodiness may stem from the increased difficulty of the 5th grade curriculum. She knows this case is just one example of many she will face this year, and she knows she must find a way to curtail the number of referrals for special education and to find a way to more effectively work with this population of students.

Questions to Consider

1. What are the issues facing Miguel that might indicate he does or does not have a learning disability?

2. What are some of the administrative and leadership concerns Susan is facing in this case?

3. Are there steps in the process that are missing or have been overlooked? What types of pre-referral interventions should be in place and documented before a referral for special education assessment should be conducted?

4. How is this particular case reflective of changes taking place overall in the district? What measures can the district put into place as it begins to experience rapid shifts in demographics?

References

Abedi, J. (2004). The no child left behind act and English language learners: Assessment and accommodation issues. *Educational Researcher, 33*(1), 4–14.

Adler, M. (2005). Programs for English language learners. In B. M. Beyer & E. S. Johnson, *Special programs and services in schools: Creating options, meeting needs.* Lancaster, PA: Pro>Active Publications.

Alexander, K., & Alexander M. D. (1998). *American public school law* (4th ed.). Belmont, CA: West/Wadsworth, An International Thomson Publishing Company.

Ali, T. (2009, January 15). Dearborn schools urged to ban Arabic. The Detroit News. Retrieved from http://www.detroitnews.com/article/20090115/SCHOOLS/901150395.

Arce, J. (2004). Latino bilingual teachers: The struggle to sustain an emancipatory pedagogy in public schools. *International Journal of Qualitative Studies in Education, 17*(2), 227–246.

Artiles, A. J., & Ortiz, A. A. (2002). *English language learners and special education: Before assessing a child for special education, first assess the instructional program.* Center for Applied Linguistics. Retrieved from http://www.misd.net/Bilingual/ellsandspedcal.pdf.

Ballantyne, K. G., Sanderman, A. R., & Levy, J. (2008). *Educating English language learners: Building teacher capacity.* Washington, DC: National Clearinghouse for English Language Acquisition. Retrieved from http://www.ncela.gwu.edu/practice/mainstream_teachers.htm

Bear, C. (2008). *American Indian boarding schools haunt many.* Retrieved from http://www.npr.org/templates/story/story.php?storyId=16516865.

Beyer, B. M., & Johnson, E. S. (2005). *Special programs & services in schools: Creating options, meeting needs.* Lancaster, PA: Pro>Active Publications.

Beyer-Houda, B. (1995). Preparing school administrators for multicultural settings. *Catalyst for Change, 24*(2): 20–22.

Blatchley, L. A. & Lau, M. Y. (2010). Culturally competent assessment of English language learners for special education services. *NASP Communique', 38*(7).

Boschee, F., Beyer, B. M., Engelking J. L., & Boschee, M. A. (1997). *Special and compensatory programs: The administrator's role.* Lancaster, PA: Technomic Publishing.

Brown v. Board of Education of Topeka, 347 U.S. 483, 74 S.Ct. 686 (1964).

Civil Rights Act of 1964, Title VI. 42 U.S.C.A. Secs. 2000D-D-1.

Cloud, N. (1988). ESL in special education. ERIC Clearinghouse on Languages and Linguistics. Washington, DC. ED303044.

Connecticut Administrators of Programs for English Language Learners (2011). *English language learners and special education: a resource handbook.* Retrieved from http://www.sde.ct.gov/sde/lib/sde/pdf/curriculum/bilingual/CAPELL_SPED_resource_guide.pdf.

Council of Chief State School Officers (2012). *Framework for English language proficiency development standards corresponding to the common core state standards and the next generation science standards.* Washington, DC: CCSSO. Retrieved from http://www.ccsso.org/Documents/2012/ELPD%20Framework%20Booklet-Final%20for%20web.pdf

Cummins, Cummins, J. (1979). Cognitive/academic language proficiency, linguistic interdependence, the optimum age question and some other matters. Working Papers on Bilingualism, No. 19, 121–129.

Equal Education Opportunities Act of 1977, Sec. 204(f). 20 U.S.C. Sec 1703.

Geraud v. Schrader, 531 P.2nd 872 (Wyo. 1975).

Hakuta, K., Butler, Y. G., & Witt, D. (2000). *How long does it take English language learners to attain proficiency?* University of California Linguistic Minority Research Institute Policy Report 2000-1. Retrieved from http://www.usc.edu/dept/education/CMMR/FullText/Hakuta_HOW_LONG_DOES_IT_TAKE.pdf.

Krashen, S. & Terrill, T. D. (1983). *The natural approach.* New York: Pergamon Press.

Learning Forward (2012). *Standards for professional learning.* Retrieved from http://learningforward.org/standards#.UfVzFdI3vbh

Morgan v. Kerrigan, 401 F.Supp. 4341 (E.D. Tex 1981).

National Center for English Language Acquisition (2011). *The growing number of limited English proficient students 1998-96/2008-09.* Retrieved from

National Institute for Urban School Improvement. Cultural factors that influence learning for ELL students. Retrieved from http://www2.sfasu.edu/enlace/Cultural%20Factors%20450%202010.pdf.

National Staff Development Council (NSDC) (2001). *Standards for staff development: Revised.* Oxford, OH: Author.

Natonabah v. Board of Education of Gallup-McKinley County School District, 355F. Supp. 716 (D.N.M, 1973).

Neill, M. (2005). Assessment of ELL students under NCLB: Problems and solutions. Retrieved from http://fairtest.org/sites/default/files/NCLB_assessing_bilingual_students_0.pdf.

Orosco, M. & Hoover, J. J. (2009). Characteristics of second language acquisition, cultural diversity, and learning/behavior disabilities. In J. J. Hoover (Ed.), *Differentiating learning differences from disabilities: meeting diverse needs through multi-tiered response to intervention.* New York: Prentice-Hall.

Samson, J. F., & Collins, B. A. (2012, April 30). *Preparing all teachers to meet the needs of English language learners: Applying research to policy and practice for teacher effectiveness.* Retrieved from http://www.americanprogress.org/issues/education/report/2012/04/30/11372/preparing-all-teachers-to-meet-the-needs-of-english-language-learners/

Spring, J. (2011). *The American school: A global context from the Puritans to the Obama era (8th ed).* New York, NY: McGraw-Hill.

Stewart, D. (1994). Immigration laws are education laws too. *Phi Delta Kappan, 75*(9): 556–558.

TESOL International Association. (2013, March). *Overview of the Common Core State Standards Initiatives for ELLs.* Alexandria, VA: Author. Retrieved from http://www.tesol.org/docs/advocacy/overview-of-common-core-state-standards-initiatives-for-ells-a-tesol-issue-brief-march-2013.pdf?sfvrsn=4

Title VI Language Discrimination Guidelines, 45 Fed. Reg. 152.52056 (1980).

U.S. Congress (1974). *Equal Educational Opportunities Act.* 20 U.S.C.A, Sec. 1703(f).

U.S. Department of Education, (2010a). *Diverse learners: Reauthorizing the elementary and Secondary Education Act.* Retrieved from http://www2.ed.gov/policy/elsec/leg/blueprint/faq/diverse-learners.pdf

U.S. Department of Education (2010b). *ESEA blueprint for reform.* Office of Planning, Education, and Policy Development. Washington, DC. Retrieved from http://www2.ed.gov/policy/elsec/leg/blueprint/blueprint.pdf

U.S. Department of Education (2010c). *Meeting the needs of English learners and other diverse learners.* Retrieved from http://www2.ed.gov/policy/elsec/leg/blueprint/english-learners-diverse-learners.pdf

U.S. Department of Education (2010d). *Obama's administration educational reform plan emphasizes flexibility, resources and accountability.* Retrieved from http://www.ed.gov/news/press-releases/obama-administrations-education-reform-plan-emphasizes-flexibility-resources-and

U.S. Government (1964). *Civil rights act.* Washington, DC: U.S. Government Printing Office.

U.S. Government (1968). *Bilingual education act of 1968. Title VII of the elementary and secondary education act of 1965 and amended in 1967.* Elementary and Secondary Education Act, 20 U.S.C., 2701 et seq.

U.S. Government (1994). *Improving America's Schools Act of 1994: Reauthorizing the Elementary and Secondary Education Act of 1965.* P.L. 103-382. Sec. 111(b).

U.S. Government (2002). *No child left behind act of 2001: Reauthorization of the elementary and secondary education act of 1965* (P.L 107-110). Washington, DC: U.S. Government Printing Office.

Zacarian, D. (2013). *Crossing language barriers.Principal, 92*(5), 34–39.

CHAPTER 6

Alternative Educational Opportunities

Introduction

THERE was a time in the not too distant past of American public education when alternative education consisted mainly of a variety of programs serving targeted groups, such as students with gifts and talents, disabilities, language barriers, teen parents, or students who were disruptive in class, at-risk of academic failure, and in jeopardy of dropping out of school. Such students were placed in specialized or alternative educational settings, which could mean: separate classrooms, small student-teacher ratio classrooms, facilities separated from other schools in a district, challenge programs such as wilderness camps and military-style boot camps, hospital and residential settings, programs in prisons, or specialized schools sponsored by intermediate school districts that might also include special education programs and classes. As these programs increased in number during the last half of the 20th century and become an accepted part of educational options, the term *alternative education* became synonymous with specialized programs and facilities serving at-risk youth within public school systems. In 1995, McNergney & Herbert defined an alternative school as, ". . . any school operating within the public school system that has programs addressing the specific needs or interests of targeted student groups" (p. 189). At that time, there were over 15,000 public alternative education programs across the nation, serving at-risk youth in highly individualized programs supported by advocates working not only with the students but providing a bridge to communication with schools, parents, social service agencies, and juvenile authorities (Barr & Parrett, 1995). As a greater variety of school funding opportunities and school selections have become available in the 1990s and early 21st century, and technology is integrated into teaching and learning, the concept of alternative education is no longer only for at-risk student groups, but instead provides alternative educational opportunities for all students.

In recent years, public and private agencies have developed non-traditional education formats such as charter schools, school choice, school/business internships and partnerships, contract schools, K–14 partnerships, school-to-work programs, or have expanded existing private educational opportunities through vouchers and tax credits. The number of children being educated through home schooling has increased, and distance education opportunities abound. Literacy programs serve adults in the community, and parents are learning side by side with their children in classrooms. All these education restructuring and reform initiatives are changing the complexion of American public education and providing a variety of choices for parents.

105

Restructuring, Reform, and Choice

Reform initiatives have taken place throughout the history of American education. The present era of educational reform began in the 1980s following publication of *A Nation at Risk* (National Commission on Excellence, 1983) and has addressed a variety of issues and ideas including inequity in educational opportunities, a mobile society, both growth and decline in student enrollment, an increasingly multicultural society, a "back to basics" movement, school restructuring, shared leadership and decision-making, curriculum development, assessment of learning, site-based management, parental involvement, school climate and culture, integration of technology into teaching and learning, teacher and school administrator preparation, and accountability on all levels. The most recent wave of educational reform addresses the continued dissatisfaction of the public related to the performance of public schools and their inability to meet the academic needs of students and skill requirements of the community and businesses. Such dissatisfaction has resulted in the development of new forms of public and private education, offering alternatives to the traditional neighborhood public school. NCLB supports educational options for parents with children in failing schools. Additional information can be found in Chapter 1 on the topics of magnet schools, charter schools, and voluntary public school choice.

Magnet Schools

Magnet schools provide an option for parents to choose a non-neighborhood public school within the same district in which their child resides. Magnet schools were designed to provide equity and choice. Following *Brown v. Board of Education of Topeka* in 1954, magnet schools began to appear, mainly in urban areas, as a means to promote integration in public schools and provide academic choice by drawing student enrollment from across a school district. These themed schools continue to serve the same purpose today in urban and suburban areas, offering students educational opportunities in specific academic content areas such as the arts, sciences, languages, business, global studies, and technology. See Chapter 1 for more information related to magnet schools and *No Child Left Behind*.

Alternative Schools

Alternative schools have also served an important role in the education of American youth. Growing from the philosophies of John Dewey and the establishment of private schools like Summerhill, alternative schools have provided educational choice options to students and parents. Alternative schools, as a part of American public education in the last half of the 20th century, have served populations of students outside of the traditional school environment. Such students have been at risk of academic failure and potentially would not be able to graduate from a traditional high school, thereby placing them in jeopardy of maintaining an independent, self-supporting life as adults due to lack of a high-school diploma or GED certificate. Alternative programs are academic, vocational, and nurturing, reconnecting students with their families and other support groups. At the same time, the programs link students with the world beyond school, offering students greater possibilities of success as contributing members of society. Generally, the programs have low student-teacher ratio classrooms, integrate learning with meaningful work, and create family-like support systems of caring adults.

Alternative education programs have also been the proving ground for emergent educational strategies later used in regular educational settings to improve teaching and learning for all students:

Through the creation and support of alternative schools, educators have experimented with such concepts as out-of-school learning, peer tutoring, cross-age grouping, challenge education, open education, school without walls, individualized continuous progress schools, traditional back-to-basics education, authentic assessment, non-graded learning, competency-based graduation requirements, school choice, and site-based decision making (Barr & Parrett, 1999, p. 126).

Some of the positive outcomes for teachers in the development of alternative education programs are distinctive teaching methods with a need-based curriculum and individualized instruction, action learning, career exploration, differentiated learning, and the integration of technology into teaching and learning. The benefits for students are a high quality of school life with individualized instruction, career exploration connecting the classroom with life beyond school, and caring support services resulting in improved student behavior, positive self-esteem, and higher academic achievement.

Schools-Within-Schools

Schools-within-schools were developed to provide alternative educational opportunities inside large public schools. In some settings the school within a school is utilized to serve at-risk students. In others, it provides the opportunity to offer smaller class sizes, individualized student advisement programs, and academic options such as global education or vocational training. Research has shown that smaller class size, individualized instruction, and parental involvement enhance academic achievement. Restructuring of traditional schools to include schools-within-schools provides school districts with the opportunity to develop smaller communities of learners within larger schools, bringing parents, teachers, and students together in developing specialized programs and student support systems directed toward improved academic success (Short & Greer, 1997).

School Choice

School choice programs offer alternative educational opportunities by allowing parents and students to choose a school within a district other than the neighborhood school. In some states school choice is permitted across district lines. These efforts have ushered in an era of marketing and competition between schools and school districts. Previously, school districts could anticipate that a captive audience of students who lived within district boundaries would be enrolling in their schools. School districts could easily project student enrollment years in advance based on community demographics and make plans for increases or decreases in the need for classroom teachers and building administrators, school expansion or decline, and budgetary projections for capital outlays such as new construction. As parents became more vocal in expressing their dissatisfaction with neighborhood schools and community populations shifted, school districts instituted school choice programs both within district and across district boundaries in an effort to maintain enrollment. See Chapter 1 for more information related to *No Child Left Behind* and school choice.

School Vouchers, Tax Credits, and Privatization

School vouchers and tax credits expand the concept of school choice beyond the boundaries of public school districts by enabling families to choose to enroll their children in private schools. The idea of using public monies to pay for education in private and parochial schools is not new. As early as the French Revolution, the Catholic Church attempted to thwart the establishment of a public school system by the French through the distribution of vouchers. More recently, states in the U.S. South used vouchers in an attempt to circumvent the Equal Protection clause of the

Fourteenth Amendment and to nullify the effects of *Brown v. Board of Education* (Alexander & Alexander, 2005, p. 196). During the last part of the 20th century, voucher plans were established in such varied locations as Wisconsin, Colorado, Florida, Vermont, Pennsylvania, Maine, Illinois Minnesota, Washington D.C., Iowa, and Ohio. By 1990, more than 20 states either passed choice legislation or were considering doing so (Association for Supervision and Curriculum Development, 1990) and others continue to join this trend, which has faced numerous legal challenges.

The Wisconsin city of Milwaukee began the modern voucher movement in 1990. Its city-wide school voucher program, available only to Milwaukee residents, was established to provide children from low-income families the opportunity to attend private or parochial schools. The Wisconsin Supreme Court found in *Jackson v. Benson* (1998) that the voucher plan did not violate the three-pronged *Lemon Test* (1971) addressing the separation of church and state under the First Amendment. Around the same time, The Supreme Court of Arizona, in *Kotterman v. Killian* (1999) found that allowing a state tax credit for donations to a school tuition organization does not violate the Establishment clause.

The Supreme Court of Ohio ruled that the Cleveland voucher plan was constitutional as it relates to the Establishment Clause. The Cleveland plan offers two types of tuition assistance to parents. The first provides tuition aid for students to attend any public, private, or parochial school of their choice. The second provides tutorial aid to children who choose to remain in a public school. The U.S. Supreme Court upheld the Cleveland voucher plan in *Zelman v. Simmons-Harris* (2002) saying that since the program allows for participation of all schools, it does not violate the Establishment Clause of the First Amendment, which prohibits the use of public funds to support religious organizations.

> *Zelman* is the final word on vouchers, the Establishment Clause, and church-state relationships. Under this decision, it would be difficult to envisage any type of government aid program, vouchers or otherwise, to church schools that would be so blatantly religious that this Supreme Court would strike it as violative of the Establishment Clause of the First Amendment (Alexander & Alexander, 2005, p. 197).

The Florida Opportunity Scholarship Program (Florida Department of Education, 2004a) allowed students attending failing schools to choose a higher-performing public school or attend a private school. Florida's McKay Scholarship Program for Children With Disabilities (Florida Department of Education, 2004b) provides opportunities to all children identified as eligible for special education services regardless of income level or residence location and allows parents to select the best learning environment for their children, public or private. In 2002, a Florida court ruled against Florida's Opportunity Scholarship Program saying that public monies may not be used to attend religious schools. The Florida Governor responded by saying,

> (T)his decision is particularly disappointing given the U.S. Supreme Court's recent decision finding Ohio's choice program constitutional. This ruling is also troubling because it suggests that the Florida Constitution requires aid programs to discriminate against parents who choose religious schools (Florida Department of Education, 2004c).

A Florida appeals court upheld the lower court's ruling in 2004 and said that the scholarship program violated the state's Constitution because it sent public money to religious institutions (Winter, 2004).

In 2004 the city of Chicago announced an initiative in which the Chicago Public Schools explored a charter school format that combined the expertise and educational personnel of private schools with that of the public schools in an effort to offer more educational opportunities for public school students. The reform plan leaned heavily on the private sector for ideas, funding, and management (Dell'Angela & Washburn, 2004; Grossman, K. N., 2004). At the time it was reported that

(B)y 2010 the mayor intends to re-create more than 10 percent of the city's schools—one-third as charter schools, one third as independently operated contract schools and the remainder as small schools run by the district (Dell'Angela & Washburn, 2004).

School choice options continue to gain proponents across the nation who endorse school selection within public school districts, vouchers, scholarships, tax credits, tutorial aid, federal grants, and restructuring.

Contract and For-Profit Schools

Private corporations and business management consultants are increasingly being hired by school districts across the nation to run individual schools or as in the case of Edison Schools to administer entire school districts. Edison opened its first schools in 1995 and has operated 130 charter and district schools serving more than 132,000 public school students in 20 states. The Edison School project addresses four major areas: (1) management of schools for school districts, (2) charter schools, (3) summer and after-school programs, and (4) achievement management solutions for school districts (Edison Schools, 2004). Contracting by public schools has allowed the expansion of for-profit businesses such as Kindercare and Sylvan Learning Centers into public education. Sylvan and other K-12 business units of Laureate Education, Inc. were sold in 2003 to a newly formed for-profit company, educate, inc. (educate, inc., 2004a). educate, inc. is now known as Educate, Inc. (2013) and is composed of Sylvan Learning Centers, Catapult Learning, eSylvan, and Connections Academy and no longer focuses exclusively on the K-12 education market, but also includes professional development tutorial services for businesses. Educate, Inc. provides tutoring and other supplemental services at learning centers, in schools, and over the Internet (Educate, Inc, 2013). Connections Academy operates K-8 virtual public schools in various states, including Colorado, Michigan, Pennsylvania, and Wisconsin (educate, inc., 2004b).

Corporate donors, philanthropists, and private foundations have joined in donating millions of dollars in support of school reform efforts. The Education Commission of the States, the New American Schools Development Corporation, and the Coalition for Essential Schools have all been beneficiaries of these donations:

> Some see these events as the falling apart of U.S. public education; others see them as the erosion of the last great monopoly since Ma Bell and the arrival, finally, of competition to the educational marketplace (Barr &Parrett, 1995).

Choice, Competition, and School Administration

School choice has resulted in greater competition among schools and school districts, which in turn has required individual schools and districts to improve their marketing skills and efforts. Additionally, school choice is introducing a new era of accountability for teachers and school administrators. When parents have the ability to move their children out of low-performing schools, it is incumbent upon school administrators and teachers to improve the quality of education being offered to students or lose the students to another school, district, or other educational option. No longer do schools have a captive audience of students who will be required to attend regardless of the quality of education.

> As options to traditional public schools continue to grow in number and popularity, the stakes of reforming public education are getting higher and the timeline for improvement is getting shorter. State legislators are sensing that parents are no longer willing to wait and see if new public school reforms are successful, adding a new urgency to education debates across the country (Hirsch and Samuelsen, 1999, p. 16).

A new era of school restructuring and reform is upon us, and it is forcing educators to view the future of American public education through a new lens.

Impact of School Choice on Financing Public Education

Funding school choice through vouchers or tax credits presents new educational opportunities for parents and students. The impact on existing public and private education structures presents a very different scenario. As students move from school to school within a district, across district boundaries, or in and out of public and private educational programs, so do the dollars, which can have both a positive and a negative impact on programs and services available to students. The impact is negligible either way unless a critical mass of students begins to transfer from a school or district. With significant student migration, schools and school districts will gain or lose funding, need to increase or decrease staff, adjust class sizes, add or eliminate programs, reconsider transportation services, and open or close schools. Any of these changes can strongly affect a school or district. Since there is no consensus across the states as to how school choice can be effectuated and what student populations school choice should serve, planning is difficult at best for schools on both sides of the issue. Some states have instituted voucher programs for only low-income students; others make choice available to all students regardless of socio-economic class, disability, or academic achievement level. There has been fear expressed by some that school choice programs draw the top academic achievers away from existing public schools and these schools are left with low-achieving student populations that require additional programs and services. The same argument has been voiced about public charter schools. Where school choice is an option it is important to monitor student population shifts. This can be accomplished through ongoing research, statistical analysis, and accountability measures associated with funding grants.

Voluntary public school choice grants are available under *No Child Left Behind* to state education agencies (SEAs) along with local school districts (LEAs) or partnerships between an SEA or LEA and another organization. Any school choice program that is proposed as part of these grants is required to promote educational equity and academic excellence. Evaluation of the program by the federal government is based on characteristics of students and indicators of student academic achievement (U.S. Department of Education, 2002; p. 83).

Charter Schools/Public School Academies

A charter school is an independent public school. Charter schools, also known as public school academies in some states, receive state funding, are open to all students, and are accountable to the state for results in student achievement. Charter schools are unique in that they are independent schools within a public school system and run much like private schools with greater flexibility in choice of programs, teachers, and administrative structures. Such schools provide yet another alternative to the traditional public school system and provide to teachers and school administrators potential for innovations not available within a traditional public school system.

The first public charter school started in 1992 in St. Paul, Minnesota, and by 2004 their numbers reached 2,900 , with the greatest concentration in Michigan, California, Texas, Arizona, Washington DC, and Florida (Alexander & Alexander, 2005; Nelson, Rosenberg & Van Meter, 2004). Statistics for the years 2009–2010 demonstrate there are charter schools in 40 states and the District of Columbia and for the years 1999–2000 to 2009–10, the number of students enrolled in public charter schools more than quadrupled from 0.3 million to 1.6 million students (U.S. Department of Education, National Center for Education Statistics, 2012). The National Alliance for Public Charter Schools (NAPCS) in a November 2011 report demonstrates the increasing growth of charter schools across the nation:

... (NAPCS) estimates that across the country more than 500 new charter schools opened for the fall of 2011 and about 150 were closed over the past year, with California leading in both categories. Overall, NAPCS estimates there are now about 5, 600 charter schools, representing growth of about 7 percent over the past year (National Charter Schools Resource Center, 2013).

The National Alliance for Public Charter Schools web site provides current data on annual yearly progress (AYP), National Assessment of Educational Progress (NAEP) performance test scores, data metrics comparing charter schools and public schools, and state-by-state district level data (National Alliance for Public Charter Schools, 2008–2013).

Charter schools have met opposition. One argument against charter schools has been the possible entanglement between church and state with public funds going to religious organizations and schools. In the *Council of Organizations of Others for Education about Parochiaid v. Governor* (1997), the Supreme Court of Michigan found the definition of public school includes charter schools and does not constitute parochiaid to religious schools. Public school funding follows a child to whichever public school the student is enrolled. This has been a point of contention among educational and political groups who contend that reduced funding impacts student achievement by reducing the amount of money available to offer educational services to students in a district. This argument is countered by the claim that since funding is provided per student for educational purposes and if a student is no longer attending a particular school, why is funding needed? The counter-response is that money is needed for specialized teachers, programs and services, staff, and administrators serving all students in a school. The quality of academic programs in charter schools has also been questioned.

Parents choose to send their children to charter schools for a variety of reasons. These reasons may actually be based on personal perceptions of differences between the school types. Reasons that influence parents and students state in choosing a charter school include: better discipline and safety; themed curricula; greater parental involvement; a more convenient location; smaller class size; better communication networks between parents, teachers, and school administrators; opportunity for improved academic achievement; or general dissatisfaction with public school systems as they are structured today. Whether these reasons are myth or reality does not negate the fact that parents are choosing to send their children to charter schools and school districts are facing increased competition as a result of choice. Schools must address public concerns and perceptions about traditional public education formats, develop marketing skills and programs to promote the positive aspects of regular public schools, and seriously address public concerns related to underachieving students, unsafe schools, aging facilities, school/parent/community relations, lack of accountability, and the influence of special interest groups on public education. The fact that virtual charter schools are now also available in several states should be a wake-up call to developers of educational policy and programs.

Funding Sources for Charter Schools

Funding provided by *No Child Left Behind* (NCLB) is unique in that it lifts restrictions on awards for the development of charter schools. NCLB provides funding options for parents of children in low-performing schools to participate in voluntary public school choice. Funding is also available to agencies that wish to establish or expand programs furnishing students and parents with greater public school choice (U.S. Department of Education, 2002). Eligibility for federal funds to the states has been extended beyond state education agencies in partnership with districts or non-profit groups or colleges to also include districts that choose to partner with other districts, nonprofit groups, or colleges in the development of a charter school. Restrictions on the number of grants that can be made and the total amount of funding each grantee may receive for charter schools have been lifted as part of NCLB (U.S. Department of Education, 2002). This particular section of the Act also stresses the development of character education promoting collaboration among school personnel, parents, and community members in the development of schools, school curricula, and special programs that emphasize citizenship, respect, responsibility, trustworthiness, justice and generosity as aspects of character development.

Home Schooling

Home schools were the earliest forms of education. Long before the establishment of public and private school systems, children were educated by parents and tutors in the household. Today, there are still parents or guardians who decide, for a variety of reasons, that they can provide a better education for their children at home than can be obtained in a public, private, or parochial school. The number of parents or guardians choosing to home-school their children has increased during the last half of the 20th century. Currently all 50 states have statutes allowing home-school education as an alternative to in-class public school instruction. However, the fact that home schooling is allowed by state statutes does not exempt children and parents from public education compulsory attendance laws. It has been clearly stated in a number of court cases that the state maintains an interest in the health, education and welfare of children and can require students to attend an accredited public or private school (Alexander & Alexander, 2005). Additionally, the social welfare of students has remained a strong consideration by the courts, whose rulings stress the importance of social interaction for all children beyond a single social unit such as the family. Kowalski (2003) states, ". . . by taking their children out of schools, home-schooling parents may be depriving them of certain resources and opportunities, such as the opportunity for peer social interaction" (p. 128). Advocates counter this claim by pointing out that home-schooled children have the opportunity to participate in the same social activities outside of school as do other children. Additionally, many states allow home-schooled children to participate in extracurricular activities offered by the schools, such as band and athletic activities. It is important for school administrators and school boards to understand the laws related to participation in these activities, particularly the rules of state athletic associations.

Each state has established its own rules and regulations related to home schooling with the state statutes falling into one of five legal categories as shown in Table 6.1. Within these categories, the rules and guidelines for home schooling vary from state to state. Some states require testing of students or submission of a portfolio to demonstrate academic achievement. Others may include requirements that home school educators follow state curriculum content standards, hold a teaching certificate or prove their ability to teach the required academic subjects, or have lesson plans, textbook selections, and supporting course materials approved by the public education agency. Additionally, parents or guardians do not always conduct home schooling. Some states allow parents to hire a certified teacher to provide home schooling or may allow more than one family of children to join group home-school instruction. Some states allow parents the option of

Table 6.1. Five Legal Categories of Home Schooling.

1. Home-school-statute states have legally defined home education and set criteria.
2. Private school states give home schools the same legal standing as private schools.
3. Approved instruction states insist on previewing the curriculum and may also require an end-of-year evaluation.
4. Equivalent instruction states may require parents to demonstrate that their curriculum is comparable or equivalent to the public schools, as defined by local school officials.
5. Constitutional guarantee state is a state whose constitution guarantees a right to home schooling with no annual evaluations or parental qualifications required (Home School Legal Defense Association, 2004).

registering their children in specific courses offered by the local accredited schools. Parents who do not feel they have the content area expertise or special equipment necessary for instruction might exercise this option. This "cherry-picking" of courses by parents can create problems for school administrators when developing class schedules or assigning teachers.

As home schooling has increased, so have the support systems for advocates of home education. Private agencies, for-profit corporations, community colleges, and school districts have developed classes for home educators. Course materials, lesson plans, and access to other instructional support are available via the Internet. The Home School Legal Defense Association actively monitors home school legislation and current court cases; provides information on home instruction, support groups, and instructional materials; and, provides the latest statistics related to home school enrollment and student academic achievement (Home School Legal Defense Association, 2004). Distance education provides another tool for home schooling, allowing students to enroll in courses taught via the Internet and landlines, an additional instructional support tool to home educators who may not have expertise in a particular subject. Complete K–8 and 9–12 diploma programs approved by some states are now available on the Internet. As dissatisfaction with traditional public education formats has increased in recent years, so have the number of parents and guardians who embrace home school options for the education of their children.

Home- Hospital- and Residential-Based Programs

Home-based educational programs are another type of instruction that can take place in home settings residential health centers, and hospitals. These programs, unlike home schooling as described above, incorporate representatives from the school, health services, or social service agencies, and might include the services of a classroom teacher, nurse, paraprofessional, physical therapist, mental health worker, or social worker. Home-based programs serve both children and family members, particularly those who are physically, socially, or culturally isolated; they provide in-home educational services to the handicapped or may address parent-child relationships and family functioning. Head Start has a home-based component and over the years programs have developed to assist parents in developing early childhood education skills and understanding the role of parents as educators. Home-based educators may assist the family in financial planning, nutrition, and access to community services. As stated by Gestwicki (1996),

> (H)ome visits offer evidence of a teacher's interest in and care for the parent's child, and an opportunity for parents to play a more comfortable and dominant role while in their home setting. For teachers, it is another chance to reach out to families and an opportunity to experience a child's home environment and relationship first hand. For children, it is a chance to build a deeper personal relationship with a teacher in a secure home setting (p. 247).

Parental involvement in the education of their children has been shown to have a positive impact on student achievement. Home-based educational programs stress education, support, and involvement of parents in acquiring techniques to stimulate learning in their children at an early age and beyond. Home-based programs create bonds between the home and school that support student learning. They have a long-term positive impact on children's attitudes regarding school and academic achievement. "Students are more likely to be successful if they see their parents as teachers, hear that their families want them to learn what their teachers teach at school, and say that the things they learn at home are important" (Epstein, 2001, p. 261).

School Administrator and Teacher Roles in Home-Based Programs

School administrators and teachers should be aware of not only the positive impact these home-based services provide to families, but also the requirement to provide these educational services under certain circumstances. Home-based instruction may be required as part of a handicapped child's individual educational plan (IEP) to remain in compliance with the *Individuals with Disabilities Education Improvement Act* or as required under *Section 504 of the Americans with Disabilities Act* for a student who is hospitalized or experiencing health problems. It may also be required in some cases related to suspension or expulsion of a student from the regular school setting, during incarceration, or residential placement of a student. A possible resource for school administrators and teachers required to offer services to students outside of the school setting is Education, Inc. (Education, Inc., 2013), which provides educational services in conjunction with school districts for children in hospitals, residential and behavioral health centers, and homebound programs.

Virtual and Blended Education

Information technology has brought the world into the classroom via the World Wide Web. Virtual field trips offer new opportunities for students to see places and visit museums around the world. It is now possible to complete a full curriculum and gain a high school diploma via the Internet. The demand for on-line courses continues to increase as students opt to take courses via the Internet and receive "virtual" credit for a course that has been approved for credit by a school district or state. Increasingly, instructional technology is utilized in classrooms across the nation to support teaching and learning. Students learn using pads, phones, pods, tablets and similar devices, using computers, and through webinars, podcasts, and video conferencing. These tools of instruction go well beyond the PowerPoint learning modules and videos regularly incorporated in classroom instruction and utilized in the past as part of on-line learning . Virtual classrooms are available to school districts through private agencies such as *Education 2020*, which has developed tutorials that can be taken at a student's own pace, labs that are hosted by a teacher inside the classroom ready to assist if students have additional questions, and courses that can be tailored to fit a district's curriculum. State educational agencies and school districts have sanctioned K–12 virtual learning toward graduation at both the elementary and secondary school levels through complete virtual instructional programs where the student never sets foot on school grounds or in blended learning programs in which virtual learning is combined with in-class instruction. Edgenuity, Inc. (2011), formally *Education 2020*, has moved forward to keep pace with the rapid changes in technology and instructional technology. Edgenuity, Inc. provides virtual instruction and professional development for K–12 students, higher education, teachers, and technical education. The company's curriculum solutions site demonstrates the variety of educational resources available including the core curriculum, career and technical education, and credit recovery. Instructional programs for incarcerated youth, English language learners, and special needs students are also available. Virtual lessons and video lessons are available for the classroom teacher to enable the teacher to move more freely through the classroom to deliver one-on-one instruction to students (Edgenuity, Inc., 2013).

Distance Education

Distance education provides students in rural schools an opportunity to engage in coursework not regularly offered in their schools. The lack of course offerings is generally due to financial constraints or lack of instructors qualified to teach courses such as advanced trigonometry, physics, or a specific foreign language. *No Child Left Behind* provides funding for distance education to rural school districts to ensure that students in isolated geographic areas have equal educational opportunities to engage in advanced placement courses, foreign language instruction,

English language acquisition, or courses regularly offered in schools across the nation. Distance learning is a resource for students and teachers alike. Distance education enables students to see and interact with instructors via satellite communication networks and the Internet. Businesses have long used telecommunication links for conferences. This same technology is available to school districts to interface with other schools, universities, businesses, learning centers, museums, and a variety of locations around the world. The merging of television, telecommunications, and computing has opened the door to education in an interactive context, where students and teachers can actively participate together in learning experiences.

> This merging of the telecommunications and computer industries should also make real-time conferencing (especially videoconferencing) a more viable form of interaction, particularly if digital televisions can be used as the conferencing device. . . . This would enhance student and teacher interaction in online courses as well as make remote guest participation easier and more interesting (Kearsley, 2000).

We have seen many changes in schools and communities around the world with the introduction of computer technologies. As the 21st century progresses, advances in the fields of technology coupled with increased access and use in schools and homes will bring many changes to the education of children and youth. It is imperative that school districts plan strategically to keep pace with the rapidly growing technologies and changes they will make in the way we teach and learn.

College- and Career-Ready Programs

A Blueprint for Reform: The Reauthorization of the Elementary and Secondary Education Act (hereafter referred to as Blueprint) was developed as part of the American Recovery and Reinvestment Act of 2009 (U.S. Government, 2009). In general, the Blueprint addresses college- and career-ready programs, English language learners, safe and healthy students, diverse learners, innovation, and preparation and accountability of teachers and school leaders (U.S. Government, 2010a):

> This blueprint builds on the significant reforms already made in response to the American Recovery and Reinvestment Act of 2009 around four areas: (1) Improving teacher and principal effectiveness; (2) Providing information to families to help them evaluate and improve their children's schools; (3) Implementing college- and career-ready standards; and (4) Improving student learning and achievement in America's lowest-performing schools by providing intensive support and effective interventions (U.S. Government, 2010a)

The Blueprint supports college- and career-ready standards, rewarding progress and success of schools in academic preparation of students and turning around the lowest performing schools in an effort to have all youth prepared with the essential academic skills needed to enter and be successful in college. The Blueprint addresses academic standards and programs at the elementary and secondary school levels, encourages the development of rigorous state-developed standards in English language arts and mathematics, better support for states, districts, and schools, and addresses the needs of low-income students, English Learners, minority students and students with disabilities. The main areas of focus are:

- College and career ready standards
- Rigorous and fair accountability and support at every level
- Measuring and supporting schools, districts, and states
- Building capacity for support at every level
- Fostering comparability and equity at every level
- Assessing accountability
- School turnaround grants (U.S. Government, 2010b).

Early College and Five Year Programs

Tech-prep School to Work programs, part of the Goals 2000: Educate America Act (U.S. Government, 1994a), had its roots in the career and vocational programs of the 1970s and early 1980s. Evolving from historical vocational programs and currently supported through the Carl. D. Perkins Career Preparation Education Reform Act of 1995 (U. S. Congress, 1995), these programs were developed to provide equal vocational education opportunities for historically underserved student populations. Part of the Act was a 2+2 program allowing student in their junior year of high school to begin a program of study eventually leading to a community college associate degree.

> Tech-prep formulates a different kind of technical education curriculum first planned for the non-college-bound student but later evolved to include all students. It consists of a planned sequence of study for a technical field over 4 years beginning in the junior year of high school. The sequence extends through the last 2 years of high school and on through 2 years of post-secondary occupational education or some type of apprenticeship arrangement of at least 2 years following secondary instruction, and culminates in certification or in an associate degree (Boschee, Beyer, Engleking, & Boschee, 1997a).

The current early-college programs and five-year programs mirror and enhance the structure of this earlier 2+2 program, creating opportunities for students to combine high school and community college courses and earn both a high school diploma and an associate degree. Like the vocational education programs of the 1970s and 1980s or the Tech-prep programs of the 1990s, these early-college programs support not only technical training in areas such as health services, construction skills, the service industry, and computer technology, but also provide the opportunity for a student to advance more quickly through high school and on to a four year college degree in a variety of academic areas.

The early-college programs depend very much on planned collaboration between K–12 schools and community colleges. This is critical to ensure that students are academically prepared to succeed in both two year community colleges and four year colleges and universities. The programs must be designed to reduce the number of remedial courses students may be required to take following graduation from high school, particularly in the academic areas of English language arts and mathematics, before moving on to regular college-level academic courses (Callan, Finney, Kirst, Usdan, & Venezia (2006). As stated in A Blueprint for Reform: Reauthorization of the Elementary and Secondary Education Act,

> Four of every 10 new college students, including half of those at 2-year institutions, take remedial courses, and many employers comment on the inadequate preparation of high school graduates (U. S. Government, 2010b)

This lack of student preparation connects directly to a need for instruction based on the K–12 state-developed and career-ready common core curriculum standards with its emphasis on mathematics and English language arts.

Adult Education

The increased number of parents who are not literate in the English language is beginning to change the complexion of instruction in school districts across the nation, particularly in areas with high immigrant populations. Schools are beginning to reach beyond the student in the classroom to provide literacy training for parents. Some schools are creating opportunities for parents to learn side-by-side with their children in the classroom. Others offer after- school, evening, and weekend classes for parents and adult community members. These efforts can have many positive results. Parents who become literate in the English language, furthering their own education and employment opportunities, also act as role models for their children. Secondly, English language acquisition allows parents to interact with school personnel in understanding and providing support to the education of their children. Implementing family education programs along with parent outreach and training assists parents in becoming active participants in the education of their children (Boschee, Beyer, Engelking, & Boschee, 1997b).

The *Bilingual Education Act of 1994* supported the correlation of materials and services to include the development of programs serving family education. Grants under this Act earmarked funds for implementing family education programs and parent outreach and training activities designed to encourage parents to become active participants in the education of their children (U. S. Government, 1994b). *The Adult Education and Family Literacy Act* (Title II of the Workforce Investment Act) authorizes funding for adult literacy education as a component of family literacy programs. The most common types of adult instruction supported through these grants are:

> adult basic education for basic literacy services for adults whose skills are below the eighth grade level; adult secondary education for services designed to prepare students to obtain a high school equivalency diploma, and English literacy services for adults with limited English proficiency (U. S. Department of Education, 2003, p. 37).

Adult education has moved beyond GED and job training, although the focus on language acquisition and employment skills has not lessened. The emphasis on broader education by K–12 school districts to adult learners has increased.

Role of the School Administrator

We have seen a variety of educational opportunities and options available to parents and students presented in previous sections of this chapter. In reviewing them, it should be obvious to that in the changing arena of education, the challenge to the public school administrator is competition, and marketing skills are one key to success. Choice programs are moving public education from a public-sector economy to a market-driven economy. Though there will still be district enrollment forecasting, it cannot always be depended upon, as in the past, for school planning, contract negotiations, and capital outlay expenditures. It will be more important than ever to collaborate with local and state government, business, industry, families, and community service agencies to ensure support for funding initiatives, coordinated services, and improved educational opportunities for all students.

Development of public relations and marketing skills by school administrators is essential to address the growing competition for student enrollment. Parents, community organizations, and businesses are calling for improved educational services for all students and assurances that students will graduate from school with the skills to perform in an increasingly competitive society. This will entail ensuring that all teachers are qualified to teach in the academic area to which they are assigned and in the incorporation of technology in instruction and learning to provide students with the highest quality education possible. Allocation of funds for professional development and regular upgrades in technology are essential to ensure that teachers and school administrators are kept current with the latest trends, research, and methodologies related to teaching and learning.

Summary

Parents have more options related to the education of their children. No longer should parents and students be held captive in a failing neighborhood school. No longer should students be instructed without the benefits of technological advances. There is greater choice and opportunity available in educational formats and settings than at any other time in the history of American education. A market economy is driving choice in educational opportunities, and the Internet has made these choices global in nature. Change is difficult. Yet, change is a constant, and we must all move, develop, and improve with change, looking toward the future and not clinging to the past. The structures of public education as we have known them have served students and the nation well. It would be disastrous not to build upon this strong foundation and to view and embrace the future of educational opportunities available to teachers and students.

Questions for Consideration

1. Describe and discuss both the advantages and disadvantages of charter schools.
2. Are vouchers and tax credits appropriate means of supporting school choice? Explain why or why not.
3. What do you envision education will look like in twenty-five years? Create a description with supporting rationale.
4. Should parental choice in educational formats be allowed or should all students be required to attend neighborhood schools? Explain and support your response.
5. Draw a comparison between NCLB and the Blueprint for Reform: Reauthorization of the Elementary and Secondary Education Act.

Case Study

Home Schooling and Public Education Programs

Teresa Salazar is the principal of Third Avenue Elementary School in City Central Public Schools, an urban district of moderate size. Like many urban districts, City Central struggles to provide for the varied learning and social needs of its students, who come from diverse linguistic, cultural, and racial backgrounds. Also similar to other urban school districts, Central City's special education classes and programs for English language learners are operating beyond full capacity, and resources are scarce. Teresa, however, has been very creative in her approach to providing the support necessary for all learners within her building. She has been able to establish partnerships with several businesses located within the city that provide the school with volunteers to serve as mentors and tutors for the students. In addition, one major corporation has donated expensive computer and technology equipment that the school would not otherwise be able to afford, and another business awarded grant monies to teachers within the school who are willing to develop and implement innovative educational programs.

Teresa has also made a concerted effort to include parents in as many aspects of school life as possible. Knowing that many parents were anxious about their own relative lack of education or difficulty communicating in English, Teresa rallied a small group of energetic teachers and active parents to help make other parents feel welcome and valuable within the school. This small initial effort has evolved into one of the district's most engaged group of parents. On any given day, mothers, fathers, and even grandparents can be found laughing and talking in the school's parent center while enjoying a cup of coffee and working on any number of projects for teachers while preschool children play at their feet. Teresa is in the process of trying to set up an arrangement by which students in the early childhood program at the local university come into the school and work with these preschool children as part of their field experience. She has also worked with the local high school principal to arrange for high school students to come to Third Avenue Elementary after school to run after-school clubs and activities. The high school students are offered service-learning credit for their effort, and both principals have been amazed at some of the interesting ideas these students have developed. Furthermore, it has solved two problems: many parents could not afford local after school care programs for their elementary school-age children, while the high school students often had nothing interesting or productive to do after school.

A new wrinkle has recently developed, however, that has left Teresa feeling irritated and impatient. A small but growing group of parents within the school's boundaries has chosen to home-school their children, citing dangerous school environments, failing academic standards, and lack of parental input into curriculum decisions. These parents banded together to provide cooperative home schooling and recently began to demand services for their children that are offered through Third Avenue Elementary. For example, one parent believes that her daughter has dyslexia and wants a full evaluation and access to specialized reading instruction through the school's resource room. Other parents want to bring their children to join the after-school clubs run by the high school students. Several parents have begun to argue that their children qualify for the school's free breakfast and lunch program as legal residents of the school zone, whether they are actually in attendance or not. The final straw for Teresa came when the parents found out about a school-business partnership grant that was awarded to the music teacher. This grant enabled him to obtain the instruments and release time necessary to create a small orchestra class for a group of interested upper-elementary students and the home-schooling parents have demanded that their children be allowed to participate.

Teresa feels that this group has, by virtue of their choice to home school their children, communicated their disdain for public education and their distrust of the local school environment. She and her staff have worked tirelessly to enhance school-community-family relationships and improve the quality of education provided to students within the school's zone. Teresa resents the fact that these parents, as home school parents, have not participated in any of the volunteer opportunities at the school or otherwise contributed to the development of the programs, but now wish to benefit from them. These parents, in Teresa's view, have repeatedly "slandered" Third Avenue Elementary as a "failing school," claiming that they are left with no choice but to home school their children. At this point, she has little sympathy for their needs and no intention of giving in to their demands.

Questions for Discussion

1. What legal or ethical principles are involved in the foregoing scenario?

2. Do these parents, in fact, have a right to the all of the services and programs they are demanding? Which, if any, are they entitled to?

3. What are some ways that Teresa, with the help of school faculty and parents, can improve the relationship with this group of parents?

4. Is this a local problem or is it indicative of a more widespread problem? What is the root cause of the growing home-schooling phenomenon?

References

Alexander, K. & Alexander, M. D. (2005). *American Public School Law* (6th ed.). Belmont, CA: Thompson West.

Association for Supervision and Curriculum Development (1990). *Public schools of choice: ASCD issues analysis.* Alexandria, VA: Author.

Barr, R. D. & Parrett, W. H. (1995). *Hope at last for at-risk youth.* Boston, Allyn & Bacon.

Boschee, F., Beyer, B. M., Engelking, J. L., & Boschee, M. A. (1997a). *Special and compensatory programs: The administrator's role.* Lancaster, PA: Technomic Publishing Co., Inc.

Boschee, F., Beyer, B. M., Engelking, J. L., & Boschee, M. A. (1997b). *Special and compensatory programs: The administrator's role.* Lancaster, PA: Technomic Publishing Co., Inc.

Brown v. Board of Education of Topeka, 347 U.S. 483, 74 S.Ct. 686 (1954).

Callan, P. M., Finney, J. E., Kirst, M. W., Usdan, M. D., Venezia, A. (2006). *Claiming common ground: State policymaking for improving college readiness and success.* National Center Report #06-1. The National Center for Public Policy and Higher Education.

Council of Organizations of Others for Education about Parochiaid v. Governor, 455 Mich. 557, 566 N. W.2nd 208 (1997).

Dell'Angela, T. & Washburn, G. (2004). *Daley set to remake troubled schools.* (2004, June 25). Chicago Tribune, pp. A1. A22.

Edgenuity, Inc. (2011). *Edgenuity, Inc: Solutions.* Retrieved from http://www.edgenuity.com/Solutions

Edison Schools (2004). *Edison schools: Company profile.* Retrieved from http://www.edisonproject.com/overview/ovO.html

educate, inc. (2004a). *Inside view.* Retrieved from http://www.insideview.com/directory/educate-inc

educate, inc. (2004b). *Connections academy.* Retrieved from http://www.connectionsacademy.com

Education, Inc. (2003). *Sylvan learning.* Retrieved from http://tutoring.sylvanlearning.com/

Education, Inc. (2013). *Home page.* Retrieved from http://www.educationinc.us/

Education, Inc. (2013). *Inside view.* Retrieved from http://www.insideview.com/directory/educate-inc

Epstein, J. L. (2001). *School, family, and community partnerships: Preparing educators and improving schools.* Boulder, CO: Westview Press.

Florida Department of Education (2004a). *Florida School Choice: Opportunity Scholarship Program.* Retrieved from http://www.opportunityschools.org/Info/OSP/

Florida Department of Education (2004b). *Florida School Choice: Opportunity Scholarship Program.* Retrieved from http://www.opportunityschools.org/Info/McKay/

Florida Department of Education (2004c). *Statement from Governor Jeb Bush regarding 8/5/2002 ruling against Florida's opportunity scholarships.* Retrieved from http://www.opportunityschools.org/Info/OSP/statement.asp

Gestwicki, C. (1996). *Home, school and community relations (3rd ed.).* Albany, NY: Delmar Publishers.

Grossman, Kate N. (2004). *Daley unveils plan to shut some schools to copy success stories.* (2004, June 25). Chicago Sun-Times, METRO, p. 20.

Hirsch, E. & Samuelsen, S. (1999). Turning away from public education. *National Council of State Legislatures,* September, 12–16.

Home School Legal Defense Association (2004). Retrieved from http://www.hslda.org/research.

Individuals with Disabilities Education Act. Pub. L. No.101-476, 20 U.S.C. Chapter 33. Amended by Pub.L. No.105-17 in June, 1997.

Jackson v. Benson, 578 N.W.2nd 602 (Wis.1998).

Kearsley, G. (2000). *Online education: Learning and teaching in cyberspace.* Belmont, CA: Wadsworth/Thomas Learning.

Kotterman v. Killian, 193 Ariz. 273, 972 P.2nd 606 (1999).

Kowalski, T. J. (2003). *Contemporary school administration: An introduction* (2nd ed.). Boston: Allyn & Bacon

Lemon v. Kurtzman, 403 U.S. 602, 91 S.Ct. 2105 (1971).

McNergney, R. F., & Herbert, J. M. (1995). *Foundations of education: The challenge of professional practice.* Boston: Allyn and Bacon.

National Commission on Excellence (1983). *A nation at risk: The imperative for educational reform.* Washington, DC: U.S. Government Printing Office.

National Alliance for Public Charter Schools (2008-2013). *The public charter schools dashboard: A com-*

prehensive data resource from the national alliance for public charter schools. Retrieved from http://dashboard.publiccharters.org/dashboard/performance/year/2011

National Association of Charter School Authorizers (2013). *Quality charter schools.* Retrieved from http://www.qualitycharters.org/index.php

National Charter Schools Resource Center (2013). *Back to school tallies: Estimated number of public charter schools, 2011–2012.* Retrieved from http://www.charterschoolcenter.org/resource/back-school-tallies-estimated-number-public-charter-schools-2011-2012

Nelson, F. H., Rosenberg, B., & Van Meter, N. (2004). *Charter School Achievement on the 2003 National Assessment of Educational Progress.* Washington, DC: American Federation of Teachers.

Section 504 of the Rehabilitation Act of 1973 as Amended through 1998. 34 C.F.R. 104.34.

Short, P.M., & Greer, J. T. (1997). *Leadership in empowered schools: Themes from innovative efforts.* Upper Saddle River, NJ: Merrill, an imprint of Prentice Hall.

U.S. Congress. House. Committee on Economic and Educational Opportunities. (1995). *Carl D. Perkins career preparation education reform act of 1995.* Hearing. 104th Congress, 1st session.

U.S. Department of Education (2003). *Guidance for the William F. Goodling even start family literacy programs.* Part B, Subpart 3 of Title I of the Elementary and Secondary Education Act (ESEA). Retrieved from http://www.ed.gov/policy/elsec/guid/evenstartguidance02.doc.

U.S. Department of Education, National Center for Education Statistics. (2012). *The condition of education 2012* (NCES 2012–045),Indicator 4. Retrieved from http://nces.ed.gov/fastfacts/display.asp?id=30

U.S. Government (1994a) *Goals 2000: Educate America act.* 20 USC 5801. Washington, DC: U.S. Government Printing Office.

U.S. Government (1994b). *Improving America's schools act of 1995. Reauthorizing the Elementary and Secondary Education Act of 1965.* (P.L. 103-382). Title VII, Part A, Sec. 7113(b)(2)(B). Washington, DC: Government Printing Office.

U.S. Government (2002). *No child left behind act of 2001: Reauthorization of the elementary and secondary education act of 1965* (P.L. 107-110). Washington, DC: U.S. Government Printing Office.

U.S. Government (2009). *American recovery and reinvestment act of 2009.* Retrieved from http://www2.ed.gov/policy/gen/leg/recovery/factsheet/overview.html

U.S. Government (2010a). *A blueprint for reform: The reauthorization of the elementary and secondary education act.* Retrieved from http://www2.ed.gov/policy/elsec/leg/blueprint/publicationtoc.html

U.S. Government (2010b). *A blueprint for reform: The reauthorization of the elementary and secondary education act.* Retrieved from http://www2.ed.gov/policy/elsec/leg/blueprint/publication_pg4.html#part4

Winter, G. (2004). *Florida court rules against religious school vouchers.* (2004, August 17). New York Times, p. 15.

Zelman v. Simmons-Harris, 536 U.S. 639, 122 S. Ct. 2460 (2002).

CHAPTER 7

Applied Educational Programs

Introduction

THERE is a growing tendency among teachers, administrators, parents, and even students involved in American public education to view the best, if not the only, path to a successful life as the attainment of a four-year college degree. Despite this general outlook, logically and factually flawed as it is, there exist in most public schools today programs that offer students, especially those in high school, opportunities for learning beyond traditional academic curricula. In fact, the inclusion of applied curricula and programs in public schools in the United States dates back to the turn of the 20th century, and debates regarding the usefulness, need, and proper venue for such programs have continued since.

This chapter will delve into the history of applied educational programs, which denote vocational, industrial arts, domestic science, technical skills training, service learning, school-to-work, and career education programs in order to understand the current status of such programs. Next, future trends in applied educational programs will be considered in terms of statistical analysis and research, conceptual models and examples of innovative programs in place throughout the country. Additionally, legal issues involved in applied educational program provision within the public school system as well as sources of funding for such programs will be discussed. Finally, administrative considerations and personnel issues will be outlined in light of the current state and future trends of these programs.

History of Applied Education Programs

At their inception, American high schools served primarily students whose families were well-off financially and socially. Curricula emphasized classical studies and liberal arts, and prior to the turn of the 20th century, fewer than ten percent of 14–17 year olds were enrolled in a school of any kind (Steinberg, 2002). However, several historical and social trends then converged during the early part of the 20th century to change the face of secondary education in the United States.

Historical and Societal Changes

Within a burgeoning economy based on industry, income provided by adolescents was no longer a necessity for many families. Additionally, as the economy moved from an agricultural to an industrial base, there were fewer opportunities for work through apprenticeships, and the need for skilled and reliable labor steadily increased as technology became more complex. Finally, child labor laws were developed out of concern for the health and safety of children and adolescents working in factories as well as the need for labor organizations to protect the security of adult employment. Along with these changes resulting from industrialization were increases in immigration and urbanization and, consequently, a rise in urban slums and substandard tenement housing, overcrowded neighborhoods, crime, and, for many, a sense of alienation and loss of community (Hunt, 1993).

Toward a New Concept of High Schools in America

These societal and cultural shifts resulted in changes in the way public education was viewed. The desire to improve living conditions for the masses and to ensure the assimilation of immigrants into American culture along with the pressing need to somehow occupy and supervise children and adolescents no longer eligible to work prompted the initiation of the first compulsory education laws in virtually every state. With these compulsory education laws came increased diversity among students attending high school, and it was thought that schools for the general public needed to involve not just intellectual and academic skills as had been the focus in previous decades, but training for work and citizenship as well. Consequently, the concept of the comprehensive high school in which general education (which later included such courses as music, art, physical education, health, and other courses designed to prepare adolescents for family, work, and leisure), college preparation, and vocational education were all offered within a single institution. The comprehensive high school, a concept which prevails today, resulted in a substantial increase of 600% in the number of students graduating from high school in a relatively short period of time (Santrock, 2003).

Early Support for Vocational Education Programs

As the concept of secondary education expanded, pressure from a variety of groups (including but not limited to local businesses, labor organizations, and women's advocacy groups) pushed schools to include training in vocational skills. Initially, vocational training programs at the secondary level were often limited to manual skills training (Kantor & Lowe, 2000); however, the programs quickly broadened in scope to include agricultural education, home economics, industrial arts, and commercial education (Kliebard, 1999). The impetus for the development and maintenance of such programs is often attributed to a need for schools to meet the needs of students with increasingly diverse needs, aptitudes, and backgrounds. However, other scholars have pointed out evidence of other motives. In their review of Kliebard's work, Kantor and Lowe discuss several, if not competing then at least divergent, views that may have led in part to the widespread appeal of vocational education. Some of these notions include the following:

- the desire of business leaders to curb the growing power of organized labor by gaining control of the labor market through publicly funded training;
- the growth of an initially small but powerful vocational education lobby group in the form of National Society for the Promotion of Industrial Education (NSPIE), later the American Vocational Association (AVA);
- the reinforcement of the American cultural values of hard work and the dignity of manual labor;
- a growing belief that schools must serve a custodial function in keeping otherwise errant youth off the streets and the corollary belief that such youth would not be capable of academic rigor and would, instead, benefit most from specific labor skills that would lead directly to employment upon graduation;

- movement toward "scientifically" oriented curricula that was utilitarian in nature and emphasized the justification of all school subjects in terms of vocational expediency;
- the idea that differentiated educational systems (e.g., college preparation, general, commercial, vocational) promoted social justice and democratic ideals by preparing all students for their probable economic futures (Kantor & Lowe 2000).

Regardless of the reasons for its enthusiastic reception across public, private, and education sectors, one point seems to be clear from comprehensive reviews of the literature on vocational education: trade and industrial education generally failed to attract large numbers of students and, for those who did graduate from such programs, the economic payoff was limited at best (Kantor & Lowe, 2000). In general, students who enrolled in high school did so in an effort to avoid factory work and manual labor, for which high school training was unnecessary as a condition for employment. Instead, increased availability of "white-collar" business and clerical occupations drew more students into the commercial education programs. Thus, commercial education programs are often considered to represent true success in the early effort to provide applied educational programs. While industrial skills were difficult to transmit in a high school classroom setting, the same setting could easily simulate the conditions and climate of an office. Thus, graduates of these programs were better trained for immediate employment and the concomitant trend of basing hiring decisions on educational credentials for business and professional occupations ensured the relevance and appropriateness of this type of training.

Overall, the shift in focus of American high schools over the past century has added fuel to the fire regarding the ultimate purpose of public education. Some, including Kliebard (1999), argue that a focus on the occupational preparation of students has undermined the humanistic conception of education and has resulted in the subordination of intellectual, moral, and democratic development. Others, such as Kantor & Lowe (2000), however, argue that the ideal of a purely intellectual and academic curriculum unconnected in any way to occupational preparation is fiction. Indeed, as these authors point out, ". . . even as kitchens, workshops, and commercial classes made their way into the high schools across the country, English, math, science, social studies, and other academic subjects did not simply disappear" (p. 138). Similarly, few if any students pursued a purely vocational course of study devoid of any core academic subjects. The longstanding and continuing debate as to the consequences of the "vocationalization" of American secondary education is one not likely to be resolved at any time but, indeed, may provide a context for understanding applied education in its present and projected forms.

Current Status of Applied Educational Programs

From the beginnings of applied educational programs, which provided training in a variety of practical skills such as farming, factory work, clerical and secretarial positions, and manual labor, student enrollment in these "tracks" steadily increased until it reached a peak between the 1960s and 1970s, after which enrollment declined until the early part of the 1990s. Existing programs seemed to lose relevance and validity as technology and an information-based economy exploded. Characterization of vocational and career education as a "dummy" track and a dumping ground for academically incapable students, prevailed in society. As a result, many students were counseled by well-intended but often misguided educators to obtain a four-year college degree (Gray, 1996). This type of thinking, however, flies in the face of a grim reality.

Research/Statistical Outlook

Data from the National Center for Educational Statistics (NCES) indicate that only about one-third of high school graduates possess the necessary coursework, grades, and test scores for success in a typical four-year college. While increased admission rates may seem to contradict this finding, Gray (1996) attributed this to a decline in the population of adolescents with a concomitant increase in the number of four-year colleges. Additionally, colleges and universities over time have reduced, and in some cases, eliminated some admission requirements (such as the requirement for foreign languages, higher level math courses, etc.) while substantially increasing the number and range of remedial courses offered. Furthermore, only 58% of students who enrolled in four-year institutions graduated within six years (NCIS, 2012). While there are varying explanations for this drop-out rate, inadequate high-school preparation and disconnection between student aptitudes and interests and the college curriculum are significant factors for some. For many who do graduate, the promise of economic security and professional status is left unfulfilled. Graduates of four-year institutions, especially those whose academic programs did not prepare them with specific job skills, face a difficult labor market, according to Gray (1996). These young adults are often underemployed (e.g., working in a job that does not require a college degree), working in jobs that are unrelated to their field of study, or struggling to find any employment at all. It is argued, therefore, that aspiration to a four-year institution is appropriate only for some students and that earning a baccalaureate degree is a one-size-fits-all solution to the future should be abandoned.

Rationale for a Renewed Approach to Applied Educational Programs

The perception of and attitude toward applied educational programs in education and society at large have engendered a view that such programs serve only to hold students back from their full potential as both learners and future wage earners. Indeed, the National Assessment of Vocational Education (NAVE, 2004) cited studies demonstrating that vocational education programs resulted in improved employment outlook in the short-term but contributed neither to academic achievement nor enrollment in post-secondary education. As a result, educators and parents alike push adolescents into college-bound educational tracks without regard to their interest, aptitude, and preparation level. School districts nationwide have allowed vocational and applied educational programs to stagnate and, in some areas, have eliminated them altogether. Such trends foster a narrow view of the purpose of public education in general and the comprehensive high school in particular, and in effect, limit the range of options for students, directly impacting their future. Fortunately, these and other issues have come to the forefront in recent years and the need to overhaul vocational education and to offer more relevant and up-to-date programs to students are now widely recognized. For the past decade, federal vocational education policy has placed priority on ensuring that secondary vocational education students are academically well prepared for careers and success in post-secondary education. For some districts and schools, meeting this objective will require substantial changes, including new policies or requirements, shifts in instructional methods, or modifications to course content.

While states vary in the content and names of applied educational programs, most fall under fairly standard categories. Table 7.1 provides an example of the broad clusters or pathways typically offered through applied educational programs, as well as common courses of study subsumed under each, the high school academic coursework typically required, and affiliated student organizations. One issue that has been noted by several researchers in the field (e.g., Drueckhammer, 2001) is that urban school districts often have more students enrolled in applied programs and more funding available, ensuring a wide range of options. These districts have increasingly reorganized their structure into academies that focus on a particular cluster. Rural districts, on the other hand, often lack both enrollment and resources, and are thus limited in the program options available. However, small suburban and rural districts are increasingly forming consortia

Table 7.1. Common Career Paths.

Career Pathway	Career Opportunities/Course of Study	Common Academic Requirements	Affiliated Student Organizations
Arts & Communications	Graphic Arts Multimedia Animation	General Math Computer Literacy Language Arts Communications	Skills USA VICA
Business Management, Marketing, and Technology	Business Management and Ownership Database Administration/Programming E-Commerce Network Administration/PC Support Entertainment/Tourism Management Real Estate/Property Management Finance Web Development	Business Business Math/Algebra Communications Economics Accounting Composition Social Studies Computer Literacy	Professionals of America Business Professions of America Skills USA VICA
Engineering, Manufacturing, and Industrial Technology	Plastics Metal Working Automation Computer Aided Drafting/Design (CAD) Industrial Electricity Electronics Welding Photonics Textiles Computer Systems Environmental Technology Building Maintenance Services Carpentry Masonry HVAC/R Plumbing Automotive Technology Collision Repair/Refinishing Technology Marine Technology Medium/Heavy Truck & Equipment Small Engine/Recreational Vehicles Aircraft/Aerospace Motocycle Technology	Algebra Geometry Triconometry Technical Writing Science	Skills VICA

(continued)

127

Table 7.1 (continued). Common Career Paths.

Career Pathway	Career Opportunities/Course of Study	Common Academic Requirements	Affiliated Student Organizations
Health Sciences	Diagnostic Therapeutic Informational Environmental	Algebra Advanced Math Biology Chemistry Language Arts Communications Computer Literacy	Health Ocupations Students of America Health Opportunities for Today and Tomorrow
Human Services	Culinary Arts/Hospitality Cosmetology Child Care Nutrition Science	Accounting Biology Chemistry Computer Literacy English Math (general, business, algebra	Skills USA VICA
Agricultural Sciences and Natural Resources	Agribusiness/Marketing Animal Science Bio-Technology Design Science Environmental Science Horticultural Science	Biology Chemistry Computer Science Earth Science Geography Intermidiate Math Language Arts Physical Science	Future Farmers of America Skills USAVICA

with other districts as well as local community colleges in an effort to expand program options and improve the quality of educational programming. Additionally, regional education centers or intermediate school districts in many states have begun to take over the responsibility of coordinating efforts within the state and overseeing program development and evaluation statewide.

Future Trends in Applied Educational Programs

After the publication of the widely read report, *Vocational Education in the United States: Toward the Year 2000* (Levesque, Lauen, Teitelbaum, Alt, & Librera, 2000), a general shift occurred in vocational education. A trend took place that shifted the focus away from preparation for entry-level jobs and toward the development of academic, vocational, and technical skills for a wider range of students and for a broader spectrum of occupational levels. Rather than offering self-contained training programs for specific jobs, vocational education increasingly utilizes career paths that encompass both scope and sequence that cover a wide range of occupations and levels of training. Using this approach, students are prepared to enter a field at a variety of levels and can see clearly where additional training and education can take them within the field. Further, more students are encouraged to participate in the programs, and the academic quality of vocational and applied programs has improved substantially. Finally, this model eliminates the "either-or" mentality that presupposes students will obtain vocational training or attend college (Lozada, 1995).

Models of Reform and Innovative Programs

The career pathways approach to vocational and applied education is not without critics. Some arguments against the approach include its implicit need for students to decide on a career path early in life and a decline of academic quality in the "applied" core content. Proponents of the approach point to statistics that indicate overall improvement in student attendance, graduation rates, GPA, standardized test scores, and subsequent employment or enrollment in post-secondary education/training. Additionally, they point out that adolescents make decisions every day that will ultimately impact their future, and that secondary students often opt for college with little if any thought as to their own career goals. Instead, they argue, career pathways are broad and flexible enough to allow students to obtain the skills necessary for a given occupation but still encourage adolescents to think about their future and to see the relevance of core academic subjects to a broad career path. Most programs offer students the option of transferring to a different career pathway or back to their home school if they feel they have made a mistake (Lozado, 1995).

In terms of the core academic subjects, programs vary the content depending upon the needs of the career path. Most other programs, however, have a single core course through which students apply the content in a meaningful way to their own career cluster. Therefore, while a high school chemistry class may be uniform in broad content, students may apply the skills and knowledge to various projects depending upon whether their focus is on cosmetology, agricultural science, or medical laboratory technology. As pointed out by Gallagher (1995), equity in academic preparation does not consist of giving the same material to all students regardless of aptitude or vocational interest. Instead, equity means giving students what is needed most to support their future aspirations (p. 217) and avoiding the mediocrity that results from trying to force all students to conform to a single academic standard.

Examples of successful programs that have combined high academic standards with occupational training and hands-on experiences are not new. In 1972, a heart surgeon Michael E. De-Bakey partnered with Baylor College of Medicine in Houston, Texas to form DeBakey High School, the first in the world to offer applied programming in health professions. Entrance to this high school was and is very competitive and graduates have a rate of enrollment in medical school significantly higher than the national average. Not all programs have such illustrious beginnings, however. A county vocational-technical center in Sussex County, Delaware had been seen by the community as more of an alternative for disruptive students than for those interested in learning job skills. Standardized test scores of the dwindling number of students enrolled were among the lowest in the state, and the curricula and technology skills of the teachers had stagnated. Then, a massive restructuring in the late 1980s brought about significant changes that resulted in opening Sussex Tech, an innovative facility serving students in grades 9–12. Currently, the entire K–12 school district has embraced the philosophy of technical education and is now Sussex Technical School District (2013). Its mission is to provide students with both rigorous academic content and training toward a specific career path, consolidated into four clusters of programming: automotive technologies; communication and information technologies; health and human services; and industrial / engineering technologies. Another example is Turner Tech, part of the Miami-Dade County School District that encompasses seven career academies and offers academically challenging curricula with innovative and hands-on technical training. The seven Academies include: Criminal Justice; Entertainment Technology; Finance; Information Technology and Entrepreneurship; Medical Science; Urban Construction, Management Technology, & Urban Planning Architecture; Veterinary Science and Agriculture Technology. This school requires students to commit to earning both a high school diploma as well as an industry-recognized certificate in one of the seven areas listed above (Turner Technical High School, 2012). All three are examples of an increasing recognition that, in order to prepare students adequately, applied educational programs must offer relevant hands-on learning experiences, direct field experiences, and real-world applications of English, math, and science (Roberts, 1999).

Another instance of innovative programming is the Gage Park High School Equipment and Technology Institute, a school-within- a-school approach to applied education. The program combines honors-level core academics with state-of-the-art technical training and a guaranteed future job. The institute is sponsored by the Associated Equipment Distributors Foundation (AED) and offers the predominantly low-income SES students an opportunity to select a career pathway along with college-level computer courses, job shadowing, corporate mentoring, and a paid internship with one of 40 participating Illinois employers during their senior year (Clark, 1999; Gage Park High School, 2013).

Eastern Technical High School in Baltimore, Maryland, revised its technical mission from the 1970s model in which it had become entrenched by combining vision and collaboration with community colleges, universities, and most importantly, dozens of major corporations. Results of this effort are clear; the percentage of Eastern Tech students meeting University of Maryland's entrance requirements rose from less than one percent in the early 1990s to 87% in 1999. The average daily attendance rate is currently reported at 97% and admission to the institute has become extremely competitive. School districts must approach such collaborations cautiously, however. The Ecole des Metiers de l'Aerospatiale de Montreal (EMAM), a high school in Montreal, Canada, is an example of what can become a highly contentious approach to applied education. In the early 1990s, high school drop-out rates in the province were as high as 40% and vocational education was underfunded and stigmatized. The school board began cooperating with the Center for Aerospace Manpower Activities in Quebec (CAMAQ), an aerospace industry group representing 13 large companies and 4 major unions, to develop a high school that would closely simulate the aerospace industry and would meet the growing demand for skilled aerospace technicians. As planning for the new high school began, funding poured in from the federal grants obtained by CAMAQ, Quebec's Ministry of Education, Montreal's school board, and equipment donations from local companies. From the outset, however, the school board was in conflict with CAMAQ over such issues as class size, manipulation of courses to meet industry hiring needs, and drug testing for incoming students. By the time the school had been in operation for three years, there had already been major changes including a replacement of the school administrator and more control over the curriculum by the companies involved. Because students had to have completed three years of secondary school before enrolling, there was little if any emphasis on academics, and students were encouraged to leave the institution to work directly for sponsor companies rather than seek further education or training. In particular, concerns among students existed about an over-reliance and tendency to capitulate to the needs of a few local companies at the expense of the best interests of its students. Nevertheless, EMAM is considered by many to be an example of an innovative approach to applied education (Litvin, 2000).

Another concern that has increasingly been raised is the influx of high-achieving students into vocational programs. The Southern Regional Education Board's High Schools that Work initiative has boosted the academic content of applied and vocational programs in hundreds of programs across more than 22 states to include college preparatory coursework, especially advanced mathematics and science courses. High-tech programs such as electronics, aviation, digital television production, computer network administration, and radiologic technology are now being offered along with more traditional vocational programs such as automotive technology. As a result, some of the brightest and most highly motivated students are now entering these programs. Critics of these programs have pointed out several issues. In some cases, the home schools of students opting for career academies lose funding from per-pupil allotments (not to mention high scores on state-mandated tests!), and increasing competition to enroll in such schools limits the opportunities of students for whom vocational education was originally designed (Ries, 2000). Nevertheless, as pointed out by Kantor and Lowe (2000), such criticisms are troubling in that they assume that certain students are bound for particular occupational destinies, and that high-level academic coursework is beyond the grasp of students traditionally enrolled in vocational programs.

It is clear that the approach to applied educational programs in the United States has been altered to meet the demands of a new century. The focus of education continues to shift toward "increasing the nation's competitiveness in international markets, reducing social waste and economic inefficiency, and training cooperative and socially-skilled workers" (Kantor & Lowe, 2000, p. 140), and, therefore, integration of core academic and technical skills and contextually-bound learning for all students will continue to prevail. What was once essentially a separate track for students needing alternatives to the traditional academic content of high school, applied educational programs have become the crown jewel of many school districts. By embedding curricular content into viable career pathways, these programs have opened doors to the future for many students of all academic abilities. This trend has extended beyond the high school into middle schools (Cutshall, 2003) and even elementary schools in the form of career pathways awareness instruction in many states. Thus, as applied educational programs become more prevalent at all levels of education, issues of funding, administration, and personnel are key to successful implementation. These issues will be explored in the sections that follow.

Legislation and Funding Sources

Once the push to develop and implement vocational training programs in the public schools gained momentum, there was a resulting need for increased funding, which, in turn, propagated mandates for vocational programming. In 1906, the National Society for the Promotion of Industrial Education (NSPIE), mentioned earlier, was organized, and a board comprised manufacturers, educators, representatives of organized labor and social workers was elected. The major political objectives of the NSPIE were to unify throughout the country the move toward vocational education and to secure federal funding. To this end, a presentation was sent to Congress that stressed the importance of vocational education to the economic welfare of the nation (Roberts, 2001). The on-going efforts of the NSPIE to secure federal funding eventually culminated in the

Smith-Hughes Vocational Education Act of 1917. This act provided federal appropriations to states to support part-time and full-time vocational education in agriculture, trades and industry education, and homemaking at the junior and senior high school levels (Drueckhammer, 2001; Kantor & Lowe, 2000).

Since the passage of the *Smith-Hughes Act*, other acts have been passed that increased funding and expanded both the scope of vocational education programs as well as the range of participants. For example, the *George-Barden Act of 1946* permitted funding for the guidance and training of participants not otherwise enrolled in school and for student organizations that related to and supported vocational education efforts. Some examples of student organizations that existed by the 1950s included: Future Farmers of America, Future Homemakers of America, Future Business Leaders of America, Distributive Education Clubs of America, Health Occupations Students of America, and Vocational Industrial Clubs of America. During this era health occupations and increased career options for women began to emerge, and an amendment to the 1946 Act specifically addressed vocational education in practical nursing (Lozada, 1999). The *Vocational Education Act of 1963* extended existing vocational programs, developed new training efforts, and encouraged research and work-study programs. In addition, this Act was the first to explicitly fund business and office occupation training (although individual courses commonly existed prior to funding), and required that a minimum of 10% of funds used for home economics programs be used to train for employment outside the home. This Act was amended in 1968 in order to allocate funds specifically for the training of those with disabilities or from disadvantaged backgrounds and extended funding to post-secondary programs (Drueckhammer, 2001).

More recently, the *Carl D. Perkins Act of 1984*, which replaced existing vocational education legislation, marked a major change in the federal funding of vocational education programs. With the passage of this Act, the focus became improvement, innovation, and expansion of programs, and existing programs in the absence of such modifications were no longer funded. This Act further sought to ensure access to vocational training to single parents, displaced homemakers, individuals with limited English proficiency, and incarcerated persons as well as to eliminate sex bias and stereotyping within vocational education and training programs (Drueckhammer, 2001; Lozada, 1999). Funds from this legislation were distributed in the form of basic grants monies available to states, which could then distribute the funds to local districts as they saw fit.

The reauthorization of this legislation became the *Carl D. Perkins Vocational and Applied Technology Act of 1990*. This Act supported the development and promotion of programs that integrate academic and technical skills at the secondary and post-secondary levels, and encouraged cooperation and articulation agreements between secondary training programs and community colleges. The 1990 Act also required states to be more accountable for the use of funds, requiring that each state develop a system of performance standards and measures for secondary and post-secondary vocational education programs as well as requiring provisions for teacher training, curriculum development, and program evaluation. The Act, re-authorized in 1998 as the *Carl D. Perkins Vocational and Technical Education Act (Perkins III)*, included a separate authorization and funding for Tech Prep, programs that focus largely on integrating academic and technical programs, infusing technical goals and instruction into a variety of career preparation pathways, encouraging the transition to post-secondary training and education, and facilitating placements into the workforce or apprenticeship training programs. Key objectives of Perkins III include:

- Ensuring that career and technical education (CTE) programs complement the academic mission of No Child Left Behind and the workforce development mission of the Workforce Investment Act.
- Helping every youth in a CTE pathway receive a challenging academic education that prepares him or her for future education and career success.

- Ensuring that every CTE pathway in secondary schools offers a smooth transition into a postsecondary program leading to a technical certificate, associate or baccalaureate degree, apprenticeship, or a job.
- Making high-quality CTE pathways widely available to both youth and career-changing adults through a variety of institutions and delivery models.
- Connecting CTE pathways to workforce investment systems to strengthen national and regional workforce quality and economic competitiveness.

Additional sources of funding include grants from foundations and corporations specifically targeted for vocational, technical, career, and applied educational programs as well as contributions from local industry and business. Grant monies are also available through various state and federal initiatives intended to boost the development of applied educational consortia and the redevelopment of programs at the local level to meet the challenge of educating and training students in the skills necessary for success in the future economy.

Administrative Considerations

School administrators play a crucial role in the successful development and implementation of applied educational programs. To begin with, school leaders must understand the purposes and objectives of such programs and must constantly look for disconnects between the inherited curriculum and ever-changing skill demands of the real world. As pointed out by Ambrosie (1998), being well-educated should not be confused with being much-schooled, and school principals must recognize that a sizeable segment of the secondary school population is affected by the choices available to them. These choices should include pursuing an occupational/technical course of study that could lead to advanced post-secondary study and/or direct entry into the job market. Thus, he argued, state and local policy notwithstanding, school principals must not abdicate their decision-making responsibility, which drives not only the day-to-day operation of the school but the overall direction a school takes.

To this end, school leaders must begin with a mission for their applied educational programs, according to Robert Kemmery, former principal of Eastern Technical High School in Baltimore, Maryland (Dembicki, 2000). In order to ensure that a vision for the school's immediate and long-term future was embraced by the faculty and presented a driving force for student achievement, Kemmery brought in workers from local business and industry. These individuals, from top executives to entry-level workers, described the company's product or service and their day-to-day roles and functions, which helped alter the mindset of high-school faculty regarding the importance and relevance of skills and courses that had carried over since the 1960s.

Kemmery (Dembicki, 2000) also believed in the importance of partnerships with local business and industry, and offered suggestions for forging such alliances. To begin with, it is important to know your school's strengths as well as the strengths of businesses in a community in order to align partnerships effectively. Next, a businesses plan should be written in which the goals, objectives, timelines, deliverables, and expected outcomes are specified. This ensures the successful continuation of the partnership if the main contacts on one or both sides leave. Kemmery also suggested that school leaders avoid approaching local businesses for money at the outset. Instead, he suggested that the focus remain on human resource help and cooperation between the school and business. As interest grows and the partnership solidifies, company funds may be directed to the program in a variety of ways. Finally, Kemmery proposed that the partnership be based on equality, i.e. with a focus on the relative advantage to both entities that will evolve as a result of the partnership. In order to find and maintain business partners for school programs, Kemmery argued that it is important to see and be seen in the community by serving on local boards (e.g., chamber of commerce, local community college board, etc.) and by attending relevant local, regional, and state business functions.

Beyond these suggestions, there are other practices school leaders and program administrators should keep in mind. As tech prep programs increase across the nation, several administrative practices are considered essential to the development and implementation of a successful program. According to Debra Bragg (2000), these include:

- Development of formal articulation between secondary and post-secondary tech prep programs, which allows for the careful alignment and sequencing of existing and emerging curricula at both levels.
- Application of career pathways that integrate core academics and technical content within the context of various career fields. Common career pathways include the following:
  —Agricultural science / natural resources science and technology
  —Arts, communications, and media technologies
  —Business and management systems / technologies
  —Health and health science technologies
  —Human and public service technologies
  —Industrial and engineering technologies
  —Transportation system technologies
- Provision of work-based learning options that foster strong partnerships with business and industry and offer high-quality learning experiences through a range of methods, such as job shadowing, mentoring, field study, and on the job training.
- Curriculum integration can be achieved through faculty collaboration and cooperative teaching and results in integration of both content and methods across disciplines.
- Professional development, a critical component of successful tech prep programs, is needed to support not only initial program implementation but development of a core curriculum, integration of instructional methods, and seamless incorporation of work-based learning. Participation in tech prep professional development must go beyond faculty members and extend to post-secondary faculty, students, parents, and representatives from business, industry, and labor.
- Program evaluation, which may be carried out by external or internal evaluators, should focus on process, outcomes, and cost-effectiveness

Although the increasing number of students enrolling in applied educational programs and continuing on into post-secondary educational programs is a testament to the success of such programs, there are administrative challenges as well. Balancing core academics with career and technical skills can be difficult in the face of pressure to elevate academic standards and student achievement scores. Furthermore, limited scheduling options can hinder efforts to provide quality work-based learning experiences and to foster collaboration and team-teaching among faculty (Bragg, 2000). A further administrative concern is providing appropriate career counseling for students at the beginning of their participation in an applied program and ensuring a mechanism for movement between and across pathways as their interests and goals change over time.

Personnel Issues

As it now stands, most states require at least a baccalaureate degree in order to obtain a teaching certificate. Some states provide teaching certificates in selected applied areas for individuals with an Associate degree or certificate as long as the individual has appropriate field experience. For example, the Texas Education Agency offers this option for teaching certification in trade and industrial education (TEA, 2012). Additional requirements that are developing across states include: increased number of teacher preparation credits (e.g., college-level coursework in instructional methods, educational psychology, professional ethics), passing performance on a national or state certification exam, and even professional or wage-earning experience in the area of expertise. With the increasing push toward integration of high-level academic content into technical and vocational training, especially high-level math and science content, there are more pressures and demands on teachers who deliver instruction in applied educational programs. A survey of 8,000 career tech teachers conducted by the Southern Regional Education Board in 1998 revealed that 45% felt they needed to update their own mathematics and science skills before they could successfully integrate such content into their existing curricula (Lozada, 1999). This means that teachers need to have the opportunity for continuing education and professional development. Additionally, teacher preparation programs will need to begin to include in their certification process more academic requirements for those seeking credentials within technical and vocational education. However, there are ways of improving the teaching methods and academic content used in applied educational settings.

A variety of products and services have been developed to meet the need for connecting applied and academic methods of instruction. For example, the Center for Occupational Research and Development (CORD) is a national non-profit organization providing innovative changes in education to prepare students for greater success in careers and higher education. CORD provides contextual learning resources, teacher workshops, a National Tech Prep Network, and information on business partnerships. CORD also assists educators in secondary schools and colleges through new curricula, teaching strategies, professional development, and facilitating partnerships with community leaders, families, and employers (CORD, 2001). Fitzgerald and Bass (1997) note that a key obstacle in the integration of academics and technical, career, and vocational training is the often adversarial relationship between teachers in these different tracks. Many schools have overcome this difficulty by bringing academic and applied program teachers together in planning committees, round-table discussions, staff development workshops, and teaching teams. Logistical difficulties with team-teaching have been overcome in some secondary schools by implementing a school-within-a-school or 'house' concept in which a school is divided into various units, each of which may (or may not) focus on a particular career pathway or program of study. Faculty form teams and meet weekly at specified times to coordinate everything from curricula to discipline policies within the unit. The smaller size and improved cohesion benefit students, and the teacher ownership of each unit allows for implementation of a shared vision. Further, while there has been a tendency of faculty and administrators alike to view academic and technical integration as important only for students enrolled in applied educational programs, teaching all academic content in an applied context and incorporating critical thinking and problem-based learning have proven beneficial for all learners.

While efforts at curriculum development and integration are problematic for staff, equally problematic is the opportunity for quality staff development, a crucial component of successful applied educational programs (Fitzgerald & Bass, 1997). Teachers must be knowledgeable about the latest technology and must know how to implement Perkins mandates that are significant departures from previous practice. Funding for staff development, however, is not enough. Teachers also need release time and stipends for participation in meaningful experiences in the form of workshops, training, and conferences outside the school or district. Furthermore, haphazard scheduling of staff development and the expenditure of time and money on sessions provided by specialists or experts can lead to frustration and resentment on the part of teachers. Instead, a systematic plan should be developed by the teachers themselves or at least with their strong input and should involve not only training in new skills and technology but provisions for ongoing support for implementation and evaluation (Joyce & Showers, 2002).

Curriculum and staff development issues aside, faculty and staff are often resistant to the idea of implementing or improving an applied educational program for a variety of reasons. Some teachers fear that restructuring existing vocational programs to meet new skill demands and mandates by various governing bodies will threaten their own job security if they have not kept abreast of developments within their area of specialty or technology in general. The support mechanisms suggested above may help alleviate these fears. Staff composition may also pose challenges to efforts at reform within a school as well. Factors such as imminent retirement and involvement with previous reform movements that were not successful can dampen the enthusiasm of otherwise active and involved teachers and can cause outright resistance in others. These difficulties can be overcome by anticipating the planning process will move in small, incremental steps and by allowing at least two years to elapse before the organization begins to fully embrace the change (Fitzgerald & Bass, 1997). Teachers can also help others spread enthusiasm for developing or implementing applied educational programs by forming professional learning communities around specific issues and finding ways to take charge of the process. Administrative support is often crucial, too, in bringing resistant teachers around. Many teachers will invest time, energy, and personal commitment to a new program only if they are convinced that it is important to the administration and will be given ample resources. Finally, providing autonomy for teachers to develop curricula and quality programs can help foster enthusiasm among vocational teachers who may feel threatened by the changes needed in their program and among academic teachers who may not initially see the relevance of such programs to their areas of expertise.

Resistance and challenge are not limited to teachers. Administrators and school counselors who define success in terms of numbers of students entering four-year colleges after graduation sometimes resent any perceived distraction from their core academic mission. Furthermore, district policy can hinder efforts of teachers to plan and implement staff development and efforts to restructure the school into units. Generating interest and enthusiasm in the larger community through publicity and business partnerships, however, can help administrators, counselors, and other teachers (as well as doubtful parents!) to see the bigger picture and recognize the value of the programs to all segments of the student population. As Fitzgerald and Bass note,

> The challenge before schools is like that facing businesses in an internationally competitive environment. Corporate executives have had to learn that former ways of organizing production- separating thinking from doing- are no longer working. Likewise, educators are learning that the separation of academic and vocational education is not effective (p. 341).

Teachers, as the implementers of applied educational programs in the schools, must take an active role in program development and evaluation, and must tailor the program to the needs of their students and community within the context of the school mission. Flexible scheduling, compensation for time, acknowledgement of effort, provision of materials, and ongoing support from administration are key elements in successful programs.

Summary

While this chapter has focused largely on the evolution of traditional vocational programs into what have come to be known variously as tech prep, career tech, occupational education, school-to-work, and vocational-technical education, other programs are increasingly interconnected in a variety of ways to applied educational programs. The Perkins Act provides a large portion of funding for such programs and has evolved over the years since its initial introduction into law. This Act has substantially and qualitatively changed the original idea of vocational education, expanding it to serve not only traditional secondary students but adults coming from a variety of circumstances. The Act has provided for single parents, displaced homemakers, individuals with limited English proficiency, students with disabilities, and incarcerated persons, and the most recent reauthorization has shaped the Act to conform to the principles of *No Child Left Behind*.

The increasing emphasis on career pathways or clusters has changed the focus of traditionally discrete courses in such areas as home economics, industrial arts, and business. These courses are often now included in one or more career pathways. For example, traditional home economics courses like sewing, cooking, and home furnishing are frequently offered under Human and Public Services or even Arts and Communications Technologies. Beyond funding, issues of personnel and administration are key elements for successful development, implementation, and improvement of applied educational programs. Teachers must be well prepared to deliver current, up-to-date technological skills instruction integrated with high-level academic core content. Academic and applied education teachers must work collaboratively on curriculum development and content integration, must be given the opportunity for collaborative planning, quality staff development, and team teaching, and need autonomy to develop and renew programs as appropriate and necessary. Administrators must recognize the need to shift attitudes and focus towards an integrated approach to education in which both academics and technical skills are seen as important student learning outcomes. Administrators also must exercise their managerial roles in providing teachers with the resources for program development and implementation. These resources include not only financial resources but release time, stipends for continuing education, professional development activities designed by the faculty, professional learning communities, and partnerships with local businesses and employers.

As vocational education moves further into the 21st century, the need for all students to learn academic content within applied contexts will increasingly drive curriculum development and educational reform. Issues of gender and social equity will continue to form the basis of challenges to the system (Werum, 2002), and economic viability in an internationally competitive market as a driving force behind American education will continue to raise pedagogical and ideological debate (Dare, 2001). One thing is certain for the moment, career- and technology-focused education is gaining a foothold in school districts across the nation, and states are increasingly mandating that district curricula include applied learning across the secondary curriculum and in some cases, across K–12.

Questions for Consideration

1. How have federal funding mandates shaped the course of vocational education in American schools over time?

2. What are some of the limitations of federal mandates and how are these seen at the level of the local school district?

3. Why is there an increasing emphasis on partnerships between schools and local business and industry?

4. How do administrative and personnel issues differ between comprehensive secondary schools and technical or career high schools? In what ways are these issues similar across settings?

5. How are career and technical applications best integrated into the middle school? Elementary school?

Case Study

Aligning the Curriculum

Mr. McCall, who has a background in electrical engineering in addition to certification in secondary education, has been involved developing career and technical education programs in several states during the past ten years. He was recently hired by Spring Valley Independent School District to restructure the vocational education program, which currently offers programs in cosmetology, auto mechanics, welding, and the construction trades. A review of the program reveals that students who enter the vocational education program are essentially in a different "track," and that the academic courses available to them tend to be general or remedial in nature. Furthermore, students involved in the current vocational education program generally have a history of poor academic performance and discipline problems, and there is a large over-representation of minorities and students of lower socioeconomic status.

In reviewing the district's public relations materials, Mr. McCall finds that a lot of attention is given to the rigorous academic standards of the district and the high rate of students who matriculate in college following graduation. Nowhere in the public relations materials does he find information about the vocational education program. In an effort to assess the attitude toward the vocational education program of students, school personnel, and community members, Mr. McCall interviews several representatives of each group. He finds a general perception that such programs are for students who otherwise would not graduate from high school, and that it is somewhat of a social stigma to be associated with vocational education. However, he is somewhat surprised to encounter several students who report having been denied the opportunity to participate in specific vocational programs by the guidance counselor. These students had been advised that their grades were good enough to get into college and that, without a college degree, they would never be able to earn a living in the future. Kathy Spencer, for example, was interested in obtaining a cosmetology license. Because she is an honor student, however, she was told that the program was completely inappropriate for her and that enrolling in the program would end her chances of being accepted by a top-tier university. Another student, Mike Abbot, is not an honor roll student but has taken advanced placement courses in science and has demonstrated a talent for computer skills. He was interested in taking auto mechanics but was given similar advice regarding his college aspirations and future.

Interviews with and observations of teachers and other school personnel reveal that there is little personal or collegial interaction between teachers of the vocational programs and regular classroom teachers. This appears to be due less to any overt hostility than to a relative lack of overlap between the academic and vocational programs as well as the physical distance between the main school and the buildings in which the vocational programs are housed. Both groups, however, seem to believe that their respective programs achieve specific but separate goals, and that students generally fit into one program or the other. Neither group seems to see any particular need to restructure the program or alter the academic curriculum in any way.

Questions for Discussion

1. What are some of the factors affecting the vocational program in Spring Valley School District?

2. What are some of the obstacles Mr. McCall faces, based on the information available?

3. What are the legal, ethical, and funding issues that must be considered?

4. How should Mr. McCall begin his effort to restructure the vocational program? What should be the main focus or goal?

References

Ambrosie, F. (1998). The forgotten standard: The value of making things. *NASSP Bulletin, 82*(589), 101–05.

Applied Academics. Retrieved from http://www.bced.gov.bc.ca/careers/aa/.

Bragg, D. D. (2000). Tech prep: Winning ideas, challenging practices. *Techniques: Connecting Education and Careers, 75*(4), 14–17.

Center for Occupational Research and Development (CORD). Retrieved from http://www.cord.org/.

Clark, C. S. (1999). Standards-Based academies: School-to-career institute offers promise as a national model. *The High School Magazine, 7*(3), 34–37.

Cutshall, S. (2003). Making the most of the middle. *Techniques: Connecting Education and Careers, 78*(1), 26–28.

Dare, D. E. (2001). Learner-centered instructional practices supporting the new vocationalism. *New Directions for Community Colleges, 115*, 81–91.

Dembicki, M. (2000). He's got the hook. *Techniques: Connecting Education and Careers, 75*(3), 28–31.

Drueckhammer, D. (2001). Vocational-Technical and career education. In G. Schroth & M. Littleton (Eds.), *The administration and supervision of special programs in education* (pp. 67–77). Dubuque: Kendall / Hunt Publishing Company.

Fitzgerald, J. & Bass, J. (1997). The frontline of reform: Teachers as implementors of school-to-work. *The Educational Forum, 61*, 336–342.

Gage Park High School (2013). Retrieved from http://gageparkhs.org/about/mission.jsp.

Gallagher, J. J. (1995). Comments of 'The reform without cost?'. *Phi Delta Kappan, 77*(3), 216–17.

Gray, K. (1996). The baccalaureate game: Is it right for all teens? *Phi Delta Kappan, 77*(8), 528–34.

Joyce, B. & Showers, B. (2002). *Student achievement through staff development (3rd ed).* Alexandria, VA: Association for Supervision and Curriculum Development.

Kantor, H. & Lowe, R. (2000). Vocationalism reconsidered. *American Journal of Education, 109*, 125–142.

Kliebard, H. (1999). *Schooled to work: Vocationalism and the American curriculum 1876–1946.* New York: Teachers College Press.

Hunt, M. (1993). *The Story of Psychology.* New York: Anchor Books.

Levesque, K., Lauen, D, Teitelbaum, P., Alt, M., & Librera, S. (2000). *Vocational education in the United States: Toward the year 2000.* National Center for Education Statistics, 2000-029.

Litvin, M. (2000). Flying High. *Techniques: Connecting Education and Careers, 75*(5), 32–35.

Lozado, M. (1995). A model reform. *Vocational Education Journal, 70*(8), 28–33.

Lozada, M. (1999). All in good time. *Techniques: Connecting Education and Careers, 74*(8), 14–19.

National Assessment of Vocational Education (2005). *Evaluation of programs: National assessment of vocational education.* Retrieved from http://www2.ed.gov/rschstat/eval/sectech/nave/index.html.

National Center for Education Statistics (2012). *The condition of education, 2011(NCES 2012-045).* U.S. Department of Education. Retrieved from http://nces.ed.gov/.

Ries, E. (2000). Making the grades. *Techniques: Connecting Education and Careers, 75*(1), 16–20.

Roberts, M. (1999). Rigor and vigor: Three schools reap results. *Techniques: Connecting Education and Careers, 74*(6), 20–23.

Roberts, M. (2001). *National Society for the Promotion of Industrial Education.* Retrieved from http://dana.ucc.nau.edu/~mr/vte591/1906.htm.

Santrock, J. W. (2003). Adolescence (9th ed.). Boston: McGraw-Hill.

Steinberg, L. (2002). *Adolescence* (6th ed.). Boston: McGraw-Hill.

Sussex Technical School District (2013). Retrieved from http://www.sussexvt.k12.de.us/district/.

Texas Education Agency (2012). Career and technical education requirements. Retrieved from http://www.tca.state.tx.us/index2.aspx?id=5351&menu_id=865&menu_id2=794.

Turner Technical High School (2012). Retrieved from http://turnertech.dadeschools.net/Index.html.

Werum, R. (2002). Matching youth and jobs? Gender dynamics in New Deal job training programs. *Social Forces, 81*(2), 473–503.

CHAPTER 8

Health and Human Services in the Schools

Introduction and Historical Perspective

COORDINATED health and human service providers made their entrance into public schools around the turn of the 20th century. The advent of child labor and compulsory school attendance laws required the intervention of health and human service workers such as nurses, social workers and counselors, to attend to the pressing needs of students and parents, both in schools and in the community. The Industrial Revolution saw a rise in the number of children working in factories. During the early 1900s, counseling services began more as vocational and occupational counseling due to the widespread use of children in industrial jobs. Social workers entered the educational scene to assist immigrant parents in understanding the compulsory school attendance laws, and they were also instrumental in assuring children attended school and families took advantage of the social services available to them. Community health nursing services also evolved around this time. The original role of community nurses was working with the high numbers of children dying from communicable diseases and keeping them out of school to prevent further infection and spread of disease. It is through these endeavors and recognition by government of the need for health services to children that the role of school nurse evolved in the early 1900s from community nurse to school nurse (Zepeda & Langenbach, 1999). In the 1930s, President Herbert Hoover called for promotion of health education for children and adolescents. The 1960s saw the passage of numerous laws related to health care delivery in schools and the community, including the *Elementary and Secondary Education Act* (ESEA, P.L. 89-10) signed into law by President Lyndon Johnson in 1965. This important legislation contained funding for services related to health and human services in schools. Title programs of this Act included support for educationally deprived children, including free and reduced price lunch in the schools, support for handicapped children, and dropout prevention in the schools (U.S. Government, 1965). Section 504 of the *Rehabilitation Act of 1973* prohibits discrimination against individuals with handicapping conditions in programs receiving federal funds (29 U.S.C. Sec. 794), and as such requires the services of health service professionals for students and adults in the schools. Public Law 94-142, the *Education for All Handicapped Children Act* (EHCA) was passed in 1975 and required collaboration among school nurses, social workers, school counselors, school psychologists, teachers, and school administrators in addressing the special needs of students with physical and learning disabilities in schools. EHCA was reauthorized as the *Individuals With Disabilities Education Act* (20 U.S.C., 1990) and reaffirmed the importance and requirement

141

of these school health and human service professionals to work together in the best interest of the child. Title I of Goals 2000 called for coordination of efforts with health and social service agencies, services to homeless children, services to neglected and delinquent youth, and services to youth in at-risk situations (20 U.S.C., 1994). Currently the work of health and human service professionals continues to be directed toward improving the overall health and life expectancy of children and adults. Healthy People 2000 and Healthy People 2010 resources are available to schools to address priority areas such as physical activity and fitness, substance abuse, violent and abusive behavior, educational and community based programs, HIV infection and sexually transmitted diseases, and nutrition among others. School nurses, counselors, and social workers, along with other health and human service professionals, have a long history of service to schools and students. All these professionals are important to the health and welfare of students, their families, and the communities they serve, playing an important role in the maintenance of a healthy school environment and support the opportunity for children and youth to learn and achieve to their highest academic potential.

Coordinated Health and Human Services

Teaming, communication, and coordination of services are the key to a service-oriented and healthy organization, i.e., one that is ready to meet the needs of the people it serves. Schools are service organizations. Development and support of a team of professionals who work together and support each other in their efforts to provide a healthy, safe, and nurturing environment for students, are essential to the creation and maintenance of a positive school culture directed toward teaching and learning. A school-based health and human services team should consist primarily of the school nurse, school social worker, school counselor, and other appropriate support staff such as the school psychologist, mental health worker, or physician. These professionals must be child advocates and dedicated to providing support for a child's physical, social, and emotional growth, which are essential to successful academic achievement. Though there is an attempt by school districts to provide the best services possible to all children, it is not always possible to have each of these professionals assigned to every school in a district on a daily basis. Social workers are often required to travel between schools serving students at multiple sites; nurses can be found working half-days at schools checking on medications and updating medical records; and school counselors may be non-existent in elementary schools while concentrating on grade point averages and college placement efforts in secondary schools. When this happens, schools are not utilizing service professionals to the best advantage of their students.

A good example of how these professionals can work together and coordinate services for the good of the child can be found in Public Law 94-142, the Education for All Handicapped Children Act (P.L. 89-10) and subsequently the Individuals with Disabilities Education Act (IDEA) (U.S. Government, 1992) and the Individuals with Disabilities Education Improvement Act (IDEIA) (U.S. Department of Education, 2003). These Acts stress the importance of collaboration in determining a child's ability or inability to achieve academically. Social workers conduct histories of children and their families, nurses develop and verify a medical history, and counselors provide a chronology of a student's social and emotional growth within the school setting. All this information is useful in determining whether a need exists for special services to help a child achieve academic success. As part of a Multidisciplinary Evaluation Team (MET) or an Individual Education Plan (IEP) team, professionals share and coordinate information for the good of the child. A coordinated school health program as described by the National Association of School Nurses (NASA, 2008) is presented in Table 8.1. More information on the coordinated efforts of these specialized teams can be found in Chapter 3, Special Education Programs in the Schools.

Outside of the MET and IEP teams, these professionals often do not communicate or see each

Table 8.1. Coordination of School Health Services.

The components of a Coordinated School Health Program include:

- *School health services:* Preventive services, education, emergency care, referral and management of acute and chronic health conditions.
- *Health education:* A planned, sequential K through 12 curriculum addressing the physical, mental, emotional, and social dimensions of health to help students develop health knowledge, attitudes, and skills.
- *Health promotion programs for faculty and staff:* Planned health promotion and disease prevention programs and opportunities for school staff.
- *Counseling psychological and social services:* Services that focus on cognitive, emotional, behavioral, and social needs of individuals and families.
- *School nutrition services:* Integration of nutritious, affordable, and appealing meals, nutritional education, and an environment that promotes healthy eating behaviors for all students.
- *Physical education programs:* A planned, sequential K through 12 curriculum that promotes lifelong physical activity.
- *Healthy school environment:* A safe physical and psychological environment that is supportive of learning.
- *Family and community involvement:* Partnerships among schools, families, community groups, and individuals.

Source: National Association of School Nurses (2008). Position statement: Coordinated school health services.

other only in passing on their way to address overloaded schedules. They do not always have full knowledge or appreciation of the similarities in duties each other performs and can become territorial, expending energy in protecting their turf or establishing authority based on the amount of time spent in a school. This can have a negative effect on the well-being of children and programs. The establishment of a coordinated health and human services team within the schools is the basis for providing essential services to students and the school. It can also be instrumental in establishing partnerships with parents and the community through outreach efforts. As pointed out by Epstein (2001), efforts to bring together the student, family, and community can have a positive influence on children as students.

School Nurse

The school nurse has duties and responsibilities within the school and coordinates with medical providers outside of the school. This includes provision of school health services, promotion of health education, performing health screenings, and supporting a healthy school environment (NASN, 2011). See Table 8.2.

The duties of the school nurse have expanded considerably since the implementation of Public Law 94-142 and IDEIA (formally IDEA). As a result of these Acts, an increasing number of students with disabilities and handicapping conditions are enrolled in the regular school setting. Many require medical or health interventions in order to remain in school the full day. As pointed out by the National Association of School Nurses (NASN), these interventions range from administration of medications to more complex procedures such as respirator care (NASN, 2004). Required health services for students with special needs have created some confusion among parents and school personnel as to the difference between medical and health services and who is or ought to be the service provider. The National Association of School Nurses (2001) adopted a position statement in June 2001 to clarify the difference between medical services and health services and to define the professional school nurse as the appropriate provider of health services in the school setting. Table 8.3 outlines the responsibilities of school nurses related to differences between medical and health services as defined by the National Association of School Nurses (2001).

Table 8.2. Role of the School Nurse.

In a coordinated school health program, the school nurse may provide leadership or play a supporting role in any of the eight components.

- *School health services:* by assessing student health status, providing emergency care, ensuring access to health care, and identifying and managing barriers to student learning.
- *Health education:* By providing resources and expertise in developing health curricula and providing health information.
- *Health promotion for faculty and staff:* By providing health information and health promotion activities, monitoring chronic conditions, and maintaining records.
- *Counseling, psychological, and social services:* By collaborating with counseling staff to identify student psychosocial problems and provide input and intervention.
- *School nutrition services:* By providing education about nutritious foods, monitoring menus and food preparation, and encouraging the inclusion of healthy foods on menus, in vending machines, and for classroom snacks.
- *Physical education programs:* By collaborating with physical educators to meet physical education goals, providing information to students about physical activity, and helping to design appropriate programs for students with special health concerns.
- *Healthy school environment:* By monitoring, reporting, and intervening to correct hazards, collaborating to develop a crisis intervention plan, and providing adaptations for students with special needs.
- *Family and community involvement:* By taking a leadership role in collaborating with community agencies to identify and provide programs to meet the physical and mental health needs of children and families.

Source: National Association of School Nurses (2008). Position statement: Coordinated school health services.

School Social Worker

School social workers play a vital role in establishing connections among the student, school, family, and community. As mentioned earlier, social workers in schools have a long history dating to the early 1900s with industrialization, the enactment of compulsory school attendance laws, and increased immigration to the United States. Many immigrant families did not understand or accept the concept of formal education and the requirement for all students to attend school on a regular basis. Thus, the social worker was cast into the role of "visiting teacher," connecting home and school in an effort to promote attendance (Zepeda & Langenbach, 1999). Renowned social worker Jane Addams established Hull House in Chicago, Illinois in the early 1900s as a means of addressing the problem of children working long hours in factories rather than attending school. Through the years, social workers have worked with schools in a variety of areas including juvenile delinquency, truancy, drop-out prevention, child abuse, alcohol and drug abuse, teen-age pregnancy, social maladjustment, poverty, and health services. As with the school nurse, the duties and responsibilities of school social workers have expanded considerably since the implementation of 94-142, IDEA and IDEIA. School social workers are members of the MET and IEP teams; develop social histories of children; interact with school nurses, counselors, psychologists, teachers, and administrators; assist families in accessing social services; and visit homes, hospitals, and prisons in service to children and youth. This list by no means comprises all the duties and responsibilities of the school social worker. As stated by the School Social Work Association of America (SSWAA) (2003),

> School social work is a specialized area of practice within the broad field of the social work profession. School social workers bring unique knowledge and skills to the school system and the student services team. School Social Workers are instrumental in furthering the purpose of the schools: To provide a setting for teaching, learning, and for the attainment of competence and confidence. School social workers are hired by school districts to enhance the district's ability to meet its academic mission, especially where home, school and community collaboration is the key to achieving that mission (SSWAA, 2003).

Table 8.3. School Nurse Role Related to 504 and IDEIA (formally IDEA).

- Assisting in identifying children who may need special educational or health-related services.
- Assessing the identified child's functional and physical health status, in collaboration with the child, parent(s)/guardian(s), and healthcare providers.
- Developing individualized healthcare plans (IHP) and emergency care plans (ECP) based on a nursing assessment.
- Recommending to the team health-related accommodations or services that may be required.
- Assisting the team in developing an Individual Educational Plan (IEP) or 504 Accommodation Plan that provides for the required health needs of the child and enables the student to participate in his or her educational program.
- Assisting the parent(s)/guardians and teachers to identify and remove health-related barriers to learning.
- Providing in-service training for teachers and staff regarding the individual health needs of the child.
- Providing and/or supervising unlicensed assistive personnel to provide specialized healthcare services in the school setting.
- Evaluating the effectiveness of the health-related components of the IEP with the child, parent(s), and other team members, and making revisions to the plan as needed.

Source: Gibbons, L. J., Lehr, K., & Selekman, J. (2013). Federal laws protecting children and youth with disabilities in the schools. In J. Selekman (Ed.), *School nursing: A comprehensive text* (2nd ed.). pp. 257–283. Philadelphia, PA: F.A. Davis & Company.

School Counselor

The school counselor provides specialized services to address the social, emotional, and mental health needs of students. Such services may be provided at the elementary, middle, and secondary school levels and include activities such as individual and group assessments, response to referrals, and interventions. Because of the specialized, individual, and group needs of students, the school counselor does not work in a vacuum. The school counselor collaborates with teachers and administrators, the school nurse, social worker, and school psychologist in addressing both student and organizational health (National Center for Chronic Disease Prevention and Health Promotion, 2004). Counselors are active member of crisis management and violence prevention teams, as well as MET and IEP teams addressing the educational and emotional needs of students with disabilities. Depending on the academic level, counselors are also actively involved in career advising, class scheduling, program development, and informational activities addressing teachers, students, parents, and school district and community members. Activities of the school counselor extend beyond the walls of the school as they regularly work in collaboration with parents, families, and community services in addressing the specific needs of students.

Additional information related to school guidance and counseling can be found in other sections of this book. Chapter 1 explains elementary and secondary education school counseling program guidelines and funding support provided under *No Child Left Behind*. Chapter 10 in its discussion of student support services provides insight into the role of the school counselor and an extensive review of guidance and counseling services in schools.

Youth At Risk

The Youth Risk and Behaviors Surveillance System (YRBS) monitors priority health and risk behaviors that contribute to the leading causes of death, disability, and social problems among young people and adults in the United States (CDC, 2012). School districts should seriously conduct dialogues with parents and community members related to the development and implementation of programs addressing risky behaviors in and out of school.

Results from the 2011 national YRBS indicated that many high-school students are engaged in priority health-risk behaviors associated with the leading causes of death among persons aged 10–24 years in the United States. During the 30 days before the survey, 32.8% of high school students nationwide had texted or e-mailed while driving, 38.7% had drunk alcohol, and 23.1% had used marijuana. During the 12 months before the survey, 32.8% of students had been in a physical fight, 20.1% had been bullied on school property, and 7.8% had attempted suicide. Many high-school students nationwide are engaged in sexual risk behaviors associated with unintended pregnancies and STDs, including HIV infection. Nearly half (47.4%) of students had had sexual intercourse, 33.7% had had sexual intercourse during the 3 months before the survey (i.e., currently sexually active), and 15.3% had had sexual intercourse with four or more people during their life. Among currently sexually active students, 60.2% had used a condom during their last sexual intercourse. Results from the 2011 national YRBS also indicate many high school students are engaged in behaviors associated with the leading causes of death among adults aged ≥ 25 years in the United States. During the 30 days before the survey, 18.1% of high-school students had smoked cigarettes and 7.7% had used smokeless tobacco. During the 7 days before the survey, 4.8% of high school students had not eaten fruit or drunk 100% fruit juices and 5.7% had not eaten vegetables. Nearly one-third (31.1%) had played video or computer games for 3 or more hours on an average school day (Centers for Disease Control, 2012).

As the above statistics show, serious concerns exist, which must be addressed by programs in the schools in conjunction with families, community resources, and government agencies.

Health and Social Issues

It is not possible to explore every situation health and human service workers are required to deal with in a school. This section will address the more common situations. Chapter 10 discusses prevention programs related to HIV/AIDS, childhood obesity, teen pregnancy, violence and crisis management, suicide, and other mental health issues.

Immunizations and Vaccinations

It is the duty and responsibility of schools to ensure that all students have the opportunity to attend school in a healthy environment, as free as possible from exposure to disease. With this in mind, every state education agency has implemented and outlined standards and requirements for immunization of children prior to admittance to public schools. To help forestall outbreaks of childhood diseases, public health services have expanded outreach programs to ensure the timely immunization of children. The United States has seen a resurgence of communicable diseases such as measles, mumps, rubella, pertussis (whooping cough), and tuberculosis. Without the safeguards of vaccinations and adequate health care, children are particularly at risk of contacting these preventable diseases. Contracting any of these diseases will interfere with a child's opportunity to learn and achieve in school. State health agencies in conjunction with state education agencies have adopted laws that require students entering into public schools to show proof of required immunizations before entry. School administrative and health service providers need to be aware of state and local regulations regarding immunizations and school attendance.

Head Lice

Occasionally, school personnel will detect one or more cases of head lice infestation among students in a school building. When this occurs, it is customary for school personnel to notify the parent(s), school district office, and local health authorities. Lice infestations occur across all race and economic groups and do not necessarily connote lack of personal cleanliness. Large-scale infestations usually occur when infested people fail to report them due to a misguided notion of a social stigma attached to the problem. Once detected, reported immediately, and treated, cases of head lice can be quickly and easily eliminated.

STD, HIV, and AIDS

Students who engage in drug abuse and are sexually active are also placing themselves at risk of contracting sexually transmitted disease (STDs), human immuno-deficiency virus (HIV), and acquired immune deficiency syndrome (AIDS).

> Estimates suggest that young people aged 15–24 years acquire nearly half of all new STDs. Compared with older adults, sexually active adolescents aged 15–19 years and young adults aged 20–24 years are at higher risk of acquiring STDs for a combination of behavioral, biological, and cultural reasons. . . . The higher prevalence of STDs among adolescents also may reflect multiple barriers to accessing quality STD prevention services, including lack of health insurance or ability to pay, lack of transportation, discomfort with facilities and services designed for adults, and concerns about confidentiality. Traditionally, intervention efforts have targeted individual-level factors associated with STD risk which do not address higher-level factors (e.g., peer norms and media influences) that may also influence behaviors. Interventions for at-risk adolescents and young adults that address underlying aspects of the social and cultural conditions that affect sexual risk-taking behaviors are needed, as are strategies designed to improve the underlying social conditions themselves (Centers for Disease Control, 2013).

> HIV is spread by sexual contact with an infected person, by sharing needles and/or syringes (primarily for drug injection) with someone who is infected, or, less commonly (and now very rarely in countries where blood is screened for HIV antibodies), through transfusions of infected blood or blood clotting factors. Babies born to HIV-infected women may become infected before or during birth or through breast-feeding after birth (Centers for Disease Control and Prevention, 2003).

It is important that the school nurse, social worker, and school counselor work in conjunction with the school administration, school board, and community in developing information sessions and literature for distribution related to these communicable diseases.

Prescription and Non-Prescription Drugs in the School

The distribution of prescription drugs in school is an important activity that should be coordinated by the school nurse or other health official. Clear guidelines and regulations must be established regarding physician prescriptions and directions, parental approval, secure and locked storage, access, distribution and observation logs, and any notes related to medical, parental, or student issues that are of concern to the health and safety of the student. In the absence of a school nurse in a building, this responsibility falls to the school administrator who may perform the duty or delegate it to another official in the school.

Non-prescription drugs also present a serious concern for faculty, staff, students, and administrators. It is difficult to know and keep track of who is carrying and using non-prescription drugs in school. What may appear to be the innocent possession and use of aspirin products, inhalants, pain relievers, allergy and cold medications, etc. for one student, may be the vehicle to illness, allergic reactions, addiction, and even death for another student. According to the Office of Applied Statistics in its 2003 National Survey on drug use and health, prescription drugs are second only to marijuana in substance abuse among youth over 12 years of age, and there has been a rise in the use of non-prescription drugs such as painkillers and over- the-counter (OTC) cough, cold, and allergy medications (U.S. Department of Health and Human Services, 2004). As anticipated, there have been changes since the 2003 report. Results from the 2010 National Survey on Drug Use and Health demonstrate the following:

- The rate of current illicit drug use among youths aged 12 to 17 remained similar from 2009 to 2010 (10.0 vs. 10.1 percent), but higher than the rate in 2008 (9.3 percent). Between 2002 and 2008, the rate declined from 11.6 to 9.3 percent
- In 2010, 10.1 percent of youths aged 12 to 17 were current illicit drug users, with 7.4 percent current users of marijuana, 3.0 percent current nonmedical users of psychotherapeutic drugs, 1.1 percent current users of inhalants, 0.9 percent current users of hallucinogens, and 0.2 percent current users of cocaine.
- Among youths aged 12 to 17, the types of illicit drugs used in the past month varied by age group in 2010. Among 12 or 13 year olds, 2.0 percent used psychotherapeutic drugs nonmedically, 1.4 percent used inhalants, and 0.9 percent used marijuana. Among 14 or 15 year olds, 6.5 percent used marijuana, 3.0 percent used psychotherapeutic drugs nonmedically, 1.2 percent used inhalants, and 1.1 percent used hallucinogens. Among 16 or 17 year olds, 14.3 percent used marijuana, 3.9 percent used psychotherapeutic drugs nonmedically, 1.3 percent used hallucinogens, 0.6 percent used inhalants, and 0.5 percent used cocaine (Substance Abuse and Mental Health Services Administration, 2011).

It is strongly suggested that school administrators and school boards review these statistics and create comprehensive district policies regarding the carrying and use of non-prescription drugs in schools and that these policies be distributed to all parents, guardians, students, faculty, and staff in the district. It is also important that the school and school districts invest in prevention programs to stem the rising tide of non-prescription drug use in schools. It is the responsibility of everyone in the school and school district to enforce any policy related to the carrying and use of non-prescription drugs in school. Chapter 9 provides information related to prevention programs.

Social Issues

Adverse social issues, like health issues, are of concern to school personnel in that they can impact the ability of students to achieve to their highest academic potential. Social issues can have their roots in school, at home, or in the community and can lead to conditions such as hunger, abuse, violence, isolation, suicide, and academic failure.

> All students can, at some time during their school years, be described as students at-risk. Whether the cause is social, emotional, cultural, physical, psychological, economic, or a language barrier, these students at one time or another are not achieving up to their academic potential and are at risk of academic failure. The results of this temporary or permanent condition can have long-term effects upon the child and can often be devastating. Results can range from lowered achievement and temporary lack of self-esteem to long-term drug and alcohol abuse and even suicide. In between these extremes, we see a variety of outward signs such as behavior problems, truancy, running away, dropping out of school, violence, sexual abuse, anorexia and bulimia, HIV, ARC, and AIDS, teen pregnancy, and a variety of handicapping conditions (Beyer, 1997, p. 343).

Drug, Alcohol, and Tobacco Use

Drug, alcohol, and tobacco use and abuse by children and teens remains a problem for parents, schools, and communities. Decades of drug abuse and tobacco use prevention programs do not seem to have made a great difference in the election by some children and youth to engage in substance abuse. The problem is evidenced in elementary, middle and secondary schools; in upper and lower-social economic classes; and in urban, suburban, and rural areas across the nation. It does not discriminate by gender, class, occupation, or educational level. Easy access by children and youth to prescription drugs used in the home such as anti-depressants, Ritalin, anxiety drugs, and over-the-counter products such as pain killers, sleep aids, glue, and aerosol products exacerbates the problem for parents, schools, and communities. School personnel have been vigilant in attempting to extinguish the source, use, and distribution of drugs in the school. They have instituted prevention programs, worked with parents and community resources, and have encouraged and supported the efforts of school counselors, social workers, nurses, teachers, and staff to eradicate this menace to the healthy physical and mental development of all students. Year after year, the Annual Phi Delta Kappa/Gallup Poll of the Public's Attitudes Toward the Public Schools lists drug and alcohol abuse by students as one of the foremost topics of public concern.

The local school board and school administrators should be instrumental, along with the support of faculty, staff, parents, and community representatives, in eradicating alcohol, drug, and tobacco use in and around schools and in implementing a substance abuse prevention program throughout a school district. Steps that should be considered in the development of such a program include:

- Involve faculty, staff, students, parents, and community representatives in program development and in the composition of a school advisory council
- Establish and advertise a clear policy
- Set and publicize standards and expectations for all students
- Develop enforcement standards and guidelines for all school personnel
- Ensure consistent enforcement
- Select or develop and implement a comprehensive K–12 substance abuse curriculum
- Provide visual and verbal reminders at all school-based events and activities.

A more in-depth discussion of substance abuse prevention programs can be found in Chapter 9.

Sexuality Education

Sexuality education in schools remains a controversial topic, and school districts across the nation have grappled with and approached the topic in a variety of ways. If or how sexuality education is implemented in the schools has most often been influenced by family and community cultural and religious norms. Education advocates and special interest groups have influenced the content of sex education programs and selection of curriculum materials. When looking at the latest statistics provided by the Centers for Disease Control, presented in the section above, Youth At Risk, it should be apparent that however and wherever sex education is conducted, it is a topic that requires elaboration. Chapter 10 provides a more extensive history of sexuality education and prevention programs related to HIV/AIDS and sexually transmitted diseases.

Teen-Age Pregnancy and Child Care in the School

Teen pregnancy is a serious concern with long-ranging effects on individuals and society. The National Education Association reports that

> (W)hile recent data shows that the U.S. teen pregnancy rates are falling, the United States has the highest rates of teen pregnancy and births in the western industrialized world, with thirty-five percent of young women becoming pregnant at least once before they reach the age of 20—about 850,000 a year. The NEA Health Information Network is particularly concerned about these numbers because teen mothers are less likely to complete high school (only one-third receive a high school diploma) and only 1.5% have a college degree by age 30.4 (NEA, 2004).

Since the 2004 report, there appears to be a positive result in efforts to reduce the number of teen pregnancies. As reported by The Center For Disease Control and prevention (2013),

In 2011, a total of 329,797 babies were born to women aged 15–19 years, for a live birth rate of 31.3 per 1,000 women in this age group. This is a record low for U.S. teens in this age group, and a drop of 8% from 2010. Birth rates fell 11% for women aged 15–17 years, and 7% for women aged 18–19 years. While reasons for the declines are not clear, teens seem to be less sexually active, and more of those who are sexually active seem to be using birth control than in previous years (NEA Health Information Network, 2010).

In the school setting, expectant students may require specialized services related to attendance, class schedules, transportation, food services, health care for both the parent(s) and infant, and child care facilities and programs.

Each year, almost 750,000 teenage women aged 15–19 become pregnant. Teen pregnancy affects the educational achievement both teens and their children; only 40% of teens who have a child before age 18 graduate from high school, and children of teen mothers are more likely to drop out of high school (NEA Health Information Network, 2010).

Some school districts provide for child-care within the district, usually assigning teen mothers to a school in the district where these facilities are available. Others may collaborate with community organizations to coordinate services among the student(s), school, and community. Schools might also consider half-day schedules as an option for teen mothers and coordinating transportation for mother and child to health centers or hospitals in the community for wellness checks. Intervention of the school social worker is essential in helping to coordinate food, health, clothing, and housing needs for the teen parent(s) and child, as well as addressing the concerns of the teen parents' extended families. The school guidance counselor can assist the student(s) in matters of academic and social concerns in the school setting. For additional information on this topic, Chapter 10 provides information on school-community based childcare services, while Chapter 9 discusses prevention programs related to unintended teen pregnancies.

Child Abuse and Neglect: Signs and Symptoms

The first step in helping abused or neglected children is learning to recognize the signs of child abuse and neglect. The presence of a single sign does not prove child abuse is occurring in a family; however, when these signs appear repeatedly or in combination, one should take a closer look at the situation and consider the possibility of child abuse. The Department of Health and Human Services, the American Medical Association, and the National Clearinghouse on Child Abuse and Neglect Information have outlined some of the commonly accepted warning signs of possible child abuse and neglect. Table 8.4 details the warning signs often associated with particular types of child abuse and neglect: physical abuse, neglect, emotional maltreatment, and sexual abuse.

It is important to note that these types of abuse are more typically found in combination than alone. A physically abused child, for example, is often emotionally abused as well, and a sexually abused child may also be neglected. The U.S. Department of Health and Human Services and the National Clearinghouse on Child Abuse and Neglect Information provide an extensive list of information and resources related to child abuse and neglect. This information can be accessed at http://nccanch.acf.hhs.gov. Law requires reporting incidents or suspected incidents of child abuse and neglect. If you do suspect a child is being harmed, reporting your suspicions may protect the child and get help for the family. It is important that all school personnel are familiar with local and state policies regarding reporting and know how to contact the local child protective service agency or police department when needed. For more information about where and how to file a report, call the Childhelp USA® National Child Abuse Hotline (1-800-4-A-CHILD®).

Table 8.4. Recognizing Child Abuse.

The following signs may signal the presence of child abuse and neglect.

The Child

- Shows sudden changes in behavior or school performance
- Has not received help for physical or medical problems brought to the parents' attention.
- Has learning problems (or difficulty concentrating) that cannot be attributed to specific physical or psychological causes
- Is always watchful, as though preparing for something bad to happen.
- Lacks adult supervision
- Is overly compliant, passive, or withdrawn
- Comes to school or other activities early, stays late, and does not want to go home.

The Parent

- Shows little concern for the child
- Denies the existence of—or blames the child for—the child's problems in school or at home
- Asks teachers or other caretakers to use harsh physical discipline if the child misbehaves.
- Sees the child as entirely bad, worthless, or burdensome
- Demands a level of physical or academic performance the child cannot achieve.
- Looks primarily to the child for care, attention, and satisfaction of emotional needs

The Parent and Child

- Rarely touch or look at each other
- Consider their relationship entirely negative.
- State that they do not like each other.

TYPES OF ABUSE

The following are some signs often associated with particular types of child abuse and neglect: physical abuse, neglect, sexual abuse, and emotional abuse. It is important to note however, that these types of abuse are more typically found in combination than alone. A physically abused child, for example, is often emotionally abused as well, and a sexually abused child also may be neglected.

PHYSICAL ABUSE

Consider Possibility of Physical Abuse When the Child:

- Has unexplained burns, bites, bruises, broken bones, or black eyes
- Has fading bruises or other marks noticeable after an absence from school.
- Seems frightened of the parents and protests or cries when it is time to go home
- Shrinks at the approach of adults
- Reports injury by a parent or another adult caregiver.

Consider Possibility of Physical Abuse When Parent or Other Adult Caregiver:

- Offers conflicting, unconvincing, or no explanation for the child's injury
- Describes the child as "evil," or in some other very negative way
- Uses harsh physical discipline with the child.
- Has a history of abuse as a child.

NEGLECT

Consider Possibility of Neglect When the Child:

- Is frequently absent from school
- Begs or steals food or money
- Lacks needed medical or dental care, immunizations, or glasses
- Is consistently dirty and has severe body odor
- Lacks sufficient clothing for the weather
- Abuses alcohol or other drug.
- States that there is no one at home to provide care.

(continued)

Table 8.4 (continued). Recognizing Child Abuse.

Consider Possibility of Neglect When Parent or Other Adult Caregiver:
- Appears to be indifferent to the child.
- Seems apathetic or depressed
- Behaves irrationally or in a bizarre manner

SEXUAL ABUSE

Consider Possibility of Sexual Abuse When the Child:
- Has difficulty walking or sitting
- Suddenly refuses to change for gym or to participate in physical activities
- Reports nightmares or bedwetting
- Experiences a sudden change in appetite
- Demonstrates bizarre, sophisticated, or unusual sexual knowledge or behavior
- Becomes pregnant or contracts a venereal disease, particularly if under age 14
- Runs away
- Reports sexual abuse by a parent or another adult caregiver.

Consider the Possibility of Sexual Abuse When the Parent or Other Adult Caregiver:
- Is unduly protective of the child or severely limits the child's contact with other children, especially of the opposite sex
- Is secretive and isolated
- Is jealous or controlling with family members.

EMOTIONAL MALTREATMENT

Consider Possibility of Emotional Maltreatment When the Child:
- Shows extremes in behavior, such as overly compliant or demanding behavior, extreme passivity, or aggression
- Is either inappropriately adult (parenting other children, for example) or inappropriately infantile (frequently rocking or head-banging, for example)
- Is delayed in physical or emotional development
- Has attempted suicide
- Reports a lack of attachment to the parent.

Consider Possibility of Emotional Maltreatment When Parent or Other Adult Caregiver:
- Constantly blames, belittles, or berates the child
- Is unconcerned about the child and refuses to consider offers of help for the child's problems
- Overtly rejects the child

Source: U.S. Department of Health and Human Services (2007). This fact sheet was adapted with permission from *Recognizing Child Abuse: What Parents Should Know.* Prevent Child Abuse America ® 2003. *This material may be freely reproduced and distributed. However, when doing so, please credit Child Welfare Information Gateway.*

Food Services

Food services in the schools have a responsibility to follow the U. S. Dietary Guideline for Americans and meet the health and nutrition needs of all students by providing access to a variety of appealing and nutritious meals (National Center for Chronic Disease Prevention and Health Promotion, 2004). Consideration should be given to dietary restrictions, cultural influences, health factors, and religious requirements in food selection and meal planning.

Cultural and Religious Considerations

Students come to school from a variety of cultural, socio-economic, and family settings. "Educational leaders . . . must be aware of the variety of cultural and religious traditions, family norms, and economic conditions that will dictate the daily routines of students as they prepare for school" (Beyer, 1995, p. 20). It is important that schools are aware of community norms so that schools can respect cultural and religious requirements in food service. Some communities and students may require vegetarian, halal, or kosher food. Religious groups may require fasting or restricted food selection on certain days or times of the year. Some students have severe allergies to foods and special considerations must be met for their health and well-being. Others may be on medically restricted diets.

Health Considerations

Childhood obesity has increased in the United States and as a result, schools and communities are seeking ways to help students eat healthy foods. Soft drink and candy machines are being taken out of schools and replaced by vending machines featuring juice, fruit, bottled water, and other nutritional snacks. On the other hand, many schools have found it financially beneficial to lease student food services to fast-food corporations such as McDonald's, Burger King, and Pizza Hut, and Domino's Pizza (Stark, 2001). Serious consideration must be given to student health issues by the local school board when making decisions regarding food and vending machine service contracts in schools.

Results from the 2007–2008 National Health and Nutrition Examination Survey (NHANES) using measured heights and weights, indicate that an estimated 16.9% of children and adolescents aged 2–19 years are obese. Between 1976–1980 and 1999–2000, the prevalence of obesity increased. Between 1999–2000 and 2007–2008, there was no significant trend in obesity prevalence for any age group . . . Among preschool children aged 2–5, obesity increased from 5.0% to 10.4% between 1976–1980 and 2007–2008 and from 6.5% to 19.6% among those aged 6–11. Among adolescents aged 12–19, obesity increased from 5.0% to 18.1% during the same period (Ogden & Carroll, 2010).

In response to this serious concern, the Institute of Medicine of the National Academies (IMNA) has developed an action plan for prevention. Table 8.7 outlines the MNA prevention

Table 8.5. Prevalence of Obesity.

In 2007–2008, the prevalence of obesity was significantly higher among Mexican-American adolescent boys (26.8%) than among non-Hispanic white adolescent boys (16.7%). In NHANES III (1988-1994) there was no significant difference in prevalence between Mexican-American and non-Hispanic white adolescent boys.

Between 1988–1994 and 2007–2008 the prevalence of obesity increased

- From 11.6% to 16.7% among non-Hispanic white boys.
- From 10.7% to 19.8% among non-Hispanic black boys.
- From 14.1% to 26.8% among Mexican-American boys.

Among girls in the period 2007–2008, non-Hispanic black adolescents (29.2%) were significantly more likely to be obese compared with non-Hispanic white adolescents (14.5%). Similarly, non-Hispanic black adolescent girls (16.3%) were more likely to be obese compared with non-Hispanic white adolescent girls (8.9%) in the period 1988–1994.

Between 1988 1994 and 2007–2008 the prevalence of obesity increased:

- From 8.9% to 14.5% among non-Hispanic white girls.
- From 16.3% to 29.2% among non-Hispanic black girls.
- From 13.4% to 17.4% among Mexican-American girls.

Source: Ogden, C. & Carroll, M. (2010). Prevalence of Obesity Among Children and Adolescents: United States, Trends 1963–1965 Through 2007–2008. Division of Health and Nutrition Examination Surveys.

Table 8.6. Confronting Childhood Obesity.

FEDERAL GOVERNMENT
- Establish an interdepartmental task force and coordinate federal actions
- Develop nutrition standards for foods and beverages sold in schools
- Fund state-based nutrition and physical-activity grants with strong evaluation components
- Develop guidelines regarding advertising and marketing to children and youth by convening a national conference
- Expand funding for prevention intervention research, experimental behavioral research, and community-based population research; strengthen support for surveillance, monitoring, and evaluation efforts

INDUSTRY AND MEDIA
- Develop healthier food and beverage product and packaging innovations
- Expand consumer nutrition information
- Provide clear and consistent media messages

STATE AND LOCAL GOVERNMENTS
- Expand and promote opportunities for physical activity in the community through changes to ordinances, capital improvement programs, and other planning practices
- Work with communities to support partnerships and networks that expand the availability of and access to healthful foods

HEALTH-CARE PROFESSIONALS
- Routinely track body mass index (BMI) in children and youth and offer appropriate counseling and guidance to children and their families

COMMUNITY AND NONPROFIT ORGANIZATIONS
- Provide opportunities for healthful eating and physical activity in existing and new community programs, particularly for high-risk populations

STATE AND LOCAL EDUCATION AUTHORITIES AND SCHOOLS
- Improve the nutritional quality of foods and beverages served and sold in schools and as part of school-related activities
- Increase opportunities for frequent, more intensive, and engaging physical activity during and after school
- Implement school-based interventions to reduce children's screen time
- Develop, implement, and evaluate innovative pilot programs for both staffing and teaching about wellness, healthful eating, and physical activity

PARENTS AND FAMILIES
- Engage in and promote more healthful dietary intakes and active lifestyles (e.g., increased physical activity, reduced television and other screen time, more healthful dietary behaviors)

Source: Copyright ©2004 by the National Academy of Sciences. All rights reserved. Permission is granted to reproduce this document in its entirety, with no additions or alterations.

plan suggestions for state and local educational authorities, health care professionals, and for parents and families. More information can be found in Chapter 10 related to childhood obesity, education, and prevention programs.

Free and Reduced Meal Programs

Too often in our society, students arrive at school hungry, and the only meal they can look forward to is what the school provides. Several federal child nutrition programs provide funds for breakfast, lunch, snacks, and sometimes dinner, so that children can be fed while they are in school, before and after school, and during the summer. Eligibility for these programs is based on a student's family income level. Funding for several other federal programs in the schools is connected to and based on eligibility for free and reduced meals. It is important that school administrators collect information related to student eligibility at the start of each school year for the purpose of securing program funding.

Food Allergies

Food allergies can be life threatening. The risk of accidental exposure to foods can be reduced in the school setting if schools work with students, parents, and physicians to minimize risks and provide a safe educational environment for food-allergic students (FAAM, 2004). School administrators and school personnel are required to be knowledgeable about and follow applicable fed-

Table 8.7. School Guidelines for Managing Students With Food Allergies.

SCHOOL RESPONSIBILITY

- Be knowledgeable about and follow applicable federal laws including ADA, IDEA, IDEIA, Section 504, and FERPA and any state laws or district policies that apply.
- Review the health records submitted by parents and physicians.
- Include food-allergic students in school activities. Students should not be excluded from school activities solely based on their food allergy.
- Identify a core team of, but not limited to, school nurse, teacher, principal, school food service and nutrition manager/director, and counselor (if available) to work with parents and the student (age appropriate) to establish a prevention plan. Changes to the prevention plan to promote food allergy management should be made with core team participation.
- Assure that all staff who interact with the student on a regular basis understand food allergies, can recognize symptoms, knows what to do in an emergency, and works with other school staff to eliminate the use of food allergens in the allergic student's meals, educational tools, arts and crafts projects, or incentives.
- Practice the Food Allergy Action Plans before an allergic reaction occurs to assure the efficiency/effectiveness of the plans.
- Coordinate with the school nurse to be sure medications are appropriately stored, and be sure that an emergency kit is available that contains a physician's standing order for epinephrine. In states were regulations permit, medications are kept in a easily accessible secure location central to designated school personnel, not in locked cupboards or drawers. Students should be allowed to carry their own epinephrine, if age appropriate, after approval from the student's physician/clinic, parent and school nurse, and allowed by state or local regulations.
- Designate school personnel who are properly trained to administer medications in accordance with the State Nursing and Good Samaritan Laws governing the administration of emergency medications.
- Be prepared to handle a reaction and ensure that there is a staff member available who is properly trained to administer medications during the school day regardless of time or location.
- Review policies/prevention plan with the core team members, parents/guardians, student (age appropriate), and physician after a reaction has occurred.
- Work with the district transportation administrator to assure that school bus driver training includes symptom awareness and what to do if a reaction occurs.
- Recommend that all buses have communication devices in case of an emergency.
- Enforce a "no eating" policy on school buses with exceptions made only to accommodate special needs under federal or similar laws, or school district policy. Discuss appropriate management of food allergy with family.
- Discuss field trips with the family of the food-allergic child to decide appropriate strategies for managing the food allergy.
- Follow federal/state/district laws and regulations regarding sharing medical information about the student.
- Take threats or harassment against an allergic child seriously.

(continued)

Table 8.7. School Guidelines for Managing Students With Food Allergies.

FAMILY'S RESPONSIBILITY

- Notify the school of the child's allergies.
- Work with the school team to develop a plan that accommodates the child's needs throughout the school including in the classroom, in the cafeteria, in after-care programs, during school-sponsored activities, and on the school bus, as well as a Food Allergy Action Plan.
- Provide written medical documentation, instructions, and medications as directed by a physician, using the Food Allergy Action Plan as a guide. Include a photo of the child on written form.
- Provide properly labeled medications and replace medications after use or upon expiration.
- Educate the child in the self-management of their food allergy including:
  —safe and unsafe foods
  —strategies for avoiding exposure to unsafe foods
  —symptoms of allergic reactions
  —how and when to tell an adult they may be having an allergy-related problem
  —how to read food labels (age appropriate)
- Review policies/procedures with the school staff, the child's physician, and the child (if age appropriate) after a reaction has occurred.
- Provide emergency contact information.

STUDENT'S RESPONSIBILITY

- Should not trade food with others.
- Should not eat anything with unknown ingredients or known to contain any allergen.
- Should be proactive in the care and management of their food allergies and reactions based on their developmental level.
- Should notify an adult immediately if they eat something they believe may contain the food to which they are allergic.

Source: The Food Allergy & Anaphylaxis Network. (FAAN)(2013). The School Food Allergy Program has been endorsed and/or supported by the Anaphylaxis Committee of the American Academy of Allergy, Asthma and Immunology, the National Association of School Nurses, and the Executive Committee of the Section on Allergy and Immunology of the American Academy of Pediatrics. FAAN can be reached at: 800/929-4040. The following organizations participated in the development of this document: American School Food Service Association, National Association of Elementary School Principals, National Association of School Nurses, National School Boards Association, The Food Allergy & Anaphylaxis Network.

eral laws including ADA, IDEA, IDEIA and Section 504, and any state laws or district policies that apply related to food allergies. Distribution of guidelines, such as those shown in Table 8.6, to school personnel and families will assist the school administrator in maintaining a safe environment for students with food allergies and help all students and families understand restrictions related to food products in the schools. The school nurse is required to maintain current medical records for all students. Nurses should also provide food allergy and allergic reaction information and training for students, faculty, and staff, including school maintenance personnel, bus drivers, and food service employees.

Physical Education Programs

Physical education programs, activities, and competition have a long history dating back to the Greeks and the birth of the Olympic Games around 800 B.C. In 17th and 18th century Europe, Rousseau and Locke supported the natural development of the child, stressing that a sound body makes a sound mind (McNergney & Herbert, 1995). During the 19th and early 20th century, the United States witnessed an evolving interest in physical education and activities starting with an emphasis on physical development and moving to sports and games, gymnastics, and finally established physical education programs in the schools. In the 1970s Title IX was implemented, ensuring equal physical education opportunities for males and females. The last half of the 20th century witnessed an emphasis on science-based movement education (Zepeda & Langenbach, 1999).

The current focus of physical education in schools has changed from games and competition to skill development, stressing motor skills, coordination, and developing life-long healthy lifestyles and habits. As stressed by the Center for Disease Control and Prevention (2013), planned physical education programs and activities foster students' physical, mental, emotional, and social development. The National Association for Sports and Physical Education (NASPE) developed the National Standards for Physical Education. These standards state that a physically educated person:

1. Demonstrates competency in motor skills and movement patterns needed to perform a variety of physical activities.
2. Demonstrates understanding of bodily motor concepts, principles, strategies, and tactics as they apply to learning and performance of physical activities.
3. Participates regularly in physical activity.
4. Achieves and maintains a health-enhancing level of physical fitness.
5. Exhibits responsible personal and social behavior that respects self and others in physical activity settings.
6. Values physical activity for health, enjoyment, challenge, self-expression, and/or social interaction (NASPE, 2013).

Adapted Physical Activities

The guidelines and implementation of P.L. 94-142 and subsequently IDEA and IDEIA have helped to make school districts and school personnel aware of the need to provided adapted physical activities for students unable to participate in regular education programs. The current movement in health education away from games and competition to health awareness and physical fitness provides for program development that can be inclusive of all students.

Comprehensive School Health Programs

The Centers for Disease Control and Prevention suggests the development of a comprehensive school health program.

Health education provides students with opportunities to acquire the knowledge, attitudes, and skills necessary for making health-promoting decisions, achieving health literacy, adopting health-enhancing behaviors, and promoting the health of others. Comprehensive school health education includes courses of study (curricula) for students in pre-K through grade 12 that address a variety of topics such as alcohol and other drug use and abuse, healthy eating/nutrition, mental and emotional health, personal health and wellness, physical activity, safety and injury prevention, sexual health, tobacco use, and violence prevention (Center for Disease Control and Prevention, 2013).

School-Linked and School-Based Health Clinics

Some schools and school districts offer health services within the schools. Traditionally, these services have included vision and hearing testing. A trend has been developing since the last part of the 20th century, to combine education, health, and human service organizations into what has become known as the "full-service school" (Dryfoos, J. G., 1994). Full-service schools are the natural outgrowth of federal laws, community demands, and recognition that physical, psychological, and social forces have an impact on the ability of children to learn. (See Chapter 10 for a more in-depth discussion of full-service schools.) In certain districts, school-linked or school-based health clinics have been established to serve the needs of students who might otherwise not have access to health care and social services. These health clinics can be found particularly in school districts serving economically disadvantaged communities. Increasingly, they also are found in middle-class communities where families are uninsured or underinsured and cannot afford or do not have access to adequate health care services for their children. In-school health clinics offer services that extend beyond vision and hearing to include dental services, immunizations, psychological services, medical examinations, sports physicals, teen pregnancy counseling, drug counseling, and HIV-AIDS and sexually transmitted disease awareness programs, among other services.

> While almost always controversial, these clinics build on a long tradition of having a school nurse in the building and relate directly to some of the major health-related dangers to healthy teenage development: pregnancy, venereal disease, AIDS, and drug and alcohol abuse. In some schools, up to 40 percent of the student body takes advantage of health services when they are available, since many of these students have no other form of health care (Barr & Parrett, 1995).

School Administrator Responsibilities

All school administrators should be familiar with federal laws and guidelines related to ADA, IDEA, IDEIA, Section 504, FERPA, and OSHA, including any state laws or district policies related to health and handicapping conditions of students and school personnel. The *Family Education Rights and Privacy Act of 1974* (U. S. Department of Education, 1974) requires that confidentiality be stressed and observed in services to students. Parents need to be kept informed of school requirements related to federal and state laws and district policies addressing the health and safety of their children. As with any educational material sent to parents and guardians, it is incumbent upon the administrator to insure that notifications regarding health issues or concerns are written not only in English but also in other language(s) prevalent in the community. Focus groups should be constituted to include family and community members in the development of health and social education programs related to students. Buildings must be clean and well maintained; sports equipment routinely disinfected and kept in good condition; halls, stairs, and walkways kept barrier free; and handicapped facilities need to be available for students and staff. Health records should be kept up to date and emergency plans developed and regularly reviewed to address serious and unexpected health and safety issues.

Maintenance of a Healthy School Environment

Environmental factors such as light, noise, air quality, and temperature can affect the physical environment of a school building and the comfort of students and staff. Environmental hazards such as chemical or biological agents are detrimental to health and safety. Dangerous social conditions, lax safety and security, and the potential for violence will affect the psychological well being of staff and students (EPA, 2013). It is the responsibility of the school administrator to address all these factors and to provide a safe and healthy environment in which all students can feel safe and have the opportunity to learn.

Coordination of Services

The school can be the key to providing information regarding health and social services available for students, parents, extended families, and community members. It is essential that educational leaders understand the importance of viewing the child as part of a family and view the family as part of a community. The school is often one of the first organizations contacted by a family when relocating. The school provides an anchor to the community and a sense of belonging for family members. In the interest of maintaining a healthy student body, the school can be the information center for families regarding not only educational services, but also health care, economic assistance, and psychological support. Health fairs, informational brochures, presentations, and workshops sponsored by the school and featuring representatives from local health and social services agencies can provide information to students, staff, and community members with an emphasis on both prevention and service delivery. Crossing bureaucratic lines and organizational boundaries and opening communication among the home, school, and community helps ease the point of entry for students and parents to local health and social services that can be provided by and in the schools. Everyone benefits from a health-conscious society—students, schools, family, and the community.

> A coordinated school health program (CSHP) model consists of eight interactive components. Schools by themselves cannot, and should not be expected to, address the nation's most serious health and social problems. Families, health care workers, the media, religious organizations, community organizations that serve youth, and young people themselves also must be systematically involved. However, schools could provide a critical facility in which many agencies might work together to maintain the well-being of young people (National Center for Chronic Disease Prevention and Health Promotion, 2004).

Funding Opportunities

Coordination of services is essential to meet the variety of health and human services requirements within a school and across a school district. The economic reality is that the per pupil allowance provided to schools does not always meet the budgetary requirements to offer and maintain programs similar to the ones reviewed throughout this chapter. External funding, particularly in the form of state and government grants, can provide extra money for health-oriented programs. The American Recovery and Reinvestment Act of 2009 provides funding opportunities to assist schools and school districts in the development and maintenance of a healthy and safe environment.

> Grantees will use funds under the Successful, Safe, and Healthy Students program to carry out strategies designed to improve school safety and to promote students' physical and mental health and well-being, nutrition education, healthy eating, and physical fitness. Grantees may support activities to prevent and reduce substance use, school violence (including teen dating violence), harassment, and bullying, as well as to strengthen family and community engagement in order to ensure a healthy and supportive school environment (The American Recovery and Reinvestment Act, 2009).

Summary

As we have seen in this chapter, health care and human service activities in the schools have evolved considerably since the early 1900s. The passing and implementation of compulsory school attendance laws brought with it the need to stem the spread of communicable disease in the schools and community. School nurses, counselors and social workers worked both separately and together in service to students, which expanded well beyond vaccinations and immunizations. Over the years, schools have been increasingly required to address not only academic programs, but health and social issues of children, youth, and adult employees as well. Legislation related to students with special needs and handicapping conditions of children and adults has widened the roles of health and human service workers in the schools. The advent of the full-service school has connected the school and community, with school-linked and school-based health clinics increasing health and human service activities in schools.

Questions for Consideration

1. Describe the components of the *Family Education Rights and Privacy Act* (FERPA). Explain the application of FERPA to health and human service programs in schools.
2. Create contingency plans for: (a) food contamination in the school; (b) a water pipe break; (c) identification of head lice; (d) measles outbreak.
3. Develop a vision, mission, goals, and objectives for a full-service school-based health clinic in the school.
4. Develop and describe the essential members, components, and activities of a coordinated health and human services team in the school. Create a plan to evaluate the effectiveness of this team.
5. Describe and develop a health and physical education activities program to address child and adolescent health concerns.
6. Describe the components of the *American With Disabilities Act* and Section 504 of the *Rehabilitation Act of 1974* that are of importance to the schools. How do these laws apply to both children and adults in schools?

Case Study

A Day in the Life of a School Nurse

For Carol Wells, a school nurse in Taylor Township Public Schools, daily life at work has become hectic. If when she first became a school nurse someone had told her what her work days would be like, she would have laughed. Carol, at this point, was not laughing. Whereas she used to split her time between two schools, spending the mornings at one and traveling to the other for the afternoon, she is now responsible for three elementary schools within the district in addition to the two middle schools. In addition, Carol's experience tells her that health concerns among the public in general, and parents of school-age children in particular, have reached an all-time high. Carol briefly reminisced about the days when she bandaged the occasional knee and called parents (one of whom was always home during the day) to retrieve feverish children from school. To think that she actually had the time to be involved in direct instruction of health classes and consult with teachers on school-health related issues seems now incredible.

Carol's daydream came to an abrupt end, however, when the first period lunch bell rang and the trail of students awaiting medication dosages began to form outside the small cubicle within the front office. She attempted to dispense the medication as quickly as possible so that the students did not miss too much of the already shortened lunch period. Schools across the district had been directed to shorten lunch hours and minimize, if not eliminate altogether, recess periods in an effort to maximize instruction time and improve student performance on state-mandated standardized tests. A double whammy, in Carol's opinion, had been dealt to the students, considering the gradual but steady increase of fattening and processed foods on the lunch and breakfast menu. As vending machines (which promised a kickback to the school for every purchase) became stationed throughout all the schools in the district, Carol was concerned about the long-term health of the students and the risk of obesity and hypertension they unknowingly faced.

Carol continued to move the students through the line as quickly as possible and marveled that so many students were taking medication. She wondered exactly how much of the apparent increase was due to over-prescribing of medication to children and adolescents. She also wondered how much was due to the fact that students are no longer allowed to take responsibility for their own dosages since doing so would mean expulsion under the district's policy of zero tolerance for drugs on school grounds. Her train of thought, however, was interrupted as the telephone rang. It was a parent calling to complain that her daughter had been sent home three days in a row with head lice and insisted that her child was getting the lice at school in the first place. Carol tried to patiently explain the district policy on head lice, and referred her to the public health information brochure, handed to her three days earlier, outlining methods for ridding the girl and the home of nits and lice eggs. The mother countered that she had read articles in a leading medical journal that invalidated such policies and indicated that head lice were in no way harmful or a public health threat. Carol reiterated the district policy and suggested that the mother write a letter to the district superintendent. Just as she was returning to the line of students, the telephone rang again. Carol decided to let the call ring back to the main office so that she could continue with her task.

She was nearing the end of the line when the telephone rang once again. This time, it was a parent complaining that a student had been seen eating a peanut butter sandwich in the school cafeteria. The parent indicated that she was well aware of the ban on all peanut products in the schools and her son, who has an allergy to peanuts, could have gone into anaphylactic shock as a result of this student's brazen disregard for the rules. Carol tried to calm the parent by reassuring her that there had evidently been no reaction and that she would reinforce the policy through the student newsletter. The parent, however, would not be consoled and informed Carol of her intention to sue the school and the offending student's parents. Carol wished her a good day and hung up. As she dispensed the last of the medication, the school principal came into the office accompanied by a father who appeared to be extremely agitated. His son had called him at work to tell him his Butterfinger candy bar had been confiscated by a lunchroom aide because it contained peanuts. Where, the father screamed, would this all end? What would the school ban next—milk products? Eggs? Dust? Bees? He ranted about how his son's rights and freedoms were being infringed upon, and threatened to sue the district for such violations. Amidst the chaos, the assistant principal approached Carol and wanted to know whether she had followed up with the students who were missing immunizations. The recently adopted requirement of the varicella vaccine had increased this task monumentally, and Carol had been inundated with calls complaining about immunizations and their possible links to a host of ills. The mere thought of all those phone calls made Carol suddenly realize she didn't feel very well. She retreated to the health station, sank onto the industrial-looking vinyl covered couch and stared listlessly for a moment at the Norman Rockwell lithograph on the wall depicting a school nurse taking the temperature of a ragtag little boy as impish faces peeked around the corner. Yes, Carol thought, her job had become more difficult over the years…but she wouldn't give it up for the world.

Questions for Discussion

1. Why is student health considered to be important to the educational process? To what extent should schools be held responsible for the health of students?

2. How can schools be sure that their health policies are based on sound and current medical evidence? When there is contradictory evidence, how should schools decide on which policy to follow?

3. Should students who are kept out of school for a significant number of days due to health concerns such as repeated bouts of head lice be offered home-bound services?

4. What are some of the legal, ethical, and moral issues related to nursing within the school context?

References

Barr, R. D., & Parrett, W. H. (1995). *Hope at last for at-risk youth.* Boston: Allyn and Bacon.

Beyer, B. M. (1997). Re-visiting reform issues in the education of Native American youth. *International Journal of Educational Reform.* (6)3, 343–348.

Beyer-Houda, B. (1995). Preparing school administrators for multicultural settings. *Catalyst for Change: Journal of the National School Development Council.* (24)2, 20–22.

Center for Disease Control (2012). *Youth risk behavior surveillance-United States, 2011.* Morbidity and Mortality Weekly Report. June 8, 2012. Surveillances Summaries, 61(4). Retrieved from http://www. cdc.gov/mmwr/pdf/ss/ss6104.pdf

Centers for Disease Control & Prevention (2003). *Division of HIV/AIDS prevention: HIV and its transmission.* National Center for HIV, STD, and TB Prevention. Last updated: September 22, 2003. Retrieved from http://www.cdc.gov/hiv/pub/facts/transmission.htm

CDC: Center for Disease Control and Prevention (2013). *Adolescent and school health: How schools cam implement coordinated school health.* Last updated September 27, 2013.Retrieved from http://www.cdc. gov/healthyyouth/cshp/schools.htm

CDC: Centers for Disease Control and Prevention (2013). *Components of coordinated school health.* Last updated February 27, 2013. Retrieved from http://www.cdc.gov/healthyyouth/cshp/components.htm

CDC: Centers for Disease Control and Prevention (2013). *How schools can implement coordinated school health.* Last updated February 27, 2013. Retrieved from http://www.cdc.gov/healthyyouth/cshp/schools. htm

CDC: Center for Disease Control and Prevention (2013). *Teen pregnancy: The importance of prevention.* Last updated November 21, 2012. Retrieved from http://www.cdc.gov/TeenPregnancy/AboutTeenPreg. htm.

Dryfoos, J. G. (1994). *Full-service schools: A revolution in health and social services for children, youth, and families.* San Francisco: Jossey-Bass.

EPA: United States Environmental Protection Agency (2013). *Healthy school environments.* Last updated May, 29, 2013. Retrieved from http://www.epa.gov/schools/

Epstein, J. L. (2001). *School, family, and community partnerships: Preparing educators and improving schools.* Boulder, CO: Westview Press, A Member of the Perseus Books Group.

Goals 2000: Educate America Act (1994). 20 U.S.C. Section 5801 et seq.

Individuals With Disabilities Education Act of 1990. 20 U.S.C. Section 1400 et seq. (1990).

Institute of Medicine of the National Academies (2004). *Preventing childhood obesity: Health in the balance.* Report Brief. September 2004. Retrieved from http://www.iom.edu/~/media/Files/Report%20 Files/2004/Preventing-Childhood-Obesity-Health-in-the-Balance/ChildhoodObesity4pagerfixforweb-pdf.ashx

McNergney, R. F., & Herbert, J. M. (1995). *Foundations of Education: The challenge of professional practice.* Boston: Allyn and Bacon.

National Academy of Sciences (2004). *Focus on childhood obesity.* Institute of Medicine of the National Academies. Retrieved from http://www.iom.edu/focuson.asp?id=22593

National Association for Sport and Physical Fitness (2013). *Moving into the future: National standards for physical education, 2nd edition (2004).* Retrieved from http://www.aahperd.org/naspe/standards/nationalStandards/PEstandards.cfm

National Association of School Nurses (2008). *Position statement: Coordinated school health services.* Retrieved from http://www.nasn.org/PolicyAdvocacy/PositionPapersandReports/NASNPositionStatementsFullView/tabid/462/smid/824/ArticleID/19/Default.aspx

National Association of School Nurses (2011). *Role of the school nurse: Position statement.* Retrieved from http://www.nasn.org/PolicyAdvocacy/PositionPapersandReports/NASNPositionStatementsFullView/tabid/462/smid/824/ArticleID/87/Default.aspx

National Clearinghouse on Child Abuse and Neglect Information (2003). *Recognizing child abuse and neglect: Signs and Symptoms.* Retrieved from http://nccanch.acf.hhs.gov

National Education Association Health Information Network. (2004). *Sexual and reproductive health.* Retrieved from http://www.neahin.org/programs/reproductive/teenpreg.htm#top

National Education Association Health Information Network (2010). *Teen pregnancy.* Retrieved from http:// crisisguide.neahin.org/reproductive/teenpregnancy.html

Ogden, C. & Carroll, M. (2010). *Prevalence of Obesity Among Children and Adolescents: United States, Trends 1963–1965 Through 2007–2008.* Division of Health and Nutrition Examination Surveys. Retrieved from http://www.cdc.gov/nchs/data/hestat/obesity_child_07_08/obesity_child_07_08.pdf

School Social Work Association of America (2003). *SSWAA's organizational mission.* Retrieved from http:// www.sswaa.org/

Stark, A. (2001). Pizza Hut, Domino's, and the public schools. *Policy Review, 108*, 59–70.

Substance Abuse and Mental Health Services Administration (2011). *Results from the 2010 National Survey on Drug Use and Health: Summary of National Findings.* NSDUH Series H-41, HHS Publication No. (SMA) 11-4658. Rockville, MD: Author. Retrieved from http://www.oas.samhsa.gov/ NSDUH/2k10NSDUH/2k10Results.htm#2.2

The Food Allergy & Anaphylaxis Network (2013). *School guidelines for managing students with food allergies* Retrieved from http://www.foodallergy.org/document.doc?id=135

U.S. Department of Education (1974). *Family Education Rights And Privacy Act.* 20 U.S.C. Sec. 1232g; 34 C.F.R. Part 99.

U.S. Department of Education (1974). *Rehabilitation Act of 1974.* (Pub. L. No. 93-112), 29 U.S.C. Part 794.

U.S. Department of Health and Human Services (2004). *2003 National Survey on Drug Use and Health.* Substance Abuse and Mental Health Services Administration, Office of Applied Statistics. Retrieved from http://www.oas.samhsa.gov/nhsda.htm#NHSDAinfo

U.S. Department of Health and Human Services (2000). *Healthy People 2000.* Center for Disease Control and Prevention. Retrieved from http://odphp.osophs.dhhs.gov/pubs/HP2000/prior.html

U.S. Department of Health and Human Services (2007). *Recognizing child abuse and neglect: Signs and symptoms.* Child Welfare Information Gateway. Retrieved from https://www.childwelfare.gov/pubs/factsheets/signs.cfm

U.S. Government (1965). *Elementary and Secondary Education Act.* (P.L. 89-10). Washington, DC: U.S. Government Printing Office.

U.S. Government (2009). *American recovery and reinvestment act of 2009: Successful, safe and healthy students.* Retrieved from http://www2.ed.gov/policy/elsec/leg/blueprint/publication_pg8.html#part8

Zepeda, S. J., & Langenbach, M. (1999). *Special programs in regular schools: Historical foundations, standards, and contemporary issues.* Boston: Allyn and Bacon.

CHAPTER 9

Prevention Programs

Introduction and Historical Perspective

A S prior chapters have documented, public schools have a long history of providing additional services to students through a variety of programs. Many mandated interventions were designed to prevent problems in the student population rather than to solve them once they appeared. For example, students' health and nutritional statuses were addressed by the national government through the Free and Reduced Lunch program. This program began in 1946 when malnutrition among school children became a national concern, after its widespread effects on physical development became apparent during the military draft for World War II (FRAC, 2004). (See Chapter 8 for more information about health programs in schools.) Alcohol prevention programs targeting school children as a primary audience date back even further, emerging from the Temperance Movement of the mid-1800s. These programs continued in the schools in some form through the post-Prohibition era to the programs in place today (Gliksman & Smythe, 1990). These two examples point out a significant feature of prevention programs implemented in the public schools: typically, they are designed to reduce or eliminate a perceived social ill believed to have national significance and far-reaching negative effects across the general, often middle-class, population.

Public schools have often been the venue for preventative programming due to a variety of factors. Public schools provide ready access to children who are a captive and, at least at younger ages, impressionable audience. In addition, it is generally seen as the mission of the public schools not only to teach academic subjects but also to socialize children and promote the development of healthy, happy, and productive citizens. Furthermore, there is an assumption underlying most of these programs that children must be targeted before they begin to develop the behavior in question, whether it is smoking, bullying, or using illegal drugs (Gottfredson, 1996). Finally, prevention programs rely on formal didactic instructional methods for dissemination of information and skills. Schools, with readily available instructors and resources necessary to implement such programs, are viewed as a logical venue for prevention education.

To gain an understanding of prevention programs in schools, it is important first to recognize that research on prevention is multidisciplinary in nature, drawing from fields as diverse as psychology, education, public health, medicine, psychiatry, sociology, social work, criminal justice, political science, law, and economics. Thus, the salient issues and trends, and conceptual frameworks for understanding prevention and evaluating the effectiveness of programming efforts vary across fields. This chapter is intended to provide a very broad overview of such programs as they relate to programs in place across the K–12 curriculum. Additionally, because there are a variety of specific prevention programs now being implemented across the nation that cover an ever-widening range of areas targeted for prevention, it is not possible to adequately cover each. Instead, prevention programs will be discussed in general terms, with characteristics of model programs highlighted for each prevention area.

In general, prevention programs that target school children and are implemented in public schools fall under the category of "primary prevention" programs, meaning that the programs are intended to decrease the incidence of the behavior in question. This category has been further divided in recent years to describe different levels of prevention based on the concept of risk. Universal prevention targets the general public or population group without consideration for risk factors, while selective prevention focuses on individuals or subgroup populations thought to have biological, psychological, or social risk factors for developing the behavior in question (Weissberg, Kumpfer, & Seligman, 2003). Both universal and selective prevention programs are found in public schools today, and as this chapter discusses the history, current approaches, and future trends of prevention programs, the reader should keep in mind the differing approaches to conceptualizing prevention. This chapter will examine the history and development of a variety of prevention programs currently in the public schools, as well.as controversies surrounding prevention programming and future trends. Finally, general administrative considerations and personnel issues will be outlined.

Substance Abuse Prevention Programs

Although efforts to implement various prevention programs in the public schools in the United States existed as early as the mid-1800s, many prevention programs did not begin in earnest until the middle of the twentieth century. Furthermore, most mandates for prevention programs surfaced in the 1980s and 1990s (Zepeda & Langenbach, 1999). For example, the passage of the *Drug Free Schools and Communities Act of 1986* (DFSCA) by the U.S. Congress provided federal funds to states, schools, and communities for the purpose of initiation and expansion of drug prevention programs. This Act, which originally operated under the *Elementary Secondary Education Act of 1964* (ESEA) as the Drug-Free Schools Program, emphasized the need to develop and implement a sequential drug-prevention curriculum, to offer parental and law-enforcement involvement, and to maintain a school-community advisory committee. When the Act later became known as the Safe & Drug-Free Schools & Communities Program under the *Improving America's Schools Act of 1994*, the emphasis shifted from a primary focus on drug prevention and intervention to include violence prevention and safety planning in schools and communities. The availability of federal funding, however, also came with increased accountability for program outcomes and required the use of proven and effective strategies. Finally, in 2001, this program was subsumed under the *No Child Left Behind Act*, and emphasized the need to target students most at risk. In addition to emphasizing drug- and violence-free schools and communities, specific language was added that addressed illegal use of alcohol and tobacco, and focused on a need to connect program planning and development efforts to student achievement, school climate, and school improvement (First District Regional Educational Service Agency, 2004).

Substance-abuse prevention programs, including programs intended to curb or eliminate the use of illegal drugs, alcohol, and smoking among school-aged children, usually take one of three forms: knowledge/information-based, affective, and social influence. Generally speaking, the earliest drug-prevention programs tended to utilize a knowledge/information approach that reflected an assumption regarding drug-abuse prevalent at the time, viz., that drug abuse resulted from a lack of knowledge about adverse consequences. It was thus thought that providing factual information about the legal, biological, and psychosocial effects of drug use to students, often through the use of scare-tactics and dramatic audio-visual presentations, would encourage the avoidance of such substances (Ringwalt, Greene, Ennett, Iachan, Clayton, & Leukefeld, 1994). This type of prevention program generally failed to demonstrate the anticipated outcome and even, according to some researchers, inadvertently increased the likelihood of drug use among some participants (Bruvold & Rundall, 1988). Affective programs were developed largely during the 1970s and early 1980s and, in contrast to the knowledge/information approach of previous efforts, were based on the assumption that drug use among students was due to personal factors such as low self-esteem, poor decision-making skills, and lack of clear personal values. It was thought, then, that by improving these interpersonal skills, even without explicit reference to drugs and other substances, students would choose to avoid them. Most recently, a social influences approach to drug prevention programs, which include some of the characteristics of both knowledge/information and affective, have been developed. The social-influence approach is based on the assumption that students use drugs and other substances due to a lack of social competence necessary to resist perceived peer and societal influence (Gliksman & Smythe, 1990; Ringwalt *et al.*, 1994).

Comprehensive reviews and meta-analyses of substance-abuse prevention programs conducted during the late 1980s and early 1990s were inconsistent but generally found little evidence of effectiveness across all three prevention approaches described above (Gliksman & Smythe, 1990; Price, Cowen, Lorion, & Ramos-McKay, 1988; Weissberg, Kumpfer, & Seligman, 2003). Inherent weaknesses in the conceptual framework of early programs were certainly to blame for at least some of the negative findings. However, a general lack of information about the consistency and appropriateness of program implementation along with a lack of consensus on appropriate outcomes accounted for at least some of the negative findings. Current trends in substance-abuse prevention programs reflect the recognition that focusing solely on the cognitive, affective, or behavioral skills of individual students ignores important environmental and contextual factors that also must be addressed. As a result, more programs are grounded in ecological—contextual theory and address the complex interactions among intrapersonal factors, interpersonal processes, institutional and community factors, and public policy (Gilchrist, 1994).

One of the most widespread substance abuse prevention programs in schools across the United States is the Drug Abuse Resistance Education or D.A.R.E. program. This program, founded in 1983 in Los Angeles, is a police officer-led series of classroom lessons that teaches children from kindergarten through 12th grade how to resist peer pressure and lead productive, drug and violence free lives (D.A.R.E., 2012). The program, which receives funding through several federal offices, is not without controversy, however. Independent research studies, conducted over several years and using a variety of methodologies, have consistently found the program to be ineffective (West & O'Neal, 2004), and even potentially harmful to some participants (Lilienfeld, 2007). Regardless of the lack of empirical support, however, the program continues to function in schools across the United States and 44 other countries, and a national D.A.R.E. Day was declared by President Barack Obama in 2010 (D.A.R.E., 2012).

Beyond the D.A.R.E. program, the United States Department of Health and Human Services—Substance Abuse and Mental Health Services Administration (SAMHSA, 2012) provides information on substance-abuse prevention programs and resources available to schools and communities for the prevention and reduction of substance abuse among youth. SAMSHA's National Registry of Evidence-Based Programs and Practices currently lists 112 interventions and programs aimed at school-aged children and adolescents (SAMSHA, 2013).

Anti-Bullying Programs

Bullying has received national and international attention in recent decades due to increased awareness of its prevalence and consequences. Bullying, according to the U.S. Department of

Health and Human Services (2013), is defined as "unwanted, aggressive behavior among school aged children that involves a real or perceived power imbalance. The behavior is repeated, or has the potential to be repeated, over time," and both victims and perpetrators of bullying may have serious, lasting problems. Bullying may take several forms, including: (1) verbal bullying such as name-calling, teasing, taunting, inappropriate sexual comments, and threatening to cause harm; (2) social bullying, including intentionally leaving an individual out, telling others not to be friends with the victim, spreading rumors, and causing public embarrassment; and (3) physical bullying, including acts of physical aggression (hitting, kicking, pinching, spitting, etc.) as well as taking or damaging the personal property of the victim. Bullying most frequently is reported to happen during school hours, often in settings with little or no supervision such as the playground, bus, or hallways, but can also occur before and/or after school hours, especially traveling to or from school. Increasingly, cyber-bullying has gained attention. This form of bullying uses electronic technology such as cell phones, computers, and tablets, and often takes place through social media sites, text messaging, chat, and other websites. This form of bullying is considered particularly destructive because it can occur any time of day or night, and when the victim is alone. In addition, cyber-bullying can be perpetrated anonymously, and harassing or intimidating messages and images can be spread quickly to a wide audience. Deleting these messages and images is difficult, and tracing the source is sometimes impossible.

According to a United States Department of Justice survey (2011), 13.2% of respondents reported having been victims of physical bullying during the previous year. Complicating the matter is that the same survey results indicated that 13% of students in grades 6–12 admit to having bullied another person, and 6% reported being both a victim and a perpetrator of bullying. Thus, one element of bullying that is gaining increasing attention and importance is the recognition that the same individuals are often both bullies and victims of bullying. Of those who experienced bullying, 25% reported being bullied for their race or religion. Bullying, according to the U.S. Department of Justice, tends to begin in elementary school and reach its highest levels during middle school, but can also occur during high school. Females tend to experience mainly verbal and social bullying, while males tend to experience both verbal and physical bullying. Victims of bullying often remain silent out of fear of retaliation or shame, and 66% of bullying victims reported feeling that the school professionals responded poorly to the situation.

According to the U. S. Department of Education (2011), 46 states have laws that address bullying, and 41 have policies regarding bullying. In addition, 36 states included provisions that addressed cyber-bullying, and 13 states specified that schools have jurisdiction over off-campus behavior if it creates a hostile school environment. And although, in this same report, U.S. Secretary of Education, Arne Duncan, is quoted as saying every state should have an effective bullying prevention program in place to protect children inside and outside of school, school districts themselves are often responsible for identifying and implementing programs to address and prevent bullying. In examining variables that appear to encourage school bullying, Allen (2010) found that poor classroom management by school personnel and lack of overall structure across the school setting were key factors. In addition, simple solutions such as zero tolerance policies were generally ineffective in the long-term for reducing or eliminating bullying behavior. Successful anti-bullying programs tend to be whole school / multidisciplinary interventions targeted at social and behavioral skills training combined with an established code of conduct with specific consequences for bullying behaviors, along with counseling, mediation, and strategic educator training (Neiman, Robers, & Robers, 2012).

While several anti-bullying programs have been developed over the years and across several nations, few systematic reviews on the effectiveness of such programs have been undertaken. However, in their meta-analysis of 44 studies on various international anti-bullying programs, Farrington & Ttofi (2010) found that, overall, anti-bullying programs were effective in reducing both bullying and victimization. Specific characteristics that had the greatest impact on reducing both bullying and victimization behaviors included parent training / meetings, disciplinary methods, and duration and intensity of the program. One of the oldest anti-bullying programs is the Olweus Bullying Prevention Program (Olweus, 2012), which has been implemented in several school districts across the U.S. and beyond. In addition, the U.S. Department of Justice maintains a model programs guide, including a section on anti-bullying programs. Programs that have been reviewed include: KiVa Anti-bullying Program, Positive Action, Success in Stages, and Steps to Respect: A Bullying Prevention Program (U.S. Department of Justice). Overall, these model programs focus on creating a schoolwide climate that builds connections, caring, and empathy while discouraging bullying and aggression.

Violence Prevention Programs

School and community violence became the focus of national attention during the 1990s, precipitated in part by several unrelated acts of and seemingly unprecedented levels of violence on public school campuses across the nation. Although the perception among educators and the public in general is that violence in the schools has increased significantly only in recent decades, school violence has existed in a variety of forms across time and location. Volokh & Snell (1998) traced the history of school violence in an effort to highlight the ambiguity involved in interpreting trends:

> We should neither minimize nor exaggerate the problem of school violence. Violence is not unique to schools, nor did it begin in the postwar era, despite the movie *The Blackboard Jungle*, which suggested that juvenile delinquency and disruption of classes was a new phenomenon. Misbehavior, violence, and disruption have been recurrent themes in schools for centuries, and school officials have rarely been happy with student behavior. American schools, historically, have also had their share of violence, sex, drugs, and gambling (p. 7).

These authors note that trends and data are also unclear regarding the age range at which violence is more prevalent (e.g., middle school versus high school), the relative breakdown of school violence between rural, suburban, and urban schools, and the incidence of victimization and weapons possession among public school students. Nevertheless, they acknowledge that there appears to be a shift toward increased severity or intensity of violence. For example, research by Sheley and Smith (as cited in Volokh & Snell, 1998 and Victory Over Violence, 2001) indicated that greater numbers of students are citing seemingly trivial occurrences (e.g., being stared at or insulted, having property stolen, etc.) as justification for shooting a classmate.

Violence prevention initially found its way into federal legislation through the *Safe and Drug-Free Schools and Communities Act* of 1994, which sought to help the nation's schools achieve a disciplined environment conducive to learning. Federal funds, available to states through grants, were earmarked for the development and implementation of effective, research-based programs designed to educate communities about violence and to eliminate violence in and around schools (Center for Effective Collaboration and Practice, 2000). In addition, the *Safe Schools / Healthy Students Initiative* is a collaborative grant program supported by three federal agencies—the U.S. Department of Health and Human Services (through SAMHSA), the U.S. Department of Education, and the U.S. Department of Justice (SAMHSA, 2013). The requirements for federal funding for violence prevention programs are similar to those for drug abuse prevention programs in that they must be effective and research-based. However, research and program evaluations investigating the effectiveness of violence prevention programs, as is true for many prevention program efforts, are limited at best, and conclusions have often been ambiguous and contradictory. Thus, Volokh & Snell (1998) have criticized the limitation of federal funding to so-called evidence-based violence prevention programs, pointing out that the causes of school violence are poorly understood and that such funding limitations may effectively prevent the development of non-approved alternative approaches that might work in specific contexts.

Current violence-prevention programs can be classified into three broad categories: school-management-based, environmental modification, and education and curricular oriented. School-management based programs tend to focus on student behavior and discipline policy. They may offer alternative school programs and encourage cooperation with local law enforcement. Environmental modification programs attempt to curb school violence by modifying the physical and/or social environment. These modifications often include the use of metal detectors, video cameras, and security guards in the school as well as reducing school and class sizes and improving the school climate. Finally, educational and curricular efforts tend to focus on knowledge and skill development, and attempt to reduce school violence by teaching empathy, anger management, social problem-solving, and nonviolent conflict resolution strategies (Frey, Hirschstein, & Guzzo, 2000; Tschannen-Moran, 2001; Volokh & Snell, 1998).

While no single approach has been found to be more effective in general than the others, specific components have been identified that seem to contribute to successful violence prevention programming. According to CECP (2000), these include having a common child-centered orientation and goals that include seeing each child as an individual, having high expectations, treating children with respect and expecting respect in return, and holding students responsible for their behavior. In addition, the importance of maintaining a positive and supportive school climate that embodies a caring learning environment, builds a sense of community, develops positive adult-child relationships, and fosters a sense of welcome and belonging (Peterson & Skiba, 2001) is emphasized. Effective programs were also identified as embracing a problem-solving approach to student behavior rather than relying on the reactive and punitive measures advocated by zero-tolerance policies, which will be discussed in more detail below. Clear, consistent, and simple expectations for students as well as staff allow for a predictable structure within the educational environment and promote a sense of stability and confidence among students. Finally, prevention and early intervention are stressed. Visible supervision of situations in which problems are more likely to arise (e.g., school entrances, lunchroom, corridors between classes, etc.) and early interventions that target students at risk for developing violent behaviors prevent the onset or escalation of problem behaviors. Furthermore, a meta-analysis conducted by Park-Higgerson, Perumean-Chaney, Bartolucci, Grimely, & Singh in 2008 of 26 randomized controlled- trial, school-based studies that were designed to reduce externalizing, aggressive, and violent behavior between the 1st and 11th grades demonstrated no significant differences between interventions, although programs that used non-theory based interventions, focused on at-risk and older children, and employed intervention specialists had stronger effects in reducing aggression and violent behavior.

In general, effective violence prevention programs identified by CEPC all strive to promote the learning and well-being of students and to foster caring, positive learning environments that provide students with the skills and supports necessary to achieve academic as well as social success. This approach stands in stark contrast to that taken by advocates of zero-tolerance policies. First implemented in the 1980s by U.S. military and customs agencies in dealing with illegal drug possession, zero-tolerance policies were mandated under the *Gun-Free Schools Act* of 1994. As a result of this mandate, students found in possession of a weapon were required to be suspended for one calendar year and referred to the criminal or juvenile justice system (Skiba & Peterson, 1999). While the original Act specified possession of firearms, the definition was later expanded to include any instrument that could be construed as a weapon. Furthermore, many school districts across the country have also invoked this policy for a broad range of offenses, often poorly defined, ranging from possession of drugs and alcohol to threats of violence to disruptive classroom behavior.

The adoption of zero-tolerance policies has resulted in rigid adherence to and strict enforcement of harsh disciplinary tactics regardless of the severity or circumstances of the behavior in question. This trend reflects a desire for expedient and facile solutions that are ultimately ineffective and often counterproductive (Holloway, 2002) to complex societal problems. Examples of fatuous situations abound in which a school's zero tolerance policy was invoked and might even be amusing if it weren't for the very real result of unjustified school expulsions, alternative education placements, criminal records, and alienation of countless students. Too often these policies have resulted in crisis-driven and coercive educational environments that foster mistrust among students and staff alike and increase the drop-out rate of students, particularly minority students and students with learning differences (CECP, 2000; NASP, 2001). Skiba and Peterson summed up the main difficulty with zero-tolerance policies in the following statement:

> Yet the indiscriminate use of force without regard for its effects is the hallmark of authoritarianism, incompatible with the functioning of a democracy, and certainly incompatible with the transmission of democratic values to children. If we rely solely, or even primarily, on zero-tolerance strategies to preserve the safety of our schools, we are accepting a model of schooling that implicitly teaches students that the preservation of order demands the suspension of individual rights and liberties. As we exclude ever-higher proportions of children whose behavior does not meet increasingly tough standards, we will inevitably meet many of those disruptive youths on the streets. In choosing control and exclusion as our preferred methods of dealing with school disruption, even as we refrain from positive interventions, we increase the likelihood that the correctional system will become the primary agency responsible for troubled youths. Ultimately, as we commit ourselves to increasingly draconian policies of school discipline, we may also need to resign ourselves to increasingly joyless schools, increasingly unsafe streets, and dramatically increasing expenditures for detention centers and prisons (p. 8).

Overall, there are certain features and characteristics that can either predispose or buffer against school violence. Factors that may predispose a school to violence among students include poor design and use of school space, overcrowding, harsh disciplinary procedures, insensitivity to multicultural factors, student alienation, rejection of at-risk students by peers and teachers, and anger or resentment among students over school routines or demands for conformity. Conversely, factors that may buffer against violence include a positive school climate, clear goals and high expectations for student performance, inclusive values and practices, high levels of school attachment among students, strong parental involvement, and provision for social development and interpersonal skill acquisition (CEPM, 2001). Finally, because there are multiple causes of inappropriate behaviors in the school setting, including behavior classified as violent, a single response or approach will probably have little overall effect in reducing or eliminating such problems. Instead, prevention programs are more likely to be effective when they comprise multiple levels of intervention and when the intensity of the intervention is appropriate for the severity of the problem (CECP, 2000).

Drop-Out Prevention Programs

Dropping out of school has been associated with a number of negative outcomes including unemployment, confinement to lower-level occupations, poverty, higher rates of health problems and criminal activity. The significant costs of school dropout rates for both individuals and society in general have become a national concern in recent years (Rumberger, 2001). Concerns center primarily around three issues. First, as the economy moves toward a higher-skilled labor force, those who fail to obtain a basic education will face greater obstacles in the labor market, resulting in limited earning potential and over-reliance on public assistance programs (Murnane & Levy, 1996). In addition, the numbers of students who are at risk of dropping out, including students living in poverty or low-income situations and who are cultural, racial, or linguistic minorities, are increasing in the public schools (Natriello, McDill, & Pallas, 1990). Finally, the push for greater accountability in the schools has resulted in a call to end to so-called social promotion, resulting in greater numbers of students who are retained in grade and who fail to pass the exit exams increasingly required for high school graduation (Amrein & Berlinger, 2003).

Although dropping out of school is generally caused by a variety of factors and circumstances (Ormrod, 2008; Santrock, 2002), there are specific individual and contextual risk factors that have been identified. School failure, including poor grades, low test scores, and retention in grade, is the most significant risk factor for dropping out of school. In fact, research has found that students who are retained in grade once are three times more likely to drop out of school than non-retained peers matched for academic ability, socioeconomic status, and ethnicity regardless of the student's age at the time of retention (NASP, 1998). Disengagement from the schooling process, which may be manifested by behavior problems, poor attendance, social isolation from peers, and a lack of involvement in school activities, even during early grades, has been associated with dropping out. Students who see their school as uncaring or non-supportive, or who view their education as irrelevant are more likely to drop out.

In addition to student characteristics, certain family, school, and community characteristics are known to put students at risk for dropping out of school as well. Students whose parents demonstrate minimal involvement with and negative attitudes toward schooling, and who place little value on school attendance and achievement are at increased risk of dropping out of school as are students who have one or more siblings who have dropped out. Schools with rigid retention policies, high teacher turn-over, large class sizes, harsh or uncompromising discipline policies, and tracking practices tend to produce greater numbers of students who drop out of school. Finally, communities that lack support systems for minority and low- income students and that do not appear to value education and staying in school have greater numbers of students who have dropped out (NASP, 1998). Although factors such as ethnicity and socioeconomic status are also associated with school dropout rates, the relationships are complex and indirect. Generally speaking, however, Latino and Native American students have the highest dropout rates, and limited economic resources predispose students to a variety of social factors that may, in turn, lead to dropping out of school (NASP, 1998).

The National Dropout Prevention Center / Network (NDPC/N) has identified strategies that are effective in reducing dropout rates including: school-community approaches, early intervention, instructional strategies and student support efforts. School-community approaches involve school improvement efforts that are designed to improve student achievement overall, especially in low-performing schools, and to reduce the achievement gap between economically disadvantaged, minority students and their more affluent, non-minority counterparts. Many experts in the field recognize the need for systemic reform in addressing complex social issues that challenge traditional school models (Martin, Tobin, & Sugai, 2002; Rumberger, 2001) while cautioning that such restructuring takes time and requires financial, administrative, and community support. In addition, school-community collaboration is needed in which everyone in a given community is held responsible for the quality of education and levels of student achievement. Finally, safe environments that are conducive to learning and that foster a sense of belonging and acceptance among students require the effort and cooperation of both school and community (NDPC/N, 2013).

Early interventions efforts include improvement in family engagement in the educational process and improved family-school communication, provision of early childhood education to children who are at risk for ultimately dropping out of school, and early literacy interventions for students who are at risk for or demonstrate difficulty with reading. Instructional strategies that reduce school drop-out rates include individualized or differentiated instruction to meet the diverse learning needs of students, as well as the use of active learning techniques and instructional technology that engage learners, emphasize authentic learning and problem-solving, and activate multiple sensory modalities. In addition, teachers who work with students at risk for dropping out need on-going professional development for peer and administrative support as well as training in innovative and effective teaching practices. Alternative educational programs and career-technical education programs can offer curricula and instruction that is perceived as more relevant to students at-risk of dropping out of school while providing a learning atmosphere designed to meet their unique academic and social needs. Additional information and examples of these types of programs can be found in Chapters 7 and 8 of this text. Finally, student support can be offered in a variety of forms. Mentoring and tutoring, service learning, and after school activities can strengthen attachments to both school and community, improve students' sense of academic and social self-worth, increase motivation and for achievement, and fill unstructured time outside of school with meaningful and engaging social interaction (NDPC/N, 2013). Additional information on student support services can be found in Chapter 10 of this book.

Prevention Programs for Health-Related Issues

In 1979, the Surgeon General's report, *Healthy People*, laid the foundation for a national health agenda that stressed the importance of prevention. The organization provides science-based, 10-year national objectives for improving the health of all Americans. Then, in 1980, *Promoting Health / Preventing Disease: Objectives for the Nation* and later, *Healthy People 2000* established a set of national objectives that has served as the basis of numerous state and community prevention programs. In the previous decade, *Healthy People 2010*, specific goals for education and school-based health programs were outlined. In particular, the number of middle, junior high, and senior high schools offering programs designed to prevent health-related problems was targeted as a specific goal. The areas of concern included injury and violence, suicide, tobacco use and addiction, alcohol and drug use, unintended pregnancy, HIV/AIDS and sexually transmitted diseases, unhealthy dietary patterns, and inadequate physical activity. In its current form, *Healthy People 2020* (HealthyPeople.gov, 2013) has as its overarching goals to: (1) attain high quality, longer lives free of preventable disease, disability, injury, and premature death; (2) achieve health equity, eliminate disparities, and improve the health of all groups; (3) create social and physical environments that promote good health for all; and (4) promote quality of life, healthy development, and healthy behaviors across all life stages. In its new framework, *Healthy People 2020* emphasizes an ecological and determinants approach to health promotion and disease prevention, recognizing that health and health behaviors are determined by influences at multiple factors, including personal (e.g., psychological, biological), organizational/institutional, environmental (social and physical), and policy levels. In addition, the organization has recognized the importance of health information technology and health communication as an integral part of the implementation and success of its objectives.

Obesity Prevention

Over the past three decades, the percentage of students who are classified as overweight, according to the definition of Centers for Disease Control and Prevention (CDC), has tripled, and in 2010 more than one third of children and adolescents were obese (CDC, 2013). Excess weight has been associated with several health-related issues including increased risk for heart disease, high cholesterol, high blood pressure, type II diabetes, obesity in adulthood, and a host of secondary health problems. Additionally, overweight students are at increased risk for developing psychological problems and disorders such as depression, eating disorders, distorted body image, and low self-esteem. Furthermore, students who are overweight are often subjected to teasing, bullying, and even discrimination (MDE, 2001). Overall, obesity has become a national concern due to the personal and economic consequences of lost productivity and increased health care expenditures (Wolf & Colditz, 1998). Several factors including those of biological, behavioral, and environmental origin have been identified that contribute to the growing incidence of obesity in the United States (CDC, 2013). While prevention programs cannot address genetic predisposition toward excess weight, such programs can effectively educate students to alter their behavior and make healthy environmental choices regarding nutrition, diet, and physical activity. More students spend increasing amounts of time in sedentary activities such as watching television, using computers, and playing video games. This, in combination with the availability of high-calorie, low nutrition foods and beverages, equals excess calories consumed against fewer calories expended (CDC, 2004; MDE, 2001). Thus, the main focus of most school-based obesity prevention programs is to increase physical activity within the schools, improve the nutritional quality of foods available through the schools, and to educate students to make healthy behavioral and environmental choices outside of school in the home and community. In addition, the CDC (2013) cited the Healthy, Hunger-Free Kids Act of 2010, which allows the United States Department of Agriculture (USDA) to develop and update federal nutrition standards for competitive foods consistent with the *Dietary Guidelines for Americans*. USDA's proposed rule, released on February 8, 2013, outlined the minimum nutrition guidelines for competitive foods and beverages outside of the federal reimbursable school meals program that are sold on school campuses during the school day. Additionally, states and local education agencies are able to adopt nutrition standards for all commercial foods in schools. This act is important because children and adolescents currently have increased access to foods at school through vending machines and other sales mechanisms that, in turn, influence the food choices and eating habits of these students.

In her guidelines for preventing childhood obesity, Misner (2003) recommended focusing on the ultimate goal—that of attaining short- and long-term improvement in health and well-being for children. Additionally, it is recommended that prevention programs maintain a health-centered rather than weight-centered approach and emphasize a whole-person approach that considers the physical, mental, and social needs equally. A framework for addressing obesity in children and adolescents begins with the need to organize a multidisciplinary decision-making team comprising health professionals, teachers, specialists, and members of the general public. This team is important to the development and implementation of any program since the effectiveness of such a prevention effort is depends on the promotion and support of healthy lifestyle choices across contexts—home, school, and community. Before program planning can begin, specific goals need to be set based upon the existing health status and needs of the students and broader community. The goals should be stated for improvement in overall health, not weight, and should include both healthy eating habits and physical activity. In addition, goals that address the development of a positive, nurturing environment also need to be stated (p. 2). The Blue Cross Blue Shield Association (BCBSA, 2010) has made several federal policy recommendations for combating childhood obesity. They include the establishment of new federal funding to support increased physical education requirements to a minimum of 30 minutes, five days per week at all grade levels, coordination of governmental and nongovernmental resources and infrastructure to reduce obesity rates among children and adolescents, and to focus on underserved and diverse communities that are disproportionately affected by obesity.

An example of a state-wide school-based prevention initiative aimed at reducing obesity among students can be seen in a consensus paper developed through a joint effort by the Michigan Department of Education, Michigan Department of Community Health, Governor's Council on Physical Fitness, Health and Sports, and Michigan Fitness Council (2001). The following recommendations for schools initiating obesity prevention programs were made by this panel as well as the American Obesity Association (2002):

- Create a safe and respectful learning environment in which students, regardless of their size, are treated with care and dignity.
- Create an environment in which students have the opportunity to be physically active by:
  —ensuring moderate to vigorous physical activity during recess for elementary and middle school students or fitness breaks for high school students;
  —incorporating physical activity into lessons and classroom procedures
  —encouraging students to walk or ride bicycles to school when and where it is safe to do so;
  —offering opportunities for competitive, recreational, and individual sports activities through interscholastic and intramural programs as well as open recreational and exercise facilities during non-school hours.
- Create a healthy nutritional environment by limiting outside vendors of foods and beverages.
- Increase student participation in physical education through improved curriculum and content.
- Strengthen the nutrition education component of the curriculum and content by teaching developmentally appropriate nutrition concepts at each grade level and infusing these concepts across curricular areas.
- Work with families to promote physical activity and healthy eating through information about community resources and healthy lifestyle choices.

Prevention of Unintended Pregnancy, HIV/AIDS, and Other Sexually Transmitted Diseases

The introduction of sexuality education programs in public schools has been controversial since their inception. Early programs tended to focus explicitly on factual information regarding sexual anatomy and the effectiveness of various forms of contraception. These programs were not only challenged by a variety of political and religious groups as promoting immorality but were also generally ineffective in curbing the increasing trend of unintended pregnancy in adolescents (Donovan, 1998; Planned Parenthood of America, 2003). By the early 1970s, legislation in 20 states abolished such programs and by the end of this decade, only three states required sex education in the schools (Kenny & Alexander, 1980). However, as HIV/AIDS became an increasing public health threat during the 1980s, it was recognized that education and prevention programs were needed in order to eradicate erroneous beliefs about the transmission of and risks factors for this and other sexually transmitted diseases (STDs). Many states began once again requiring sexuality education programs in addition to instruction on AIDS and other STDs (Donovan, 1998).

The prevention and education programs of the 1980s improved on earlier approaches to sexuality education by incorporating communication skills such as negotiation strategies and refusal. These programs were somewhat more successful in outcome than earlier efforts (Planned Parenthood of America, 2003), but their modest success was short-lived in many areas of the country. The 1990s brought once again a political and religious backlash against such programs, and there was a significant push for state legislation and local school boards to significantly limit the instructional content. Pressure to limit prevention programs to teaching abstinence until marriage and to avoid any discussion or instruction on contraception beyond failure rates gained momentum during the 1990s, especially at the local level where challenges to district sexuality education policies have steadily increased (Donovan). Although these challenges have continued to the present time, there have been improvements in the effectiveness of sexuality education and prevention programs as indicated by program outcome evaluations. National statistics indicate a steady downward trend in unintended pregnancy rates since 1990 among adolescents across demographic sectors (National Center for Health Statistics, 2004).

According to Advocates for Youth (2008), there are characteristics associated with effective sexuality and HIV prevention programs. Successful programs:

- Focus on one or more specific behaviors that lead to unintended pregnancy or sexually transmitted infections, including HIV.
- Deliver and consistently reinforce a clear message about abstaining from sexual activity and/or using condoms or other forms of contraception. This appears to be one of the more important characteristics distinguishing effective from ineffective programs.
- Provide basic, accurate information about the risks of teen sexual activity and about ways to avoid intercourse or to use methods of protection against pregnancy and sexually transmitted infections.
- Include activities that address social pressures that influence sexual activity.
- Provide examples of and practice with communication, negotiation, and refusal skills.
- Incorporate behavioral goals, teaching methods, and materials that are appropriate to the age, sexual experience, and culture of the students.
- Employ teaching methods designed to involve participants and have participants personalize the information.
- Are based on theoretical approaches that have been demonstrated to influence other health-related behaviors and identify specific important sexual antecedents to be targeted.
- Select teachers or peer leaders who believe in the program, and then provide them with adequate training.
- Last a sufficient length of time (i.e., more than a few hours).

In general, a review of programs by Kirby *et al.* (1994) found that, compared with less effective programs, those with successful outcomes were less general and more focused on specific behaviors. In addition, more effective programs presented a clear stand and focused on explicit behavioral values and norms. Interestingly, many program advocates and researchers no longer view abstinence-based and responsibility-based prevention efforts as mutually exclusive, and acknowledge that some of the backlash was and is due to poorly articulated program goals and a general failure to correct the misperception that comprehensive programs do not include abstinence (Donovan, 1998). Most recently, the importance of incorporating social norms in sexuality education and prevention programs has been recognized. This approach addresses commonly held misperceptions regarding the frequency with which certain behaviors occur in the population (Planned Parenthood, 2003). In other words, adolescents are more likely to overestimate the extent to which their peers are engaging in sexual intercourse for a variety of reasons including perpetuation of the perception through media and "locker-room" talk. This approach has been successful in correcting misperceptions regarding the prevalence of other risky behaviors including drinking and substance use.

Prevention of Suicide and Other Mental Health Problems

Between the years 1960 and 1990, the rate of suicide among adolescents aged 15 to 19 years tripled, and the rate of suicide among children between the ages of 10 and 14 years has increased 120% since 1980 (Kalafat, 2003). This alarming trend has given rise to national concern over suicidal behavior among children and adolescents, and has prompted research to better understand the risks factors within the individual as well as environmental and contextual risk factors associated with this behavior. Effective interventions have been sought for students in crisis, and there has been a substantial movement to develop and implement school-based prevention programs in an effort to curtail the trend. For example, in 1999, the *Surgeon General's Call to Action to Prevent Suicide* resulted in the drafting of a national agenda to reduce suicide rates among all

Americans, including children and adolescents (US Department of Health and Human Services), and a revised version was drafted in 2012 which expanded the goals and objectives for reducing and preventing suicide. A framework for immediate action known as AIM—Awareness, Intervention, Methodology—was developed through a process of consensus using expert opinion and evidence-based findings. Awareness involves increasing public knowledge regarding suicide as a public health concern. This knowledge includes:

- Risk factors associated with suicide
- Effective prevention strategies
- Resources within the community for suicide prevention programs as well as assessment and treatment programs for associated mental and substance abuse disorders

Among other recommendations, interventions relevant to schools include:

- Institute training for all human services professionals including teachers in suicide risk assessment and recognition, treatment, management, and after-care interventions.
- Develop and implement effective training programs for families and natural community helpers (such as educators, coaches, religious leaders, etc.) on how to recognize, respond to, and refer individuals showing signs of suicide risk.
- Develop and implement safe and effective programs in educational settings for youth that address adolescent distress, provide crisis intervention, and incorporate peer support for seeking help.
- Enhance community care resources by increasing the use of schools as access and referral points for mental and physical health services and substance abuse treatment and provide support for individuals who survive the suicide of someone close to them.

Methodology recommendations seek to advance the science of suicide prevention through research designed to improve understanding of risk and protective factors associated with suicide as well as research investigating the effectiveness of suicide prevention programs, clinical treatment for suicidal individuals, and culture-specific interventions.

Risk factors have been identified that are associated with suicide. However, the importance of these risk factors and combinations of factors vary by age, sex, and ethnicity. Furthermore, educators are cautioned that some lists of warning signs of suicide are overly general and may be counterproductive if applied broadly in a general education setting, where such signs may be a relatively normal response to distress (Vieland, Whittle, & Garland, 1991). Nevertheless, it is important for educators, including teachers, coaches, administrators, and others who work directly with students to be aware of the following risk factors:

- Previous suicide attempt
- Psychological disorders, particularly mood disorders such as depression and bipolar disorder
- Co-occurring psychological disorders and alcohol and/or substance abuse
- Family history of suicide
- Feelings of hopelessness or isolation
- Aggressive or impulsive tendencies
- Loss of a relationship
- Physical illness
- Easy access to lethal methods, especially guns
- Influence of significant people who have died by suicide (e.g., family members, peers, celebrities) either through personal contact or media representations
- Cultural or religious beliefs that validate the practice of suicide

- Local epidemics of suicide
- Victimization by peers (Russell, 2003).

In addition to the risk factors listed above, the Surgeon General and National Action Alliance for Suicide Prevention (2012) also identified individuals who engage in non-suicidal self-injury, individuals in justice or child welfare settings, and members of the lesbian, gay, bisexual, and transgendered (LGBT) populations as having an increased risk for suicidal behaviors. However, suicide risk and high levels of stress are often attenuated by protective factors (Doan, Roggenbaum & Lazear, 2003; Kalafat, 2003) that can be enhanced in home, school, and community settings. These protective factors include:

- Academic success
- Attachment to school and positive relationships with peers and adults within the school
- Social involvement and participation
- Easy access to effective and appropriate care for mental, physical, and substance abuse disorders
- Restricted access to highly lethal methods of suicide
- Family and community support
- Learning skills in communication, problem-solving, conflict resolution, and non-violent methods of handling disputes
- Cultural and religious beliefs that discourage suicide and support self-preservation instincts

School-based suicide prevention programs generally fall into one of three categories, developed by the Institute of Medicine (1994). Universal prevention programs, which are aimed at the entire school population rather than specific subgroups or individuals. These programs focus on creating competent school communities that enhance protective factors that promote general well-being in students as well as comprehensive prevention programs that specifically address prevention of suicide among students. This is a particularly important function since suicide is generally not the result of a single, isolated event or stressor. Instead, it is often linked in complex ways to other problems such as substance abuse, frequent and severe victimization or intimidation by aggressive and violent students, and limited social competence (Kalafat, 2003). Selective prevention programs focus on specific subgroups of students who are considered to be at heightened risk for suicide. Finally, indicated interventions are those that focus on individual students who have been identified through screening, self or others as having suicidal thoughts or plans. Current comprehensive school-based suicide prevention programs are primarily focused on improving the ability and readiness of peers and so-called school gatekeepers (administrators, faculty, staff) to recognize potential for suicide in students, respond appropriately, and obtain help for the individual (CDC, 1992; Kalafat, 2003). The CDC (1992), through an analysis of effective school-based comprehensive suicide prevention programs, has identified many common strategies that are well aligned with the awareness and intervention recommendations of AIM, discussed previously. In general, these programs involve several components:

1. Training for school gatekeepers in the recognition of suicide risk in students, appropriate initial responses to students with suicidal thoughts or plans, and referral to the appropriate professional or agency.
2. General suicide education to provide basic information to students regarding the facts about suicide, alert them to warning signs, and provide information about how to seek help for themselves or others.
3. Screening programs to identify high-risk students in order to provide selective and indicated interventions appropriately.

4. General prevention programs designed to foster self-esteem, school attachment, and social competency among students, especially those with high risk for suicide. Activities can include peer support programs and life skills training.

5. Information for parents regarding risk and protective factors and the importance of restricting access to lethal means of suicide, especially firearms and drugs.

6. Intervention plans to cope with the crisis that may result from the suicide of one or more students. The main purposes of the intervention plan are to prevent additional suicides from occurring as a result (sometimes referred to as suicide clusters) and to help students cope with feelings, which may range from grief and a sense of loss to anger and a sense of betrayal. It is important, however, to avoid sensationalizing the suicide or glorifying the victim since this could have unintentional reinforcing effects on vulnerable students (CDC, 1992; Kalafat, 2003).

Student Intervention and Crisis Management

Crises in schools can result from any number of factors ranging from student violence, accidental injury, substance abuse, and suicide. Even when a crisis does not occur on school property, the aftermath of personal, local, or national tragedies can and do affect the behavior and needs of students in the school setting. Although crises are, by their very nature, unforeseen, and it is thus impossible to have a plan of action for every conceivable crisis, there are general steps that schools can take to prepare for such occurrences and ensuring that they are handled in the most effective and appropriate way possible. One method that has been effective in dealing with crises in schools is to have in place a well-trained, prepared crisis intervention team comprising individuals with diverse backgrounds. Team members should include the school administrator, guidance counselor, school psychologist, school social worker, school nurse, and selected teachers (Doan, Roggenbaum, & Lazear, 2003). Although the crisis intervention team may include members of the community as it is determined to be necessary and appropriate, schools are cautioned to avoid replacing school personnel with outside experts. School personnel are critical to crisis intervention and management because they have ongoing relationships with, and knowledge of, students, their families, and the community. Thus, school personnel are in prime position to understand the evolving needs of students and their families during and after a crisis. Finally, school personnel work together regularly and are able to plan, coordinate, evaluate, and revise efforts on an ongoing basis. Therefore, outside experts should be included on crisis intervention teams on a consultation, short-term, or case-specific basis (Office for Victims of Crime, 2003).

Regardless of their professional roles within the school, OVC (2003) recommends that the following team roles be assigned:

- *Crisis Team Chairperson:* Responsible for convening scheduled and emergency team meetings, ensures that necessary resources are available within the school for each team member to perform assigned duties, and communicates with the larger district crisis intervention team. This role is often (but not always) filled by the school administrator.
- *Assistant Team Chairperson:* Assists the chairperson in all functions, and takes over the role of chairperson in their absence.
- *Coordinator of Counseling:* Responsible for the ongoing training of crisis team members and other school personnel, and identifies counseling resources within the community and arranges for these resources in the event of a crisis. Also determines the extent of counseling services needed by students and staff during and after crises.
- *Staff Notification Coordinator:* Establishes, coordinates, and initiates a fan-out system for contacting crisis team members and general school staff when school is not in session. Also

establishes a plan to efficiently spread important information to staff during school hours.

- *Communications Coordinator:* Responsible for conducting direct in-house communication, screening incoming calls, and maintaining a log of all calls related to the crisis. Develops a notification protocol for communicating information regarding the nature, severity, and extent of the crisis. In the case of a single or very limited number of crisis victims, relatives and close friends should be identified and, if necessary, be referred for additional counseling (CDC, 2002).
- *Media Coordinator:* Maintains ongoing communication with police, emergency services, hospital representatives, and the district office in order to maintain information current. Handles all media requests for information and, in cooperation with district officials, prepares statements for the media and community.
- *Crowd Management Coordinator:* Responsible for managing movement during a crisis. Establishes and monitors plans for possible scenarios that may require evacuation, additional security measures, or restriction of access to areas within the building. Must also plan for the safe and organized movement of students under a variety of circumstances.

OVC (2003) recommended that schools determine in advance which types of crises require a team response versus those that might be better handled through other means. Some general categories have been identified that usually require and are best handled by a crisis team approach. These include: (1) the death of a student, staff member, or member of the community whose death affects a significant portion of the student body; (2) a major environmental disaster such as a flood or fire; (3) situations in which there is a real of potential threat to the physical safety or emotional well-being of students.

Current Controversies and Future Trends

A primary controversy surround school-based prevention programs is the extent to which, if at all, such programs belong in the public schools. Ideologically- and politically driven criticism of program goals, content, and methods of delivery aside, there are many justifications for the continued development, implementation, and evaluation of such programs. To begin with, students spend more time at school than any other single environment outside the home (Doan, Roggenbaum, & Lazear, 2003), and are often more likely to seek the confidence of assistance from school staff and peers (CDC, 1992). Finally, schools are the primary, if not sole, institutions within a community charged with the responsibility to educate and socialize children and adolescents of all backgrounds and environments. As such, schools provide a logical setting for universal prevention programs and are often in the best position to identify students at risk of problem behaviors and provide or make arrangements for selective and indicated interventions (Kalafat, 2003). In fact, research has demonstrated the efficacy of multi-year, multi-component programs that integrate universal, selective, and indicated intervention approaches across community, school, and family settings (Catalano, Berglund, Ryan, Lonczak, & Hawkins, 2002). Thus, school-based prevention programs connect with families and communities are justified and represent the future direction for prevention initiatives.

One of the most serious issues facing prevention program efforts is the relative lack of evidence on which they are based. Although the general characteristics and components of programs thought to be effective are identified in part through careful program analysis, the effectiveness of specific prevention programs is based on expert opinion or political ideology, with little external evidence of long-term outcomes (Gorman, 2003). Thus, there is substantial need for more rigorously controlled evaluations of programs. In particular, program evaluations need to define the outcomes more clearly and develop the means to evaluate long-term outcomes. Beyond reliance upon outcome measures, process measures of both program quality and fidelity of implementation need significantly more attention, and more needs to be understood about mediating and moderating variables that influence program effects in large systems such as schools (Weissberg, Kumpfer, & Seligman, 2003). In addition, in light of the limited funding of schools and the ever-present threat of budgetary cutbacks, cost-benefit analyses as well as cost-effectiveness evaluations of prevention programs are also important for resource allocation (Caulkins, Rydell, Everingham, Chiesa, & Bushway, 1999). Finally, the existence of a specific need for such programs must be carefully undertaken before the adoption and initiation of such programs in order to ensure that time and resources are well spent (Brown, 1997; Flannery, 1998).

Regardless of the area of prevention, there are some general practices that are associated with successful prevention programming. Efforts at prevention programming should be based on sound theories of child and organizational development (Bronfenbrenner & Morris, 1998). In addition, although effective programs designed to reduce specific behaviors are focused on well-articulated goals and limit program content to information necessary to achieve the goals (Donovan, 1998), there is a growing recognition of the interrelationship among problem behaviors. Comprehensive prevention and health promotion programs can be implemented that address individual, environmental, and contextual risk factors and promote protective factors through coordinated efforts (Dryfoos, 1997; Jessor, 1993). Furthermore, it is now well understood that one-time workshops are not effective for long-term behavioral change and this is true for prevention programs as well. Prevention programs need to be developed in such a way that it is implemented on a continuing basis over a wide age range. Thus, programs are more likely to result in behavioral changes if they are tailored to meet the cultural, community, and developmental needs of the participants and involve coordinated components that address appropriate aspects of prevention at all ages (Weissberg, Kumpfer, & Seligman, 2003).

Administrative and Personnel Issues

For any school-based prevention program, administration and personnel are essential to its success. As mentioned previously, prevention programs must be selected on the basis of their ability to effectively produce clearly stated goals and outcomes, and these goals and outcomes must align with the needs of the intended participants. Needs for various prevention measures differ across student populations and depend upon the prevalence of risk factors for the behavior in question, the developmental level of the students involved, the community and cultural values regarding the issue, and the general school climate (Kalafat, 2003; Weissberg, Kumpfer, & Seligman, 2003). In order for any prevention program to be effective, there must be buy-in from the administration and staff as a whole that there is a need for prevention, and that it is a priority within the school to maximize the intended program effects (Doan, Roggenbaum, & Lazear, 2003). Once a program has been selected, staff needed to implement the program must be selected, trained, and supported on an ongoing basis through professional development, collaboration, planning, and self-monitoring. The administrator must ensure that the quality and integrity of the program are maintained by monitoring the implementation process and providing ongoing professional development opportunities and support to program staff.

Administrators are ultimately responsible for the selection of staff members to be involved in program development, implementation, and evaluation, and these professionals must possess exceptional interpersonal skills. Program staff must also be selected on the basis of their ability to convey program content in a meaningful, empathetic, and effective manner using a variety of interactive teaching methods. Furthermore, the administrator must be able to effectively communicate the goals and intended outcomes of school-based prevention programs to families as well as community members, to respond to questions about the program, and to involve them in appropriate ways at all levels of planning. Finally, administrators must realize that prevention programs do not stand alone and are only effective to the extent that positive outcomes extend beyond the program and into the various contexts in which program participants live and function. Therefore, administrators and school staff need to establish and maintain a positive school climate in which all students are members of a community. They must then connect the school community to that of the larger community through a variety of methods including service learning and mentoring opportunities through well-planned and integrated program delivery.

Summary

As we entered the 21st century, there was a growing recognition among educational researchers and practitioners alike of the need to expand traditional concepts of schooling in order to meet the changing needs of students. Increases in rates of substance use, suicide, disease and illness, student drop-out rates, and violence within and beyond the school underscore the obligation of schools, in cooperation with families and communities, to provide for basic safety and social needs of students before academic success can be expected (Maslow, 1943). Although prevention programs are not new, and are not without controversy, the development of effective prevention models and strategies for all areas of prevention have evolved substantially from the early initiatives, which tended to be isolated and sporadic, and often without theoretical or empirical support. Current model programs attempt to integrate universal, selective, and indicated prevention approaches across a continuum of developmental levels, and attempt to minimize risks while enhancing the social skills of program participants. While there is still a need to establish rigorous evidence for the effectiveness of these programs, program evaluation efforts have been improving, and prevention science will hopefully continue to guide the direction of future policy and institutional practices.

Questions for Consideration

1. What are some ways in which the prevention needs of a particular school or district are evaluated? How should these be prioritized?
2. Why would a narrow content focus and the presentation of clearly defined behavioral values and social norms result in greater effectiveness in sexuality education and prevention programs?
3. How can crisis intervention teams prepare for the vast array of circumstances and situations schools potentially face today? What is the administrator's role in preparing the crisis intervention team?
4. To what extent are schools responsible for enhancing protective factors among students? How can this be achieved?

Case Study

Zero Tolerance?

In the middle of the afternoon on what seemed to be a relatively calm day at Smith Middle School, Mrs. Wall, the 8th grade science teacher, enters the office with a student and demands to see the school principal, Mr. Jennings. As the two are ushered in to his office, Mr. Jennings can see that Mrs. Wall is holding what appears to be a hunting knife in one hand. The student, Ricky Tan, is not familiar to Mr. Jennings, and he appears to be very frightened. Mrs. Wall states that the student brought the knife into her fifth period science class and that she expects that he be expelled from school. Mr. Jennings dismisses Mrs. Wall so that she can return to her classroom and asks Ricky to wait in his office as he retrieves his permanent record. Upon review of the permanent record, Mr. Jennings finds that Ricky enrolled at Smith Middle School in January of the previous year, having just immigrated from Vietnam with his family. He has been receiving ESL services but is still far from proficient in English. His report cards reflect adequate progress in all academic areas, and qualitative notes made by last year's teachers indicate that he is a pleasant, cooperative student who tries hard to succeed. Ricky has no record of any discipline problems, and he rarely misses school.

Five years ago, the school district implemented a zero tolerance policy for weapons on school grounds, and there is no mistaking that the hunting knife qualifies as such. Mr. Jennings contacts Ricky's father and asks him to come to the school. As Mr. Jennings tries to explain to Ricky that he has violated a school rule and that there are serious consequences for bringing weapons to school, he is surprised when Ricky insists that he was told to bring the knife to school by Mrs. Wall for a class assignment. While Mr. Jennings is certain that this could not possibly be true, he is uncertain whether Ricky is purposefully lying or whether his limited English skills are causing some kind of misunderstanding.

Mr. Jennings sends a paraeducator to Mrs. Wall's classroom so that she can come back to the office to discuss the issue. When asked about Ricky's statement, Mrs. Wall responds that the assignment was to bring in a tool for discussion. Further investigation reveals that Ricky, whose knife is nearly identical to one shown in the textbook, asked his father for permission to take the knife to school based on the assignment. He kept the knife, which was in a leather sheath, in his backpack throughout the day and took it out only when, at the beginning of science class, the students were instructed to lay their tools out on their desks. Ricky had opened his textbook to the page with the picture of the knife with his right next to it. When Mr. Tan arrives at school, it is clear that he has very limited English skills. After a brief verbal exchange in Vietnamese between Ricky and his father, Mr. Tan tries to communicate in English that he had given his son permission to take the knife, which he uses as a tool, for the class assignment. He is confused as to what his son has done wrong.

Questions for Discussion

1. What are the legal and educational issues involved in this case?

2. What are some of the ethical considerations?

3. Does the principal have any option other than to seek expulsion for this student? If so, what are they?

4. What are the implications for adhering to the zero tolerance policy? What are the implications for making an exception?

References

Advocates for Youth (2008). *Characteristics of effective sexuality and HIV prevention programs.* Retrieved from http://www.advocatesforyouth.org/topics-issues/sexeducation/832?task=view.

Allen, K. P. (2010). Classroom management, bullying, and teacher practices. Professional Educator 34(1) 1–15.

American Obesity Association (2002). *Childhood obesity.* Retrieved from http://www.obesity.org/subs/childhood/prevention.shtml.

Amrein, A. L, & Berlinger, D. C. (2003). The testing divide: New research on the intended and unintended impact of high-stakes testing. *Peer Review, 5*(2), 31–32.

Blue Cross Blue Shield Association (2010). *Federal policy recommendations for combating childhood obesity.* Retrieved from http://www.bcbs.com/why-bcbs/childhood-obesity-prevention/Childhood_Obesity_Recommendations.pdf.

Brown, B. S. (1997). Drug abuse prevention needs assessment methodologies. *National Institute on Drug Abuse (NIDA) resource center for health services research.* Retrieved from http://www.nida.nih.gov/about/organization/DESPR/HSR/da-pre/Brownprevention.htm.

Bronfenbrenner, U., & Morris, P. A. (1998). The ecology of developmental processes. In W. Damon (Series Ed.) & R. M. Lerner (Volume Ed.), *Handbook of child psychology: Vol. 1: Theoretical models of human development (5th ed.),* pp. 993–1028. New York: Wiley.

Bruvold, W. H.., & Rundall, T. G. (1988). A meta-analysis and theoretical review of school-based tobacco and alcohol intervention programs. *Psychological Health, 2,* 53–78.

Caulkins, J. P., Rydell, C. P., Everingham, S. M. S., Chiesa, J. R., & Bushway, S. (1999). *An ounce of prevention, a pound of uncertainty: The cost-effectiveness of school-based drug prevention programs.* Santa Monica, CA: RAND.

Catalano, R. F., Berglund, M. L., Ryan, J. A. M., Lonczak, H. S., & Hawkins, J. D. (2002). Positive youth development in the United States: Research findings on evaluations of positive youth development programs. *Prevention & Treatment, 5*(15). Retrieved from http://journals.apa.org/prevention/volume5/pre0050015a.html

Center for Disease Control and Prevention (2013). *Childhood obesity facts.* Retrieved from http://www.cdc.gov/HealthyYouth/obesity/facts.htm.

Center for Effective Collaboration and Practice (2000). *Goals and purpose of Safe and Drug-Free Schools and Communities Act.* Retrieved from http://www.air-dc.org/cecp/resources/safe&drug_free/goals_and_purpose.htm.

Clearinghouse on Educational Policy and Management (2001). *Trends and issues: School safety.* Retrieved from http://cepm.uoregon.edu/trends_issues/safety/#04.

Drug Awareness and Resistance Education (2012). Retrieved from http://www.dare.com/home/about_dare.asp.

Doan, J., Roggenbaum, D. J., & Lazear, K. (2003). *Youth suicide prevention school based guide.* Tampa, FL: Department of Child and Family Studies, Division of State and Local Support, Louis de la Parte Florida Mental Health Institute, University of South Florida.

Donovan, P. (1998). School-based sexuality education: The issues and challenges. *Family Planning Perspectives, 30*(4), 188–193.

Dryfoos, J. G. (1997). The prevalence of problem behaviors: Implications for programs. In R. P. Weissberg, T. P. Gullotta, R. L. Hampton, B. A. Ryan, & G. R. Adams (Eds.), *Healthy children 2010: Enhancing children's wellness,* pp. 17–46. Thousand Oaks, CA: Sage.

Farrington, D. P. & Ttofi, M. M. (2010). *School based programs to reduce bullying and victimization.* Unpublished final grant report from the United States Department of Justice (Document No. 229377). Retrieved from https://www.ncjrs.gov/pdffiles1/nij/grants/229377.pdf.

First District Regional Educational Service Agency (2004). *History of the Safe & Drug-Free Schools and Communities Program.* Retrieved from http://www.first-district.resa.k12.ga.us/drugfree/history.htm.

Flannery, D. J. (1998). *Improving school violence prevention programs through meaningful evaluation.* New York: ERIC Clearinghouse on Urban Education. ERIC/ CUE Digest Number 132.

Food Research and Action Center (2004). *National School Lunch Program.* Retrieved from http://www.frac.org/html/federal_food_programs/programs/nslp.html.

Frey, K. S., Hirschstein, M. K., & Guzzo, B. A. (2000). Second step: Preventing aggression by promoting social competence. *Journal of Emotional and Behavioral Disorders, 8*(2), 102–112.

Gilchrist, L. D. (1994). Current knowledge in prevention of alcohol and other drug abuse. *Research and intervention: Preventing substance abuse in higher education.* Washington, DC: United States Department of Education. Retrieved from http://www.ed.gov/pubs/PreventingSubstanceAbuse/Current.html.

Gliksman, L., & Smythe, C. (1990). A review of school-based drug education programs: Do we expect too much? In R. C. Engs (Ed.), *Controversies in the addictions field* (pp. 175–183). Dubuque: Kendall-Hunt.

Gorman, D. M. (2003). Prevention programs and scientific nonsense. Policy Review, 117, 65–75.

Gottfredson, D. C. (1996). School-based crime prevention. In L. W. Sherman, D. C. Gottfredson, D. L. MacKenzie, J. Eck, P. Reuter, & S. Bushway (Eds.), *Preventing crime: What works, what doesn't, what's promising.* A report to the United States Congress. Prepared for the National Institute of Justice.

Holloway, J. H. (2002). The dilemma of zero tolerance. *Educational Leadership, 59*(4), 84–85.

Institute of Medicine (1994). *Reducing risk for mental disorder: Frontiers for preventive intervention research.* Washington, DC: National Academy Press.

International Campaign for Victory Over Violence (2001). The challenge. Retrieved from http://www.vov1. com/TheChallenge.html.

Jessor, R. (1993). Successful adolescent development among youth in high-risk settings. *American Psychologist, 48*, 117–126.

Kalafat, J. (2003). School approaches to youth suicide prevention. *American Behavioral Scientist, 46*(9), 1211–1223.

Kenny, A.M., & Alexander, S. J. (1980). Sex/family life education in the schools: An analysis of state policies. *Family Planning/Population Reporter, 9*(3), 44.

Kirby, D., Short, L., Collins, J., Rugg, D., & Kolbe, L. (1994). School-based programs to reduce sexual risk. *Public Health Reports, 109*(3), 339–361.

Lilienfeld, S. O. (2007). Psychological treatments that cause harm. *Perspectives on Psychological Science, 2*, 53–70.

Martin, E.J., Tobin, T. J., & Sugai, G. M. (2002). Current information on dropout prevention: Ideas from practitioners and literature. *Preventing school failure, 47*(1), 10–17.

Maslow, A. (1943). A theory of human motivation. *Psychological Review, 50*, 370–396.

Michigan Department of Education Office of School Excellence (2001). *The role of Michigan schools in promoting healthy weight: A consensus paper.* Retrieved from http://www.emc.cmich.edu/pdfs/ Healthy%20Weight.pdf.

Misner, S. (2003). *Guidelines for childhood obesity prevention programs: Promoting healthy weight in children.* University of Arizona Cooperative Extension. Retrieved from http://ag.arizona.edu/pubs/ health/az1317.pdf.

Murnane, R. J., & Levy, F. (1996). *Teaching the new basic skills: Principles for educating children to thrive in a changing economy.* New York: Free Press.

National Association of School Psychologists (1998). *Position statement on student grade retention and social promotion.* Retrieved from http://www.nasponline.org/information/pospaper_graderetent.html.

National Association of School Psychologists (2001). *Zero tolerance and alternative strategies: A fact sheet for educators and policymakers.* Retrieved from http://www.naspcenter.org/factsheets/zt_fs.html.

National Dropout Prevention Center / Network (2013). *Effective strategies.* Retrieved from http://www. dropoutprevention.org/modelprograms.

Natriello, G., McDill, E. L., & Pallas, A. M. (1990). Schooling disadvantaged children: *Racing against catastrophe.* New York: Teachers College Press.

Neiman, S., Robers, B., & Robers, S. (2012). Bulling: A state of affairs. *Journal of Law and Education 41*(4), 604–648.

Office for Victims of Crime (2003). *School crisis response initiative.* Retrieved from http://www.ojp.usdoj. gov/ovc/publications/bulletins/schoolcrisis/welcome.html.

Olweuas Bullying Prevention Program (2003, 2012). Retrieved from http://www.clemson.edu/olweus/.

Ormrod, J. E. (2008). *Educational psychology: developing learners.* New York: Pearson.

Park-Higgerson, Perumean-Chaney, Bartolucci, Grimely, & Singh (2008). The evaluation of school-based violence prevention programs: A meta-analysis. *Journal of School Health, 78*(9), 465–479.

Peterson, R. L., & Skiba, R. (2001). Creating school climates that prevent school violence. *The Clearing House, 74*(3), 155–163.

Price, R. H., Cowan, E. L., Lorion, R. P., & Ramos-McKay, J. (1988). *14 ounces of prevention: a casebook for practitioners.* Washington, DC: American Psychological Association.

Ringwalt, C. L., Greene, J. M., Ennett, S. T., Iachan, R., Clayton, R. R., & Leukefeld, C. G. (1994). *Past and future directions of the D.A.R.E. program: An evaluation review.* Retrieved from http://www.ncjrs.org/txtfiles/darerev.txt.

Rumberger, R. W. (2001, January). *Why students drop out of school and what can be done.* Paper presented at the conference Dropouts in America: How severe is the problem? What do we know about intervention and prevention?, Boston: Harvard University.

Russell, S. T. (2003). Sexual minority youth and suicide risk. *The American Behavioral Scientist, 46*(9), 1241–1258.

Santrock, J. W. (2002). *Adolescence.* New York: McGraw-Hill.

Skiba, R., & Peterson, R.(1999). The dark side of zero tolerance: Can punishment lead to safe schools? *Phi Delta Kappan.* Retrieved from http://www.pdkintl.org/kappan/kski9901.htm.

Substance Abuse and Mental Health Services Administration (2012). *Prevention of substance abuse and mental illness: what we are doing.* Retrieved from http://www.samhsa.gov/prevention/.

Substance Abuse and Mental Health Services Administration (2013). *National Registry of Evidence-Based Programs and Practices.* Retrieved from http://www.nrepp.samhsa.gov/SearchResultsNew.aspx?s=b&q=substance+abuse

Substance Abuse and Mental Health Services Administration (2013). *Safe Schools and Healthy Students SS/HS Initiative.* Retrieved from http://www.sshs.samhsa.gov/default.aspx.

Tschannen-Moran, M. (2001). The effects of a state-wide conflict management initiative in schools. *American Secondary Education, 29*(3), 2–32.

United States Department of Education (December, 2011). *U.S. Department of Education releases analysis of state bullying laws and policies.* Retrieved from http://www.ed.gov/news/press-releases/us-education-department-releases-analysis-state-bullying-laws-and-policies.

United States Department of Health and Human Services (2013). *Bullying: know the facts.* Retrieved from http://www.stopbullying.gov/index.html.

United States Department of Health and Human Services—Centers for Disease Control and Prevention (2004). *Defining overweight and obesity.* Retrieved from http://www.cdc.gov/nccdphp/dnpa/obesity/defining.htm.

United States Department of Health and Human Services Center for Diseases Control and Prevention (1992). *Youth suicide prevention programs: A resource guide.* Retrieved from http://www.phppo.cdc.gov/cdcRecommends/.

United States Department of Health and Human Services—Office of Disease Prevention and Health Promotion (2001). *Healthy People 2010, Volume I, 2nd ed.* Retrieved from http://www.healthypeople.gov/Document/tableofcontents.htm#volume1.

United States Department of Health and Human Services—Substance Abuse and Mental Health Services Administration (2004). *SAMHSA Model programs: Effective substance abuse and mental health programs for every community.* Retrieved from http://www.modelprograms.samhsa.gov/template_cf.cfm?page=model_list.

United States Department of Health and Human Services—Substance Abuse and Mental Health Services Administration (2004). *School violence prevention.* Retrieved from http://www.mentalhealth.org/schoolviolence/.

United States Department of Health and Human Services (1999). *The Surgeon General's call to action to prevent suicide.* Washington, D.C.: U. S. Public Health Service. Retrieved from http://www.mentalhealth.org/suicideprevention/calltoaction.asp.

United States Department of Health and Human Services Office of the Surgeon General and National Action Alliance for Suicide Prevention (2012). *2012 National strategy for suicide prevention: goals and objectives for action.* Retrieved from http://www.surgeongeneral.gov/library/reports/national-strategy-suicide-prevention/full-report.pdf.

United States Department of Health and Human Services (2013). *HealthyPeople.gov 2020 Topics & Objectives.* Retrieved from http://www.healthypeople.gov/2020/topicsobjectives2020/default.aspx.

United States Department of Justice (October 2011). *OJP Fact sheet.* Retrieved from http://www.ojp.usdoj.gov/newsroom/factsheets/ojpfs_bullying.html.

United States Department of Justice (n.d.). Office of Juvenile Justice and Delinquency Prevention: OJJDP Model Programs Guide: Bullying. Retrieved from http://www.ojjdp.gov/mpg/programTypesDescriptions.aspx.

Vieland, V., Whittle, B., Garland, A. (1991). The impact of curriculum-based suicide prevention programs for teenagers: an eighteen month follow-up. *Journal of the American Academy of Child and Adolescent Psychiatry, 30*, 811–815.

Volokh, A., & Snell, L. (1998). *School violence prevention: Strategies to keep schools safe (unabridged).* Policy Study No. 234. Retrieved from http://www.rppi.org/education/ps234.html.

Weissberg, R. P., Kumpfer, K. L., & Seligman, M. E. P. (2003). Prevention that works for children and youth: An introduction. *American Psychologist, 58*(6/7), 425–432.

West, S. L. & O'Neal, K. K. (2004). Project D.A.R.E. outcome effectiveness revisited. *American Journal of Public Health, 94*(6), 1027–1029.

Wolf, A. M., & Colditz, G. A. (1998). Current estimates of the economic cost of obesity in the United States. *Obesity Research, 6*(2), 173–175.

Zepeda, S. J., & Langenbach, M. (1999). *Special programs in regular schools: Historical foundations, standards, and contemporary issues.* Boston: Allyn & Bacon.

CHAPTER 10

Student Support Services

Introduction

THE current student population in American public schools is diverse. The multifaceted cultural, ethnic, and linguistic backgrounds, abilities, skills, needs, and assets of students have all but eliminated any notion that appropriate curricula and well-trained faculty are all that is necessary for academic achievement. Rather, a wide range of services is needed in the schools to ensure that all students achieve academic success. Beyond academic achievement, however, it is widely recognized that schools serve a broader function than mere training of the mind. Schools are the primary institutions through which children are socialized, and education is often viewed to be as oriented to promoting democracy as it is to fostering academic competence (Ornstein & Hutchins, 1998). Furthermore, schools often aspire, through mission statements and district philosophies, to educate the whole child in such a manner as to encourage the development of life-long learning. These are ambitious and laudable goals considering the diversity within the student population. Given the violence, substance abuse, as well as social and economic instability facing families, schools and communities today, it is not difficult to understand that schools must reach beyond core content to provide the services and support that are needed.

Many students, including those who have attained high levels of academic achievement, benefit from and need various forms of support within the school setting. Student support is somewhat of an ambiguous term that has come to have different meanings depending upon the context in which it is used, and is sometimes confused with other terms such as special education support and supplemental services. The Office of Student Services (OSS), previously known as the National Center for Research in Vocational Education (NCRVE) defines student support as those services provided by educational institutions to facilitate learning and the successful transition from school to work, military, or further education of all students (Maddy-Bernstein & Cunanan, 1995). Services that support student learning and successful participation in the larger community may include, but are not limited to, student advising, mentoring, partnering with the local community, tutoring, before- and after-school programs, and child care. It should be noted at this point, however, that these distinctions are somewhat arbitrary. In reality, there is tremendous overlap both in terms of the nature of support services available through the schools and community as well as the interaction and interdependence of these services within the larger context of school-community partnerships. Each of these areas of support will be addressed below, including the history of and funding for the service. In addition, general administrative and

189

personnel issues will be discussed, and the current status and future directions of these services will be outlined.

Guidance Counseling

Historical Overview

Guidance counseling in the schools is not a new phenomenon. Public schools have offered guidance services in one form or another for well over a century, but there have been notable shifts in the focus of counseling services provided to students. In order to understand the current status and future directions of counseling programs in the schools, the history of such programs must first be examined (Gysbers, 2001). The first wave of guidance programs was prompted by the relatively sudden influx of large numbers of students into high schools caused by industrialization (see Chapters 6 and 8). The primary focus of early guidance programs was to help students match their skills to available job options. Vocational guidance services soon expanded to educational guidance and the placement of students into appropriate tracks that would destine them for college, business, or vocational work. The progressive social reform movement of the time, the introduction of vocational preparation programs into secondary schools, and the burgeoning field of psychometrics established career counseling as a scientifically respectable and educationally necessary service (Johnson & Johnson, 2003; Pope, 2000). With the ebb and flow of prevailing philosophies of education over time, the focus of school-based guidance counseling shifted. The 1940s brought new theories and conceptualizations of counseling as a profession, marking a relatively dramatic shift away from the predominantly vocational and psychometric approaches of earlier decades. School counselors began to deal with the emotional and social development of children and adolescents, providing both individual and small group counseling as well as directly impacting and participating in curriculum reform. With the onset of the Cold War came a realization that guidance counselors could also play a strategic role in improving the academic achievement of students, especially through assessment and guidance to appropriately challenging math and science courses. During this time, counselors also played a key role in attempting to lower the drop-out rate (Johnson & Johnson, 2003; Zepeda & Langenbach, 1999). In addition, the school counselor was increasingly called upon to guide students in decisions regarding higher education and to help them obtain necessary financial assistance (Pope, 2000). Such counseling was limited to secondary schools.

It wasn't until the 1960s that counseling programs at the elementary level became commonplace in public school settings. The foundation for elementary school counseling had been set in the 1920s by William Burnahm's pioneering work emphasizing the importance of establishing a positive school climate. However, it was the shift toward developmental approaches to education during the 1960s and 1970s that ultimately solidified the role of the school counselor at all levels of education (Faust, 1968). Eventually this shift resulted in a differentiation of the role and responsibilities of guidance counselors and the services they provided for different levels of education. At all levels, however, there has been a steady increase in the scope and variety of responsibilities of these professionals that mirrored the social conditions of the time. During the 1970s and 1980s, for example, school counselors became drug and child abuse prevention specialists. Later, they began to focus on helping children deal with divorce and social alienation and, out of necessity, played crucial roles in drug, AIDS, and suicide prevention. The past twenty years have required counselors to shift their attention to issues of violence as they help children, families, and school staff deal with school violence, bullying, terrorism, and death. Despite these additional responsibilities, school counselors have been expected to maintain their traditional roles as academic, career, and vocational counselors as well (Johnson & Johnson, 2003). This can be seen in the critical role school counselors have been required to assume in not only helping students and the school as a whole deal with the pressure of high-stakes testing but also to assist in raising test scores (Green & Keys, 2001).

Current Practice

According to Johnson & Johnson (2003), frustration due to conflicting role expectations from administrators, teachers, and parents (Maddy-Bernstein, 1995) and a lack of professional identity plagued school counselors as more and more responsibilities were added to their role within the school setting. A paradigm shift for the practice of school counseling, however, came about when the profession began to define itself by not *what* school counselors do *per se* but *how* they facilitate academic success among students and prepare them for successful transitions to work or higher education. Thus, the current model of school counseling focuses on students and seeks to demonstrate program efficacy in terms of student growth in career, personal, social, and especially academic achievement domains (American School Counselor Association [ASCA], 2008). Traditionally, school counselors focused their services on small subgroups of students, for example, assisting high-achieving students in securing entry into universities or providing social-behavioral interventions for high-risk students. More recent approaches to school counseling, in contrast, stress the full integration of counseling services into the academic mission of the school with equitable access for all students. This model, referred to as a comprehensive school counseling program, is based on four interrelated components:

- Foundation
- Delivery Systems
- Management Systems
- Accountability

School Counseling Programs

The foundation of school counseling programs rests on a clearly articulated philosophy that guides the development, implementation, and evaluation of the program. It is rooted in the academic mission of the school and strives to identify and deliver the knowledge and skills all students should acquire. The delivery system of the school counseling program is grounded in the school's philosophy and mission, and describes the activities, interactions, and methods to be used. The delivery system often includes plans for a guidance curriculum, individual student planning, responsive services such as consultation, referral, etc., and administration and management of the program. The management system addresses the goals and organizational structure of the school counseling program for each year. An advisory council is appointed, comprising students, parents, teachers, counselors, administrators, and community members, whose task is to review the results of the program and to make recommendations for the following year. Recommendations are based on careful analysis of data describing student needs and achievement, and are specified in an action plan for every desired competency and result. Rather than merely documenting the counseling processes and services delivered, as had been the traditional approach, the accountability focus of comprehensive school counseling programs is the demonstration of its effectiveness in improving student outcomes in achievement, career, and personal-social domains. The time necessary for successful program delivery should be analyzed both in terms of the counselor's time and the school calendar. The ASCA (2008) recommends that 80% of the school counselor's time be spent in direct service to students. With this in mind, the comprehensive model of school counseling emphasizes the integral role of school counselors in carrying out the school's mission and improving student outcomes. Non-counseling duties such as student registration, discipline, classroom and detention room coverage, and test administration, for which school counselors have long been responsible, should be reassigned in order to take full advantage of the special skills and training of these professionals.

Emerging Models of Guidance Counseling

While no one can predict exact outcomes, there are some assumptions about the future roles of school counseling programs within the changing landscape of public education. Several authors have identified similar themes regarding counseling's future. Technology, global economics, diversity within the population, emphases on standards and competencies, and emerging paradigms for understanding change have become and are predicted to continue to shape public education in general, and school counseling in particular (Adelman & Taylor, 2002; Wickwire, 2002). Of particular importance is the growing dissatisfaction with, and inappropriateness of, the traditional school model in meeting the learning needs of students in the 21st century, with a concomitant emphasis on expanding the function, services, and boundaries of the school setting into the greater community (Bemak, 2002). Perhaps the only certainty is that school counselors, both individually and as a profession, must move outside of the narrow confines of the traditional counselor role and take on key leadership roles in school reform efforts and shaping the future of public education in general (Adelman & Taylor, 2002; Gysbers, 2002). Wickwire (2002) summed up the direction for the future of school counseling programs in the following statement:

> Counselors are ultimately responsible for futures in the counseling profession, although factors in the external environment may play major roles. Counseling futures could range from obliteration to modification to renaissance, depending, in part, on the posture and action of those in the profession. Focused convergent and divergent study and action regarding possible, probable, and preferred futures is recommended. This attention is best directed through a proactive approach to defining and creating demonstrable, marketable results that meet client needs. Counselors will make the final choice regarding survival, maintenance, or enhancement of the counseling profession (p. 15).

In her introduction to a special issue on the role of school counseling in the 21st century, Dahir (2009) notes that "school counselors must be prepared to provide leadership in the schools in order to ensure that human relationships are nurtured, that diversity is valued, and that every student receives an equitable and quality education; school counselors must be social justice advocates who ensure that academic, career, and interpersonal success is woven into the fabric of education for every student" (p. 3). Dahir & Stone (2009) compare the skills required during the 20th century, which focused largely on counseling, consultation, and coordination, to new skills that will be needed in the 21st century, including leadership, social justice advocacy, use of technology, assessment and use of data, cultural mediation, and the ability to serve as a systemic change agent.

Mentoring

The origins of the word *mentor* can be traced back to Greek mythology when Athena takes on the male form of Mentor in order to watch over and guide Odysseus's son Telemachus (Homer, trans. 1967). Modern connotations relevant to this chapter include that of teacher, coach, and guide. Mentoring programs have taken on a variety of forms and have been established at all levels of education (Hansman, 2002). Mentoring has generally been shown to have positive effects in reducing a multitude of risk behaviors among children and adolescents, and has been beneficial to many students in terms of academic, social, and career guidance. This section will explore the history and current practice of mentoring in its various forms within the K–12 environment.

Volunteer Adult-Student Mentoring

The need for guidance and adult role models among students is not, as is often assumed, limited to students who are at risk for various behaviors such as dropping out of school, joining neighborhood gangs, or becoming sexually promiscuous. Although these students certainly can benefit from a positive and supportive relationship with a caring adult, mentoring can benefit many other students as well. Students who are academically gifted or talented can benefit from the experience and encouragement of an adult with similar interests. Students interested in a particular career path benefit from the guidance and insights of an adult who has traversed the inroads to that career. Mentoring relationships can assist students with special needs, who are learning English, or who have recently immigrated to the United States with interpersonal and social skills. Students experiencing social or academic difficulties can benefit from the encouragement of an adult who is personally involved in their success (Northwest Regional Educational Laboratory (NWREL, 2001). Even students experiencing loneliness, epidemic among children of prosperity, according to Peter (2000), in the absence of any other difficulty or need can benefit from the friendship and advocacy of an adult mentor.

According to NWREL (2001), the social and economic conditions of the last few decades have resulted in children and adolescents being isolated from traditional support systems such as extended family, stable neighborhood communities, and family friends. Mentoring programs are increasingly seen as a versatile and relatively inexpensive means of addressing the academic, career, and personal development needs of all segments of the student population at all levels of education. While research on the effectiveness of mentoring is generally positive (Foster, 2001; Hancock, 2003; Jucovy, 2000), there are some limitations. Mentor relationships that are volunteer-based may not be as enduring as those that form naturally, and the students who need mentors the most are frequently the same students who have difficulty developing and maintaining trust. However, these limitations can be reduced or eliminated by providing a solid infrastructure for the mentoring program.

In-school mentoring programs are more likely to succeed when potential mentors are provided with orientation and training prior to being matched carefully with a student based on common interests (Herrera, Sipe, & McClanahan, 2000). The age, sex, and ethnicity or race of the mentor have been shown not to be a significant predictor in the success of the relationship. Instead, a strong commitment to the program the matched student, and having interests in common are key elements of a successful pairing. As pointed out by Jucovy (2001), however, mentoring children and adolescents is not always easy, and volunteers cannot simply be paired with a student and then left to their own devices. Ongoing training and support should be provided to volunteers through mentor support groups, administrative monitoring of mentor relationships with students, ongoing training in a variety of topics related to child development, risk behaviors, cultural sensitivity, goal setting, etc., and mentor recognition activities. Finally, there must be an understanding that, like all relationships, mentoring relationships take time to develop, and volunteers must be patient and persistent in establishing trust with students through regular and sustained contact (Foster, 2001).

Peer Mentoring

Although there is little doubt regarding the positive outcomes of volunteer adult-student mentor relationships, students also have a tremendous effect on each other and on the school climate in general (Stader & Gagnepain, 2000), especially during adolescence when students look more to each other for guidance than to adults (Muss, 1996). As a result, peer-mentoring programs have become popular within schools across the nation. At the high school level, Stader & Gagnepain (2000) report on the use of peer mentoring in improving the academic and social needs of entering students who were paired with junior and senior student volunteers. The program grew from an initial rate of 40% of freshmen seeking a mentor to approximately 95% of freshman participating in the program after five years. Shifting from an academic tutoring to a social adjustment and responsibility focus, and asking for upper-classmen volunteers rather than recruiting honor students impacted the growth of the program. Providing time during school hours for both training of peer mentors and for contact between mentoring teams proved important for the growth and success of the program. Training for peer mentors included discussion centering around a variety of adolescent concerns, appropriate counseling techniques, active listening skills, goal setting, and information on when to involve the school guidance counselor.

Peer mentoring has also been used successfully at the middle and elementary school levels for improving academic achievement, homework and assignment completion, critical thinking, conflict resolution, and interpersonal skills. Peer mentoring can also reduce acting-out behaviors, and has been used successfully to facilitate transitions from one level of schooling to the next (Gensemer, 2000). Regardless of the age or focus of the peer mentoring program, the National Peer Helpers Association (NPHA, 2002) makes several recommendations for developing such programs. These are easily adapted to in-school peer mentoring programs and include start-up, implementation, and maintenance components, each of which is outlined in Table 10.1.

Cross-age Student Mentoring

A variation of peer mentoring that has shown tremendous success, especially in the domain of academic achievement, is cross-age peer mentor programs. This model of mentoring pairs an older student with a younger one in need of individual support (National Youth Network, 1999). Studies of cross-age peer mentoring have generally shown positive effects for the student being mentored as well as the mentor in terms of self-esteem. Students who receive mentoring from an older student benefit from the experience, knowledge, and skills of the older student, and often find it easier to establish trust and open communication with someone closer to their own age who has similar concerns. Older students serving as peer mentors for younger students develop stronger leadership skills and have fewer school problems themselves as a result (Gensemer, 2000). In fact, students who have had difficulty themselves with behavior or academic achievement should not necessarily be excluded from becoming peer mentors. Some research has indicated that these students will benefit from becoming a role model for younger students and actually demonstrate improvement in achievement or behavior as a result (Gumpel & Frank, 1999). Cross-age mentoring, like all peer mentoring programs, requires thoughtful planning based on the needs of the students being served and careful implementation with appropriate and on-going training and support for student mentors.

Formal Mentoring Programs

Formal mentoring programs differ from the above to the extent that they are usually available through non-profit organizations or through state and national programs. As such, they often have the ability to secure financial support and institutional support. These formal mentoring programs have become involved with school-based programs, independent living skills programs, court-mandated programs, and recreational or community-based programs. Religious organizations, corporations and businesses, and social organizations are increasingly providing support and encouragement for members and employees to volunteer as mentors for young people with a variety of needs. Additionally, older students are increasingly volunteering to become mentors to younger students in fulfillment of service learning requirements (Office of Educational Research and Improvement (OERI, 1993). Some well-known formal mentoring programs are listed:

Table 10.1. Components of In-School Peer Mentoring Programs.

Start-up	Planning	• Rationale based on needs assessment • Clear purpose • Specific goals and objectives • Procedures to be followed • Methods to ensure compliance
	Commitment	• Administrative and community support • Program advisory committee • Resources
	Staffing	• Positive rapport with peer mentors • Continuing education and training relevant to program goals • Commitment to principles of peer mentoring • Clear understanding of student needs and program goals and the ability to communicate these to peer mentors, other staff, and community members • Time to plan, train, evaluate, and supervise
Implementation	Screening and Selection	• Establish selection criteria for peer mentors • Establish volunteer procedures
	Training Characteristics	• Reflects program purpose and goals • Takes into account age, needs, and characteristics of population served • Uses appropriate materials and methods • Includes demonstration, skill development, practice & critique • Is on-going
	Training Elements	• Role of the peer mentor • Confidentiality / liability issues • Communication skills • Problem-solving / decision making strategies • Issues / topic relevant to purpose
Maintenance	Evaluation	• Process evaluation • Evaluation of the program's impact • Outcome evaluation
	Long-range Planning	• Staff Supervision • Peer ownership • Long-term program goals

- *Big Brothers / Big Sisters of America:* Founded in 1904, this national organization provides individual mentoring to children and adolescents with a variety of needs through community volunteers. The goal of the program is to help children to reach their potential through professionally supported one-to-one relationships, and the vision of this organization includes contributing to brighter futures, better schools, and stronger communities for all (2013).
- *One Hundred Black Men of America, Inc.:* This non-profit organization, established in 1963, comprises men in business, industry, public affairs, government, and the professions. The mission of the organization is to improve the quality of life within communities and to enhance the educational and economic opportunities for all African Americans. Through mentoring, members of the organization strive to guide youth in life experiences, foster a positive self-perception and self-respect, encourage excellence in education, and foster the development of lifelong goals (2013).

- *National Mentoring Partnership:* This organization advocates for the expansion of mentoring programs and offers resources for mentors and mentoring initiatives nationwide. In 1990, the founders of this organization became concerned that increasing numbers of children and youth felt a lack of care from adults in their lives and believed that future economic opportunities were beyond their reach. The goal of the organization is to provide children and youth with much needed connections to caring adults who can be role models of opportunity by overcoming barriers to mentoring in local communities (2013).

School-Community Partnerships

Schools have long been considered central to the community in that they have served not only as the formal institutions of learning but as recreation facilities, meeting houses, election sites, and centers of community involvement. However, in recent years schools in certain locations have faced increasing problems associated with social isolation and a deteriorating sense of community values among students, limited financial and human resources, and disconnection between various service organizations and educational service providers. As a result, there has been a growing interest in renewing community involvement in education and forging partnerships between schools and communities (Pardini, 2001). This is being accomplished in a number of ways, and there are accepted means of connecting schools and the educational process to the larger community. These include development of full-service schools, formal school-business and community partnerships, service-learning opportunities for students, and extension of academic learning experiences into internships and field-based learning as well as out-of-school learning opportunities. Each will be discussed in the following sections.

Service Learning

According to the National Service-Learning Clearinghouse (2013), service learning is "a teaching and learning strategy that integrates meaningful community service with instruction and reflection to enrich the learning experience, teach civic responsibility, and strengthen communities." The idea of developing citizenship through public education can be traced back to the days of Thomas Jefferson, who believed that civic responsibility and the knowledge, skills, and behaviors that underlie democracy must be explicitly taught (Cogan, 1999). Currently, however, concerns regarding apparent apathy and cynicism among students and a concomitant shift away from the ideals of democratic citizenship toward that of consumerism and economic competitiveness drive home the need to educate students regarding their rights and responsibilities as citizens of a broader community. To this end, many schools have begun to implement service learning opportunities and even to require service learning as a condition for high-school graduation. There have been critics of service learning who take issue with this practice for a variety of reasons. The argument that required service learning in the schools undermines the very essence of volunteerism and reduces the likelihood of students volunteering in the future is to a large extent unfounded according to both field and experimental studies (Stukas, Snyder, & Clary, 1999). And while some argue that service learning requirements are the results of a liberal, left-wing agenda, others argue just as forcefully that such requirements are a means of perpetuating an established social structure and thus inhibit critical analysis of these same democratic ideals. Perhaps more importantly, though, it is claimed that service learning requirements detract from the primary mission of the schools- to impart core content knowledge and skills (Cogen, 1999).

Service learning can be distinguished from volunteering in that the former links academic content to actual practice and outcomes or effects within the context of the greater community. For example, a volunteer effort to increase voter registrations in poor urban neighborhoods might stress the service aspects of the activity (Allen, 2003; Lickteig, 2003). However, a seemingly similar service learning project would focus on constructing a deeper understanding of the process underlying the activity. In this example, understanding of the importance of active civic engagement in the political process is critical, as is analyzing the effects on local, state, and national decision-making when systematic efforts are undertaken that encourage marginalized segments of the community to participate. Overall, service learning in schools embodies the following:

- Positive and meaningful experiences that are relevant to the individual learner.
- Cooperative rather than competitive experiences that promote teamwork and citizenship.
- Experiences that address complex issues in real-life settings rather than simplified problems in isolation.
- Engages problem-solving in the specific context of service activities and community challenges rather than generalized or abstract concepts from a textbook.
- Promotes deeper understanding and critical analysis.
- Supports social, emotional, and cognitive learning and development across K–12 educational levels (National Service-Learning Clearinghouse, 2013).

Internships and Field-Based Learning

Beyond service learning, students benefit from experiencing real-world applications of content knowledge in a variety of settings through internships and field-based experiences. Internships and field-based experiences are increasingly used by secondary schools as a way of connecting school and work (refer to Chapter 7 of this text for more information on school-to-work initiatives). Student internships, usually offered during the last two years of high school, however, go beyond exposing students to the world of work. These opportunities allow students to see direct applications of academic knowledge and skills to a particular occupation, while they forge positive relationships with role models and potential mentors within a given field. In addition, many students experience for the first time genuine success in school as they complete personally meaningful projects, and it is through such experiences that some students are finally able to develop and express special interests and talents (Littky & Allen, 1999; Markham & Lenz, 2002). Students who have historically been academically successful also find such experiences challenging and rewarding as they hone their knowledge and skills to a greater degree and meet higher expectations than had previously been placed on them. Through internships and field-based learning experiences, schools are often able to combine some of the most important aspects of student support services including mentoring, tutoring, student advising, and individualized learning plans in an effort to make school relevant and bring meaning to academic content areas. As schools and school districts search for an alternative to the large, impersonal secondary schools that are failing so many students, Steinberg, Almedia, & Allen (2003) have identified four types of innovative programming that seem to produce strong results, especially for students at risk for a variety of problems. Three of the four are directly related to internships and field-based learning experiences, including:

- Reinvented high schools in which small, highly focused and rigorous learning environments use curriculum, staff, community resources, and time in a radically different way in order to better address the development and intellectual growth of students and engage them in work relevant to them and meaningful to the greater community.
- Education/employment blends for adolescents through instructional arrangements that combine academic learning, technical training, and professional or work-based experience.

- Extended learning opportunities that make creative use of time and resources outside the school building and school day to engage students in intensive learning.

School-Business Partnerships

According to Weinberger (1992), school-business partnerships began to flourish in the 1980s, especially under the Reagan administration, which challenged business and industry leaders to develop a working relationship with every public and private school in America. Since then, school-business partnerships have taken on increasing importance in terms of providing educational opportunities and services for students. Through such partnerships, volunteers from business and industry have served as tutors, mentors, and instructors for a variety of school-based programs. Resources in the form of equipment and small grants have been provided to schools and school faculty for the development and implementation of programs designed to improve the academic achievement of students. Local businesses have served schools by providing field-based experiences and internship sites for countless students. Yet, as businesses and corporations have responded to this challenge, the school-business partnership movement has not been without criticism or justifiable concern.

Critics of business-school partnerships argue that such sponsorship of schools has led to the infiltration of corporate values at the expense of democratic educational ideals (Lickteig, 2003). Furthermore, collective responsibility for the funding of public schools has gradually shifted away from taxpayers while state and federal education budgets have also been reduced, leaving schools in a quandary as to how to fund the programs and services that are increasingly necessary for achieving state achievement standards and benchmarks. This deterioration in the traditional approach to public school funding, according to some, is a direct result of greater value being placed on commercialism, consumer spending, and short-term profits driven by corporate values than on the long-term investment in the education of future citizens. In this environment schools are left with little choice but to seek external funding for services and equipment, often through major corporations, and these corporations are often quite interested in supporting schools—if there is a possibility that doing so will increase profit margins. Thus, school-business partnerships have become increasingly controversial as students, essentially captive as an audience, are targeted as a lucrative consumer group and exposed to advertising through commercial broadcasts, web browsers, food services, and vending machines placed in the schools by corporations (Stark, 2001). (See Chapters 8 and 9 for more information on nutrition, obesity, and related health concerns.) Although these contracts often provide schools with financial incentives, Manning (1999) suggests that what may seem like a huge sum of money amounts to little when analyzed more carefully within the context of long-term gain and the price of a child's mind. Perhaps the most significant criticism of the subsidization of schools by business and industry is concern over the selling of education in the name of global economics and world competition. As humanities and liberal arts within public education are replaced with functional literacy and job skills, and as students are prepared not to be valuable, contributing members of society but producers and consumers of goods and services, the long-standing goals of public education can be subtly replaced by values of materialism and expected product consumption. Administrators and educational decision-makers should enter into partnerships with businesses cautiously, critically examining the motives, incentives, and potential long-term outcomes for all involved (Giroux, 1999).

Full-Service Schools

According to Tagle (2003), "[Communities] are finding ways to transform public schools into more than just facilities for academic learning and exploring how other local institutions can play a role in providing academic and nonacademic supports for students before, during, and after school hours. They are, in essence, creating unified and local visions for the way children and youth learn and develop by redefining the ways schools, community-based organizations, and other stakeholders work and collaborate" (p. 46). Basically, this describes the concept underlying the full-service school, a relatively recent and innovative way to meet the needs of students and ensure their success in both school and community. While there was a time when schools and the larger community typically enjoyed a symbiotic relationship, the past several decades have increasingly seen the separation of these two entities in both roles and services provided. Additionally, full-service schools differ from the community schools of the past in that they have come about in response to two needs, according to Lawson (1999). First, more children and youth are entering school with physical and mental health needs that cannot be met by the schools and yet often interfere with academic success. Additionally, fragmentation and lack of communication among community service agencies have led to a need for increased cooperation and integration of services.

Although research investigating outcomes and cost-effectiveness of such programs is sparse and not necessarily generalizable from one community to another, there have been program evaluations in which positive outcomes have been reported for full-service schools. Some of these include gains in achievement, improved attendance rates among students, lower rates of behavior problems and suspensions from school, reduction in high-risk behaviors, improved access to services, greater parent involvement, and lower rates of neighborhood crime and mobility (Dryfoos, 2002). Thus, this innovative approach to education seems to hold a lot of promise for restructuring education and service delivery to meet the changing needs of society. But concerns do exist regarding the development, implementation, administration, and staffing of full-service schools. In her discussion of full-service schools, Dryfoos (2002) indicates that, while different models of full-service schools are available, in general, the primary responsibility of the school is to provide high-quality education. Everything else, including health services, mentoring, counseling, family services, extended school-day activities, crisis intervention, and recreation are the responsibility of the community service agencies involved directly with the school (Dryfoos, 1994). While use of a wrap-around service model (CEPC, 2002; Stevenson, 2003) for individual students and their families can facilitate communication and cooperation among the various agencies involved, disputes involving the use of time, space, funds, other resources, and staff can develop. Issues of confidentiality and authority must also be considered in all decision-making processes. In addition, conflicts over roles and responsibilities as well as philosophical orientation can arise, especially when community service staff and school personnel hold similar professional titles and skills as is the case of psychologists, counselors, social workers, and other related service personnel. These conflicts can be avoided through clear program goals and role expectations, trust and professional collaboration, and a focus on the needs of students. Another issue is a tendency, if services are not properly aligned and fully integrated at the planning stage, for an attitude to develop that the community service agencies involved are there to "fix" the school or solve its problems. Administrators are cautioned that every service and program offered through full-service schools should be evaluated carefully in order to ascertain whether it will truly benefit students and the extent to which there may be duplication of efforts (Dryfoos, 2002; Pardini, 2001).

Perhaps the most pressing challenge for successful full-service schools is the sustainability of their programs. The intense amount of planning, cooperation, and collaboration that must go into a successful program is hardly worth the time and effort if the program is not likely to survive through changing local demographics, shifting social context and the inherent vicissitudes of the local, state, and national political climate. Tagle (2003) identifies three factors that are the foundation for sustained policy and practice of full-service schools. First, public engagement in the development, implementation, and evaluation of the program is crucial. In this context, the public should include all members of the community (parents, residents, school and community service agency personnel, and those who have not traditionally had a voice in community matters) as well as organized stakeholder groups and educational policymakers. Furthermore, specific program goals must be developed and an acceptance among the larger community of responsibility for the education and welfare of its children and youth must be fostered. Overall, full-service schools require tremendous up-front planning as well as oversight and direction. To reach true integration of school and community services requires a high level of commitment and collaboration among all agencies involved, and public engagement is both a requirement for and a result of these initiatives.

Before and After School Programs

Economic and social conditions within the United States have changed dramatically over the past few decades. In general, the workday is longer now, and the number of households in which either a single parent heads the family or both parents work outside the home has steadily increased. In direct contrast, however, schools have generally kept the same calendar and hours that have been in place for generations, leaving many students with significant amounts of unstructured and, more importantly, unsupervised time. With the prevalence of risk-behaviors in children and adolescents generally increasing (see Chapter 9), there is a need for communities and schools to engage these students in meaningful activities and extend learning opportunities into out-of-school time (Walker & Hackman, 1999). And yet, only in the past fifteen years has this need resulted in formal legislation, program initiatives, and funding (Rinehart, 2003). In general, school-age care programs offer safe and healthy environments for children before and after school and are usually provided by commercial child-care businesses, religious organizations, local governments, school-business partnerships, and school districts themselves. School-age care programs can qualify for funding by U.S. Department of Health and Human Services grant programs and often emphasize arts and recreation, although some also provide homework help, tutoring, and supplemental reading and math instruction (see Chapter 1 for information on funding available through NCLB).

More and more attention, however, is being paid to these programs as a greater understanding regarding the social and cognitive learning of students develops and the recognition and acceptance of a community's responsibility to provide for the education and welfare of its youth increase. Custodial services that merely assure safety of children during out-of-school hours are no longer considered adequate, and a variety of creative and innovative approaches to out-of-school learning opportunities and programs have been developed. Noam (2003) has identified several levels of programming that connect the diverse worlds of school, family, and community in which children live and learn. The lowest of these levels, described as self-contained programs, make little or no attempt to collaborate with schools at the interpersonal, curricular, or systemic level. The focus is often, if not always, on arts and recreational activities, although time and location for homework completion may be set aside. The next level, described as associated programming, makes an attempt to offer academic services but is more focused on tutoring students separate from the school's curriculum and methods. This failure to connect school-age care efforts with instruction taking place during the school day can be attributed to poor communication between the school and the program providers, who in any case are often not sufficiently trained to provide deep or connected learning experiences.

The highest program levels, to which schools and communities should aspire, are the coordinated and unified levels, according to Noam (2003). Coordinated school age care describes program efforts directly tied to the curricular mission of the school and facilitated by an education coordinator or school-program liaison. This individual is a presence in the school, has frequent and direct contact with classroom teachers, and is responsible for aligning the school-age care program with the school's standards and curriculum through projects and supplemental curricula. Integrated programming is represented by efforts through which the school-age care program and the school relate on a curricular, interpersonal, and systemic level. At this level, clear curricular continuities exist as the school-age care program and school itself share staff, space, and procedures. Projects are usually very school-focused, since classroom activities are meaningfully connected to out of school learning. Finally, the highest level, described as unified programming, is nearly indistinguishable from school because its instructional approach truly represents an extended school day and a seamless integration of program efforts at the curricular, interpersonal, and systemic levels. At this time, the programming level is largely a goal toward which schools and communities should aim (Noam, 2003).

When the term "school-age care" is used, the age ranges of 5–12 are often invoked in the public mind. However, there is a growing recognition of the needs of students in the middle adolescent years (13–18), who often have too much time and money but too little supervision and support during out-of-school hours. Adolescents can benefit from program efforts that are aimed to capitalize on the human capacity for intrinsically motivated learning and the developmental needs for increased social contact with peers in a safe and risk-free environment. These needs are increasingly met through the provision of services during out-of-school time that may be aligned with the mission and standards of the schools but employ methods and materials far removed from teaching associated with the typical school-day. Surfing the internet, discussing popular books, films, music, and other media, visiting museums, and even navigating the rocky interpersonal social dimensions of adolescence through role-play and dialogue are examples of free-choice learning (Dierking & Falk, 2003) that hold great appeal to this group of adolescent students.

In general, communities and schools must begin to recognize or perhaps reaffirm their understanding of education as a deeper and more engaging process than mere schooling. Schools and communities in collaboration must utilize out-of-school time as a means of helping adolescents find connection and relevance among the various worlds in which they live and learn. Teenage students will benefit from opportunities to participate in programs that increase their general knowledge of the world and that enable them to build skills and competencies in areas, especially arts-related, that have been devalued or eliminated entirely as a result of the current standards-based reform movement (Friedman, 2003). Thus, while schools often espouse a belief in the value of, and a mission to, develop life-long learning, the latter will not be accomplished without collaboration between schools and communities and access to funding to provide for the free-choice learning of its youth.

Child Care Services

There are few if any student support services that seem to generate as much controversy as that of school-based child care services for parenting students. Luscher (1998) argues that the controversy surrounding the provision of such services as well as the manner in which child care services are delivered to parenting students is the result of a culture imbued with what she terms white, middle class values and role expectations. These services are provided, according to Luscher, in a manner that reinforces society's notions of adolescent pregnancy and motherhood as unacceptable and irresponsible, and conveys the attitude that those in need of such services are likely to be neither responsible nor successful as parents or as students. Yet, child-care services are a necessary support service that enables parenting students, especially mothers, to complete their education and experience a sense of achievement and value around their roles as both parent and student. Communities in general can benefit from integration of school-based child-care programs with other support service initiatives, because infants and toddlers receive quality care and adolescent parents remain in school and attain knowledge and skills necessary for employment. Parenting students have the benefit of quality care for their children and the opportunity for parent education, and all students have the opportunity to observe and learn about human development through service-learning projects completed through on-site child-care facilities (Reagan, 1997). Furthermore, there is little evidence to support the argument that provision of such services serves to encourage other students to take a cavalier attitude toward the consequences of parenting during the teen years. On the contrary, participation of non-parenting students in academic and service learning projects within on-site childcare facilities has been shown to correlate with decreased levels of teen pregnancy and childbirth (Santrock, 2003). Overall, society cannot afford to withhold care and educational services that are necessary for the healthy growth and development of its children in order to punish or otherwise discourage what may be considered irresponsible and burdensome outcomes of immoral behavior. These adolescents and their children will only flourish and become productive members of the community if they are accepted and cared for by a compassionate society.

Peer Support Programs

While it is now clearly understood that schools alone cannot be held solely accountable for the growth, development, and learning of students, there still remains a tendency to think of educators and service providers as responsible for fixing the problems and difficulties that children and adolescents face today. However, one very powerful source of support that is often left untapped at all levels of education is that of students themselves. Students are capable of producing outstanding results with other students through peer- and cross-age mentoring and tutoring as described above. Student participation in peer mediation and peer arbitration can also be a significant factor in reducing a variety of social problems within the school such as bullying, risk-taking behaviors, and alcohol and drug use (Stacey, 2002). Through peer counseling, conflict resolution, active listening, advising, education, and friendship initiatives (Cowie & Wallace, 2002), students are able to effectively reach out to each other and support the needs of fellow students in a way that is not possible for adults and professionals. Furthermore, through peer support programs, the social climate of the school is positively impacted at its foundation as students themselves establish and reinforce a caring and supportive atmosphere and answer to each other when problems arise. However, in order for peer support programs, especially those aimed at mediation and arbitration, to be successful within the school, administration, faculty, and staff must have a clear understanding of the processes involved and the expected outcomes in terms of academic performance and interpersonal skill development. Through this mechanism, students are empowered to solve their own disagreements without adult intervention (but not adult supervision) (Gihooley & Scheuch, 2000) and to take on the responsibility for and ownership of the general success of the collective student body.

Administrative and Personnel Considerations

The traditional school organization is gradually giving way to less rigid, formal structures that reflect the changing values, expectations, and contexts of society in general. The traditional roles of teacher and administrator, and even the preparation for these roles, must change in accordance with this trend. To begin with, school administrators must be prepared in methods of collaborative educational leadership that fosters voluntary commitments, allows for a sense of empowerment among various constituents, and is focused on context rather than rules and policy. Furthermore, school administrators must become well versed in the causes, correlates, and effects of poverty, and must learn to foster resiliency among students through family-centered practice and advocacy for students with special needs and who are at risk for developing problem behaviors (Lawson, 1999). Ensuring that school faculty and staff, related service personnel, community-based service providers, and volunteers from the community as well as student volunteers receive appropriate and on-going training and support is paramount to the provision of quality student support service programs. Furthermore, knowing the needs of the students and community at large as well as having well-articulated program goals will enable school administrators to choose programs, services, and partnerships wisely and to conduct appropriate program evaluations in order to ensure program efficacy and sustainability. School administrators and personnel need to constantly update knowledge about various program options, available funding sources, and potential collaborative efforts within the community in order to maximize the academic, interpersonal, and career development of its students at all levels of education.

Summary

There is a general recognition that traditional models of schools and all they entail, from teacher-centered instructional practices to top-down, administration-driven decision-making processes, are no longer a viable option for meeting the academic, interpersonal, and vocational needs of students in a rapidly changing society. On one hand, it is becoming increasingly accepted that schools cannot bear the sole responsibility for the education and development of the country's youth and that strong communication and collaboration among schools, communities, and families are needed to provide education in a complex, multifaceted society. On the other hand, the battle cry of current education reform efforts is that of accountability, meeting standards, and closing the achievement gap that exists between various sectors of the student population. The logical conclusion from both standpoints is that there must be financial, logistical, and community support for the programs and services needed by students to attain success in the various domains traditionally addressed by public schools and to become productive members of society. These support programs and services must be student-centered and developed to meet specific needs within the student body. Integration rather than division of funding, resources, and space is a necessary component for the sustainability of support programs, and public acceptance of the responsibility for the education and development of society's youth must be realized through community engagement, public policy, and state and federal legislation. That is, education policy and legislative mandates regarding the progress and outcomes of public school efforts must be integrative and supportive in nature rather than divisive and punitive. Educational leaders and policy makers must eschew the ideological absolutes inherent in either-or propositions (Glickman, 2003) and engage students, parents, local educators, and community members in contextually-bound educational decisions that result in the development, implementation, and evaluation of appropriate support programs and services for today's youth and tomorrow's future.

Questions for Consideration

1. What are some of the positive and negative aspects of school-business partnerships? How can schools and communities ensure that students benefit from such collaborations?
2. What are some of the advantages of adult-student mentoring over peer-mentoring programs, and vice versa? How should school leaders determine the best mentoring model for a particular school or district?
3. Should schools attempt to attain the unified level of out-of-school programming for its students? If so, how can this be accomplished? If not, what are the reasons?
4. In what ways do student support services overarch special education services, gifted and talented initiatives, programs for English language learners, alternative educational oppor-

tunities, applied educational programs, and traditional health, nutrition, and physical education programs in the schools? How have legislative mandates, public policy, and available funding sources served to facilitate or inhibit integration of services aimed at supporting the academic, interpersonal, and vocational needs of students?

Case Study

Tragedy at Holly Heights High School

Holly Heights is a small, affluent community outside of a large urban area on the west coast. Most of the residents believe that the community is a safe and healthy place to raise children, and there are plenty of parks, playgrounds, and student-friendly hang-outs around the town. Most of the students who attend Holly Heights High School are from well-educated families who are occupied in high-earnings professions. In general, the school has performed well on state-mandated standardized tests as well as other indicators of success such as the number of students taking advanced placement courses, average SAT scores, graduation rates, rates of student matriculation to four-year institutions, parental involvement, and school engagement of students. In fact, Holly Heights has more academic clubs, interscholastic sports teams, and social organizations than any other high school in the region. The school, however, is not perfect, and there are problems despite the advantages most students have. Divorce rates within the community are slightly higher than average, and many students in the schools have to deal with issues stemming from parental separation, divorce, remarriage, and blended families. In addition, some of the students seem to have far too much money at their disposal and not enough supervision due to their parents' long working hours and professional career aspirations. Students also frequently report feeling intense pressure from their families to excel in academics and athletics, and to take on leadership roles in various student organizations. Also a certain degree of hostility exists between affluent students who drive expensive sports cars or SUVs to school and brag about their parents' connections to social and political leaders within the community and beyond, and the relatively disadvantaged students.

Tim Reynolds is the most senior of three school counselors at the high school and, as such, is currently the department chairperson. The counselors are responsible for duties such as academic advising, dealing with minor issues of student discipline, and maintaining permanent record files. In addition, the counselors regularly conduct individual and small-group counseling sessions on issues such as peer pressure and social skills in addition to running various support groups for students dealing with divorce, substance abuse within the family, learning disabilities, and attention deficit disorder. The counselors actively work with teachers in integrating prevention of alcohol, tobacco, and drug use into the curriculum in addition to serving as faculty sponsors for student organizations such as Students Against Drunk Driving (SADD). While district schools, in compliance with a board of education decision, stopped offering sexuality education five years earlier, the school counselors provide individual counseling and referrals related to sexuality issues. Overall, Tim is pleased with the programs they have in place and feels that his department is a successful model of comprehensive school counseling.

Another successful academic school year was coming to a close. Most of the pressures associated with standardized testing, college admissions, and even athletic competitions had ended, and the faculty and students alike were anxious for summer break. The front office was relatively quiet as the school principal, school psychologist, and one of the school counselors were at the district administration building participating in a complicated IEP meeting. Suddenly, chaos erupted as a sophomore burst into the main office screaming that her best friend had taken an overdose of a drug and was sick. Everyone within earshot including Tim and another counselor,

Janet, ran out of the office, following the student to the far end of the east wing of the school. Lying unconscious on the floor of the girls' restroom was a sophomore student whom Tim recognized as Vicky Taylor. Although he did not know the student well, he remembered her from a divorce support group he had conducted the previous year. She hadn't said too much during the group sessions, but she did share that she often felt alone since her father moved out of the home to a nearby city and her mother began working longer hours to make ends meet.

Tim and the others rushed to her side, and from the chalky color of her skin and the dilation of her pupils, he knew they would need to get her to a hospital immediately. The situation grew immediately worse as Tim realized that, in their panic, the front office had been left empty and no one had remained behind to contact emergency personnel. He shouted to the school secretary, Nancy, to return to the office and call 911. In an instant, he knew he'd made a mistake and ran out of the girls' restroom to make the call himself from the much-closer telephone in the athletic director's office. He was immediately engulfed by a flood of students entering the corridor from the gymnasium, as the bell sounded ending fifth period, but fought his way through the mass of students. After placing the call, he ran back to the restroom to find a crowd of students blocking the restroom entrance. The assistant principal was trying to get the students to move away, but they seemed to only push farther in, straining to see what was going on. Tim and the assistant principal, after several minutes and with help from other teachers who had also come to see what was happening, were able to clear the immediate area. Crowds of students and teachers, however, remained in the corridor despite the bell signaling the beginning of 6th period. Janet, the other counselor, had located an empty pill bottle under a sink in the corner of the restroom. The label on it indicated that it had contained a strong sedative prescribed for Vicky's mother, although there was no way to tell how many pills Vicky had taken and whether the overdose had been an accident or a suicide attempt. After what seemed an eternity, the emergency medical technicians arrived on the scene. Nancy, leaving the front office empty again, led them to the east wing where they had to push their way through the remaining throngs of students and teachers. More valuable time was wasted as a teacher was sent to the nearest computer, again in the athletic director's office, to obtain the emergency contact information for Vicky.

As the ambulance left the school parking lot, Tim wasn't sure if he should follow in his own car to the hospital or whether he should stay behind and get everything back under control. He was somewhat relieved when he saw the assistant principal drive off behind the ambulance. Although he was on the school and district crisis management team, he felt at a total loss. The school's crisis plan, which he had helped to develop, was now several years old. He hadn't reviewed the plan all year, and wasn't sure himself who was supposed to have taken responsibility for what action. He knew, however, that there had been several breaches of the plan, which could have serious consequences. Then, what seemed to be a worst-case scenario suddenly became even more serious as Tim re-entered the office. Janet, the other school counselor on the scene, informed him that several sophomore girls had just come to the office to report what they knew about the situation. They believed that Vicky had attempted to commit suicide because she had recently become the target of vicious gossip and unrelenting teasing at school that began when, in trying to become more popular with the boys, she engaged in sexual behavior with some members of the football team. Allegations of sexual harassment on school property as well as physical intimidation and threats emerged.

Questions for Discussion

1. Could this situation have been prevented? If so, what were some of the potential warning signs that the school counselors should have noticed?

2. When this crisis happened, the faculty was unprepared and valuable time was lost in getting emergency personnel to the scene. What should have been done differently?

3. What should the school faculty in general, and the school counselors in particular, do next? How should the school deal with the girls' allegations?

4. Could this crisis be an isolated event within the school, or do you think it may be a manifestation of a deeper problem within the community? If you believe the latter, what should the long-term plan be in addressing the problem?

References

Adelman, H. S., & Taylor, L. (2002). School counselors and school reform: New directions. *Professional School Counseling, 5*(4), 235–248.

Allen, R. (2003). The democratic aims of service learning. *Educational Leadership, 60*(6), 51–54.

American School Counselor Association (2008). The ASCA national model: A framework for school counseling programs. Retrieved from http://www.ascanationalmodel.org/.

Bemack, F. (2002). Paradigms for future school counseling programs. In C. D. Johnson & S. K. Johnson (Eds.), *School counseling programs: Brining futuristic approaches into the present* (pp. 37–49). Greensboro, NC: CAPS Publications.

Big Brothers Big Sisters of America (2004). Retrieved from http://www.bbbs.org/site/c.9iILI3NGKhK6F/b.5962335/k.BE16/Home.htm.

Center for Effective Collaboration and Practice [CEPC] (2002). *Introduction to wrap-around.* Retrieved from http://cecp.air.org/wraparound/materials.html.

Cogan, J. J. (1999). Civic education in the United States: A brief history. *International Journal of Social Education, 14*(1), 52–64.

Cowie, H., & Wallace, P. (2000). *Peer support in action: From bystanding to standing by.* London: SAGE Publications.

Dahir, C. A. (2009). School counseling in the 21st century: Where lies the future? Introduction to the special section. *Journal of Counseling and Development, 87*(1), 3–5.

Dahir, C. A. & Stone, C. B. (2009). School counselor accountability: The path to social justice and systemic change. *Journal of Counseling and Development, 87*(1), 12–20.

Dierking, L. D., & Falk, J. H. (2003). Optimizing out-of-school time: The role of free-choice learning. In G. G. Noam (Series Ed.) & K. J. Pittman, N. Yohalem, & J. Tolman (Vol. Eds.), *New directions for youth development: Vol. 97. When, where, what, and how youth learn: Blurring school and community boundaries* (pp. 75–88). San Francisco, CA: Jossey-Bass.

Dryfoos, J. G. (1994). *Full-service schools: A revolution in health and social services for children, youth, and families.* San Francisco, CA: Jossey-Bass.

Dryfoos, J. G. (2002). Full-service community schools: Creating new institutions. *Phi Delta Kappan, 83*(5), 393–399.

Faust, V. (1968). *The counselor-consultant in the elementary school.* Boston: Houghton Mifflin.

Foster, L. (2001). *Effectiveness of mentor programs: A review of the literature.* (Report No. CRB-01-004). Sacramento, CA: California Research Bureau. (ERIC Document Reproduction Service No. ED463511).

Friedman, L. (2003). Promoting opportunity after school. *Educational Leadership, 60*(4), 79–82,

Gensemer, P. (2000). *Effectiveness of cross-age and peer mentoring programs.* U.S. Alabama. (ERIC Document Reproduction Services No. ED438267).

Gihooley, J., & Scheuch, N. S. (2000). *Using peer mediation in classrooms and schools: Strategies for teachers, counselors, and administrators.* Thousand Oaks, CA: Corwin Press.

Green, A., & Keys, S. (2001). Expanding the developmental school counseling paradigm: Meeting the needs of the 21st century student. Professional School Counseling, 5(2), 84–95.

Giroux, H. A. (1999). Schools for sale: Public education, corporate culture, and the citizen–consumer. *The Education Forum, 63*(2), 140–149.

Gumpel, T. P., & Frank, R. (1999). An expansion of the peer-tutoring paradigm: Cross-age peer tutoring of social skills among socially rejected boys. *Journal of Applied Behavior Analysis, 32*(1), 115–118.

Gysbers, N. C. (2001). School guidance and counseling in the 21st century: Remember the past into the future. *Professional School Counseling, 5*(2), 96–105.

Gysbers, N. C. (2002). Comprehensive school guidance programs in the future: Staying the course. In C. D. Johnson & S. K. Johnson (Eds.), *School counseling programs: Brining futuristic approaches into the present* (pp. 145–154). Greensboro, NC: CAPS Publications.

Hancock, K. (2001). The case for in-school mentoring. *Education Canada, 43*(1), 24–25.

Hansman, C. A. (2002). Mentoring: From Athena to the 21st century. In C. A. Hansman (Ed.), *Critical perspectives on mentoring: Trends and issues.* Washington, DC: Office of Educational Research and Improvement.

Herrera, C., Sipes, C. L., & McClanahan, W. S. (2000). *Mentoring school-age children: Relationship development in community-based and school-based programs.* Washington DC: Office of Educational Research and Improvement.

Johnson, S., & Johnson, C. D. (2003). Results-based guidance: A systems approach to student support programs. *Professional School Counseling, 6*(3), 180–184.

Jucovy, L. (2000). *The ABCs of school-based mentoring.* (Technical Assistance Packet No. 1). Portland, OR: Northwest Region Educational Laboratory. (ERIC Document Reproduction Service No. ED449433).

Jucovy, L. (2001). *Supporting mentors.* (Technical Assistance Packet No. 6). Portland, OR: Northwest Region Educational Laboratory. (ERIC Document Reproduction Services No. ED470759).

Lawson, H. A. (1999). Two new mental models for schools and their implications for principal's roles, responsibilities, and preparation. *NASSP Bulletin, 83*(6), 8–27.

Lickteig, M. K. (2003). Brand-name schools: The deceptive lure of corporate-school partnerships. *The Educational Forum, 68* (1), 44–51.

Littky, D., & Allen, F. (1999). Whole-school personalization, one student at a time. *Educational Leadership, 57*(1), 24–28.

Luscher, K (1998). Contested scripts: The education of student-mothers in childcare schools. *Educational Studies, 29*(4), 392–410.

Maddy-Bernstein, C., & Cunanan, E. S. (1995, November). Improving student services in secondary schools. *Office of Student Services, 7*(2). Retrieved October 3, 2004 from http://vocserve.berkeley.edu/briefs/Brief72.html.

Manning, S. (1999). Students for sale. *Nation, 269*(9), 11–16.

Markham, T., & Lenz, B. (2002). Ready for the world. *Educational Leadership, 59*(7), 76–79.

Muss, R. E. (1996). *Theories of adolescence.* New York: McGraw-Hill.

National Service-Learning Clearinghouse (2013). Retrieved from http://www.servicelearning.org/what-service-learning.

National Mentoring Partnerships (2013). Retrieved from http://www.mentoring.org/.

National Peer Helpers Association (2002). *Programmatic standards checklist.* Retrieved from http://www.peerhelping.org/NPHAPublications/standardshtml.htm.

National Youth Network (1999). *What is peer mentoring?* Retrieved from http://www.ncjrs.org/html/youth-bulletin/9907-4/contents.html.

Noam, G. G. (2003). Learning with excitement: Bridging school and after-school worlds and project-based learning. In G. G. Noam (Series Ed.) & K. J. Pittman, N. Yohalem, & J. Tolman (Vol. Eds.), *New directions for youth development: Vol. 97. When, where, what, and how youth learn: Blurring school and community boundaries* (pp. 121–138). San Francisco, CA: Jossey-Bass.

Northwest Regional Educational Laboratory (2001). *Student mentoring.* Retrieved from http://www.nwrel.org/request/sept98/article2.html.

One Hundred Black Men of America, Inc. (2013). Retrieved from http://www.100blackmen.org/mentoring. aspx.

Ornstein, A. C. & Hutchins, F. P. (1998). *Curriculum: Foundations, principles, and theory*, 3rd ed. Boston: Allyn & Bacon.

Pardini, P. (2001). School-community partnering. *School Administrator, 58*(7), 6–11.

Peter, V. J. (2000). Loneliness: The bane of children of prosperity. *Momentum, 41*(4), 14–17.

Pope, M. (2000). A brief history of career counseling in the United States. *The Career Development Quarterly, 48*(3), 194–211.

Reagan, G. (1997). Enhancing teen parenting skills through practical experiences in a public school child care setting. Nova Southeastern University. (ERIC Document Reproduction Service No. ED414065).

Rinehart, J. (2003). A new day begins after school. *Principal, 82*(5), 12–16.

Santrock, J. W. (2003). *Adolescence.* Boston: McGraw-Hill.

Stader, D., & Gagnepain, F. G. (2000). Mentoring: The power of peers. *American Secondary Education, 28*(3), 28–32.

Stark, A. (2001). Pizza Hut, Domino's, and the public schools. *Policy Review, 108*, 59–70.

Stacey, H. (2000). Mediation and peer mediation. In H. Cowie & P Wallace (Eds.), *Peer support in action: From bystanding to standing by.* London: SAGE Publications.

Steinberg, A., Almedia, C., & Allen, L. (2003). Multiple pathways to adulthood: expanding the learning options for urban youth. In G. G. Noam (Series Ed.) & K. J. Pittman, N. Yohalem, & J. Tolman (Vol. Eds.), *New directions for youth development: Vol. 97. When, where, what, and how youth learn: Blurring school and community boundaries* (pp. 29–44). San Francisco, CA: Jossey-Bass.

Stevenson, R. A. (2003). Wraparound services. *School Administrator, 60*(3), 24–25.

Stukas, A. A., Snyder, M., & Clary, E. G. (1999). The effects of "mandatory volunteerism" on intentions to volunteer. *Educational Horizons, 77*(4), 194–201.

Tagle, R. (2003). Building learning-centered communities through public engagement. In G. G. Noam (Series Ed.) & K. J. Pittman, N. Yohalem, & J. Tolman (Vol. Eds.), *New directions for youth development: Vol. 97. When, where, what, and how youth learn: Blurring school and community boundaries* (pp. 45–58). San Francisco, CA: Jossey-Bass.

Walker, J. D., & Hackman, D. G. (1999). Full-service schools: Forming alliances to meet the needs of students and families. *NASSP Bulletin, 83*(6), 28–37.

Weinberger, S. G. (1992). How to start a student mentor program. Bloomington, In: Phi Delta Kappa Educational Foundation. (ERIC Document Reproduction Service No. ED348621).

Wickwire, P. N. (2002). Current trends and their implications for futures in the guidance profession. In C. D. Johnson & S. K. Johnson (Eds.), *School counseling programs: Bringing futuristic approaches into the present* (pp. 3–16). Greensboro, NC: CAPS Publications.

Zepeda, S. J., & Langenback, M. (1999). *Special programs in regular schools: Historical foundations, standards, and contemporary issues.* Boston: Allyn & Bacon.

No Child Left Behind Act of 2001:
Reauthorization of the Elementary and Secondary Education Act of 1965

Title I: Improving The Academic Achievement of the Disadvantaged

- Improving Basic Programs Operated by Local Educational Agencies
- Reading First
- Early Reading First
- William F. Goodling Even start Family Literacy Program
- Improving Literacy through School Libraries
- Education of Migratory Children
- Prevention and Intervention Programs for Children and Youth Who are
- Neglected, Delinquent, or At-Risk
- National Assessment of Title I, Title I Evaluation and Demonstrations
- Close-Up Fellowship Comprehensive School Reform
- Advanced Placement
- School Dropout Prevention
- General Provisions

Title II: Preparing, Training, and Recruiting High Quality Teachers and Principals

- Teacher and Principal Training and Recruiting Fund, Grants to States
- School Leadership
- Advanced Certification/Credentialing
- Early Childhood Educator Professional Development
- Mathematics and Science Partnerships
- Troops-to-Teachers

- Transitions to Teaching
- National Writing Project
- Civic Education
- Teaching of Traditional American History
- Teacher Liability Protection
- Enhancing Education Through Technology
- Ready-to-Learn Television

Title III: Language Instruction For Limited English Proficient and Immigrant Students

- Language Instruction for Limited English Proficient and Immigrant Students

Title IV: 21st Century Schools

- Safe and Drug-Free Schools and Communities
- Gun-Free requirements
- 21st Century Community Learning Centers
- Environmental Tobacco Smoke

Title V: Promoting Informed Parental Choice and Innovative Programs

- Innovative Programs
- Public Charter Schools
- Credit Enhancement Initiatives to Assist Charter School Facility Acquisition, Construction, and Renovation
- Voluntary Public School Choice
- Magnet Schools Assistance
- Elementary and Secondary School Counseling
- Partnerships in Character Education
- Smaller Learning Communities
- Reading Is Fundamental-Inexpensive Book Distribution
- Gifted and Talented Students
- Star Schools
- Ready to Teach
- Foreign Language Assistance
- Physical Education
- Community Technology Centers
- Educational, Cultural, Apprenticeship, and Exchange Programs for Alaska Natives, Native Hawaiians, and Their Historical Whaling Partners in Massachusetts
- Arts in Education
- Parental Assistance Information Centers
- Women's Educational Equity

Title VI: Flexibility And Accountability

- Improving Academic Achievement, Accountability, Grants for State Assessments and Enhanced Assessments
- Funding Transferability for State and Local Educational Agencies
- State Flexibility Authority ("State-Flex")
- Local Flexibility Demonstrations ("Local-Flex")
- Rural Education Initiative: Small, Rural School Achievement
- Rural Education Initiative Rural and Low-Income Schools
- General Provisions, National Assessment of Education Progress

Title VII: Indian, Native Hawaiian, And Alaska Native Education

- Indian Education
- Native Hawaiian Education
- Alaska Native Education

Title VIII: Impact Aid Program

- Impact Aid

Title IX: General Provisions

- General Provisions
- Unsafe School Choice Option

Title X: Repeals, Redesignations, And Amendments To Other Statutes

- McKinney-Vento Homeless Education Assistance Improvements

Source: U. S. Government (2002). *No child left behind act of 2001: Reauthorization of the elementary and secondary education act of 1965.* (P.L 107-110). Washington, DC: U.S. Government Printing Office.

ESEA Reauthorization:
A Blueprint for Reform of the Elementary and Secondary Education Act

Blueprint Proposal:

Accountability

- Asking states to set standards that prepare students for college and careers.
- Creating a fair accountability system that recognizes and rewards growth and progress.
- Providing flexibility to state and local educators to innovate and create local solutions.
- Focusing rigorous, meaningful interventions and support for the lowest performing schools that also have not demonstrated any progress.
- Recognize and reward schools that increase student achievement and close achievement gaps—and recognize and reward districts and states that turn around their lowest-performing schools.
- Give the majority of schools and districts the flexibility to use a wide variety of data to design their own improvement plans to increase achievement and close gaps.
- Challenge schools that have achievement gaps that aren't closing or low student achievement that's not improving to use data-driven, evidence-based interventions.
- Require states to identify the bottom 5 percent of their schools that haven't made progress and turn them around using one of four models.

A Complete Education

- Literacy
- Science, Technology, Engineering, and Mathematics (STEM)
- Ensure a Well-Rounded Education
- College pathways and accelerated learning
- Activities to strengthen a complete education

College and Career Ready Standards and Assessment

- Rigorous college-and career-ready standards
- Rigorous fair accountability and support at every level
- Measuring and supporting schools, districts, and states
- Building capacity for support at every level
- Fostering comparability and equity
- Assessing achievement

Diverse Learners

- Education for students with disabilities
- Education for English learners
- Education for migrant students
- Education for homeless children and youth
- Education for neglected and delinquent children and youth
- Education for Indian, Hawaiian Native, and Alaskan Native students
- Education for rural students

Early Learning

- Continued Title I support of preschool
- Birth-through-college-to-career-agenda
- Comprehensive education reforms
- Encouragement for innovation in early learning
- Joint professional development
- Expanding administrator's knowledge of early learning
- Support for teachers of young children
- Seamless transitions and improved coordination
- Strengthen literacy and STEM P-12 plans
- Increased learning time for young children
- Comprehensive early learning assessment systems

Families and Communities

- Supporting comprehensive district approaches to family engagement
- Enhancing district capacity around family engagement
- Providing a new Family Engagement and Responsibility Fund
- Identifying and supporting best practices
- Successful, safe, and healthy students program
- Promise Neighborhoods Program
- 21st Century Community Learning Centers
- Better information for families about their children's schools
- Better information for families on teacher and principal effectiveness

- Family notification
- Effective teachers engaging families
- Effective leaders engaging families
- Family literacy
- Meaningful high-quality choices

Public School Choice

- Support effective public school choice
- Supporting effective charter schools
- Promoting public school choice
- Continuing the Magnet Schools Assistance Program

Reward Excellence and Promote Innovation

- Fostering a Race to the Top
- Supporting effective public school choice
- Promoting a culture of college readiness and success
- Supporting, recognizing, and rewarding local innovations
- Supporting student success

Rural Schools

- Dedicated formula funding
- Level playing field in competitions
- Greater flexibility with funds
- Improve the teaching corps
- Change teacher quality rules so they work better for rural schools
- Flexibility in interventions
- Cuts red tape
- Turnaround options
- Technology
- School and community collaboration
- Autonomous public schools

Science, Technology, Engineering, and Mathematics Education

- Targeted supports to teachers and schools
- Fostering innovation
- Enhancing partnerships
- Improving assessments
- Other subjects in accountability systems
- Recognition and rewards
- Strengthening preparation programs
- Relevant professional development and collaboration time

Supporting Teachers

- Increasing funding
- Responding to teachers' voices
- Sharing responsibility
- Improving evaluations
- Rewarding success
- Focusing on growth
- Supporting teachers in closing gaps
- Improving achievement through flexibility
- Increasing collaboration time
- Holding preparation programs accountable
- Funding relevant professional development
- Improving principal leadership

Turning Around Low Performing Schools

- Transformation model
- Turnaround model
- Restart model
- School closure model

Source: This publication is in the public domain and may be reproduced in whole or in part. It comprises proposals from A Blueprint for Reform: The Reauthorization of the Elementary and Secondary Education Act, U.S. Department of Education, March 2010. To read the full text, visit www2.ed.gov/policy/elsec/leg/blueprint. For more information, go to www.ed.gov or call 1-800-USA-LEARN.

**Comparisons Between NCLB and the Blueprint for Reform
Based on Information from: A Blueprint for Reform**

Core Policies to Maintain in ESEA Reauthorization

- Disaggregation and focus on improving performance of all groups of students.
- Focus on equity.
- Standards-base reform and accountability.

NCLB: Accountability

- "Race to the bottom" for state standards.
- Focus on proficiency; schools making progress can still be "failing."
- Many ways to "fail," no recognition for success.
- Exclusive focus on tests, narrowing of curriculum.
- Mandated SES and choice.
- Over-identifies schools.
- Allowing persistently low-performing schools to avoid real change.
- Punitive/labels without support.
- All consequences focused at the school level.

Blueprint for Reform: Accountability

- States adopt college- and career-ready standards.
- Differentiation of schools based on student growth and school progress.
- Real rewards for high poverty schools, districts, states showing real progress especially in serving underserved populations and closing achievement gaps.
- Development and support the use of assessments.

217

- Look beyond assessments in determining what a school needs, including attendance, conditions of learning, course completion to paint a fuller picture of a school.
- Allow use of additional subjects.
- Additional resources for developing a well rounded curriculum.
- More flexibility around best how to serve schools; no mandated or SES choice.
- Targets more limited portion of schools for significant intervention.
- Meaningful change in persistently low-performing schools.
- Meaningful investment in low-performing schools.
- Holding every level of the system responsible for improvement and support.

NCLB: Teachers and Leaders

- Not focused enough on the profession and teacher voice.
- No acknowledgement or support of teacher collaboration.
- Equitable distribution requirements not meaningful.
- Ignored need for better school leaders.

Blueprint for Reform: Teachers and Leaders

- Utilize surveys of teachers (around working conditions, professional development, and support) and surveys for conditions for learning that include teacher perspective.
- Invest in expanded learning time programs that provide more time for educators to plan and collaborate.
- Greater focus on getting great teachers where they are needed most.
- Invest in preparing and improving better leaders.

Blueprint for Reform: Broad Principles

- Make accountability about more than test scores for most schools.
- Fund development of measurement systems around conditions of learning.
- Greater opportunity and structures for positive adult-student relationships.
- Funding for providing comprehensive services so that students are safe, healthy, able to focus on learning.
- Encourage funding equity

Source: U.S. Department of Education (2010). *ESEA reauthorization: A blueprint for reform. NCLB and the Blueprint* Powerpoint nclb_and_blueprint.ppt. Retrieved from http://www2.ed.gov/policy/elsec/leg/blueprint/index.html

BONNIE M. BEYER is currently a Professor of Educational Administration and Coordinator of Educational Leadership Programs at the master, education specialist, and doctoral levels in the College of Education, Health and Human Services at the University of Michigan-Dearborn. She has served as the Associate Dean and Coordinator of Academic Services of the previous titled School of Education. She has taught and conducted research on organizational leadership and development, K–12 school leadership, school and administrative law, special programs in schools, public relations, and curriculum development. Her education experience prior to the university setting includes administration of both regular and special education programs in public, private, and parochial schools. Dr. Beyer has published in national and international journals, presented at state, national, and international conferences, and is the author of numerous articles, book chapters, and books on special and compensatory programs in schools.

EILEEN S. JOHNSON is an associate professor in the Department of Organizational Leadership at Oakland University where she teaches courses in curriculum and staff development, ethics and philosophy of educational leadership, learning theories and psychological issues in education, and research methods. A former public school teacher, school psychologist, and educational diagnostician, she continues to provide consultation services on issues of student learning in private and public educational settings. Dr. Johnson has published and made presentations at state and national conferences in her areas of research and interest.